WEIGHING IN

CALIFORNIA STUDIES IN FOOD AND CULTURE
Darra Goldstein, Editor

WEIGHING IN

OBESITY, FOOD JUSTICE, AND THE LIMITS OF CAPITALISM

Julie Guthman

UNIVERSITY OF CALIFORNIA PRESS

Berkeley   Los Angeles   London

University of California Press, one of the most distinguished
university presses in the United States, enriches lives around
the world by advancing scholarship in the humanities, social
sciences, and natural sciences. Its activities are supported by
the UC Press Foundation and by philanthropic contributions
from individuals and institutions. For more information, visit
www.ucpress.edu.

University of California Press
Berkeley and Los Angeles, California

University of California Press, Ltd.
London, England

Library of Congress Cataloging-in-Publication Data

Guthman, Julie.
  Weighing in : obesity, food justice, and the limits of
capitalism / Julie Guthman.
     p.   cm.
  Includes bibliographical references and index.
  ISBN 978–0-520–26624–7 (cloth : alk. paper)
  ISBN 978–0-520–26625–4 (pbk. : alk. paper)
  1. Obesity, Social aspects.   I. Title.
  RA645.O23G88   2011
  362.196′398—dc22

                                        2011003848

Manufactured in the United States of America

20   19   18   17   16   15
10   9   8   7   6

To Mom, for Sierra

CONTENTS

ACKNOWLEDGMENTS

This book was conceived several years ago and emerged in part from several small research projects, some of which were supported by the University of California at Santa Cruz's Committee on Research and Social Science Division. I am thankful for this support. I am also thankful to Sarah Yahm and Amy Morris, graduate students who helped out with this earlier research.

Sometime in 2004, my colleague Melanie DuPuis and I first pounded out an article that became the backbone of this book. This book would not exist without her insights and encouragement. I am grateful, too, to Lené Whitley-Putz, who worked as the course assistant when I first taught the Politics of Obesity class in 2005. Her provocations and the course responses convinced me that there was a bigger story to tell. The book began to take form at a residential workshop at UC's Humanities Research Institute at UC Irvine in the fall of 2006. True to the intent of these workshops, those ten weeks away from my usual responsibilities provided the space and conversation to launch the project.

Over the years a number of people provided ideas that came to matter in this text, among them Joe Bryan, Mike Goodman, Jessica Hayes-Conroy, J. P. Jones, Jake Kosek, Katie LeBesco, and Kimberly Nettles. Amy Ross was especially influential with her always trenchant insights, this time about the conflation of self-care and philanthropy. Likewise, conversations with Becky Mansfield about the human body as a site of both ecological transformation and biopolitical discourse helped me see how to meld two very different approaches. I met Anna Kirkland, whose perspectives are quite close to my own, late in the process. Apparently, we were thinking and writing similar things at the same time; I worry she is underacknowledged in the text.

It was not until late in the project that I realized I was following a science studies approach of sorts. Scientists I interviewed and with whom I discussed the project were extremely generous with their comments and resources. Several coffees and email discussions with Katherine Flegal of the Centers for Disease Control and Prevention were particularly useful, as were my discussions on endocrine disruption with Retha Newbold of the National Institute of Environmental Health Sciences and Bruce Blumberg of UC Irvine. The Science and Justice Working Group at UC Santa Cruz was also influential in the development of my thinking.

Colleagues who commented on draft chapters and otherwise substantially supported the project include Alison Alkon, Charlotte Biltekoff, Aaron Bobrow-Strain, Melissa Caldwell, Carolyn de la Pena, Melanie DuPuis, Ryan Galt, and Paul Robbins. Sharing pieces of this work at the Environmental Politics Colloquium at UC Berkeley, the UC Multicampus Research Program on Food and the Body, and BFP (an informal working group) was tremendously useful for working through key ideas. Talks in geography departments at the Universities of Minnesota, Georgia, and British Columbia, Penn State, and Clark sharpened my thinking. I am extremely grateful to be part of all of these intellectual communities.

The manuscript itself was profoundly transformed and improved thanks to the tough love of two reviewers. I owe Susanne Friedberg and Becky Mansfield a huge debt of gratitude for their detailed in situ comments and broader pushes to align my abundant arguments. Other close friends and family generously read and commented on nearly finished chapters in ways that made the text more readable: Jerry Kohn, Michael McCormick, Andrea Steiner.

At UC Press, Jenny Wapner was an extraordinarily gifted and kind hands-on editor whose deep engagement in the project made her comments so very useful. I was really sad when she left the press and I particularly appreciate her continued support thereafter. In Jenny's wake, Sheila Levine and the production staff handled the manuscript with aplomb. I wish to thank Madeleine Adams for her superb work during the copyediting phase. I'd be remiss if I didn't mention Peter Wissoker, formerly at Cornell University Press, who encouraged the project and gave terrific feedback at the book's most inchoate stages. Thanks to Debora Pinkas for important advice.

The Community Studies Department at UC Santa Cruz played an enormous role in the shape, direction, and completion of the book, for better or for worse. For better, I've had the good fortune to work with some of the smartest and most engaged undergraduates one could find. They have been my muses and inspirations for much of what is in this book and have shaped my thinking as much as they say I have shaped theirs. I hope they will forgive me for using their comments and ideas as rhetorical devices. For worse, I have written this book during a sustained effort by some in the university's administration to eliminate the department, allegedly for budgetary reasons, although many observers would argue that it reflects the unfortunate neoliberalization of the university. As I write this, I do not know the final outcome. The stress of simultaneously putting this book together and trying to keep this groundbreaking department alive was too much to bear at times. Nonetheless, it gave me a newfound understanding of social movement strategy, which is in some sense a subtext of this book. Special shout-outs to Mary Beth Pudup and Andrea Steiner for being the best of colleagues in the worst of times. I have learned a great deal from working with them. And many thanks to Joan Peterson for steadfast commitment to the department and our students.

My parents and brother deserve thanks for providing love, confidence, and a good amount of fodder to pull off a book as provocative as this. My very deepest gratitude is to the two people I most love to live with, Michael and Sierra McCormick. Michael, I couldn't do it without you. Sierra, I will miss you very much when you go off to college. Be good, and I hope this book doesn't embarrass you.

CHAPTER 1

Introduction

What's the Problem?

A PERSONAL PROLOGUE

This book begins with me, even though starting this way makes me profoundly nervous. Over the years I've learned that just about all scholars have autobiographical connections to their research, although the connections don't always matter. I have an urge to come clean with mine, because I do have a personal stake in my arguments. Here at the outset I'm going to admit that I'm a foodie, and I'm going to have to convince you that I'm not a hypocrite. I'm going to admit that I'm not very thin, and I want to convince you that the current public conversation about obesity is wrongheaded. I'll even admit that I'm fairly privileged and still find much to fault in contemporary capitalism. In fact, the topics in this book come full circle for me. It all begins with my father.

My father was a "health food nut" long before natural foods were popularized. A sickly, bedridden child, in 1945 he moved to California as a young adult in search of the California dream and its promises of health. His first business was a health food store in Pasadena. Over the years, he followed and even befriended many of the health food gurus of the day, including Jack LaLanne, Paul Bragg, and John Robbins. He never met a dietary restriction he didn't like, constantly badgered his loved ones about weight and eating habits, and, while he valorized the "natural" above all, he too readily conflated the natural, the healthy, and the aesthetic. My father went from being a sickly, bedridden child to a singular specimen of physical health in adulthood, overcoming all odds of early death through his unflagging daily practices of rote exercise and orthorexic eating. (*Orthorexia* is a neologism that refers to self-imposed strictures concerning what foods one eats—a discipline now quite fashionable.) At the age of eighty-five, he refused one bite of (as I recall, additive-free, organic) ice cream with his one beloved grandchild (my daughter) providing the temptation. He deemed this one bite poison and, as with many of his other refusals, took obvious pleasure in the denial. He died a year later in a bizarre accident, an apparent result of his Alzheimer's-diminished cognitive abilities and an ironic ending to a life defined by efforts to ensure longevity.

As for me, well, I drank raw milk as a kid, ate lots of meat (because at the time he thought it was healthy), and was allowed ice cream only once a year. If I wanted a treat, I had to eat carob-chip whole wheat cookies made with honey, which in the mid-1960s were truly awful, or our homemade peanut butter "candy" made of natural peanut butter, honey, and dried milk. When our family ate out, we never went to McDonald's or anything like it but ate at those late-1960s hippie restaurants that dotted Los Angeles, including the one where a famous scene in the movie *Annie Hall* was filmed. Early on I discovered how dietary strictures provoke desire, and I came to love Wonder Bread, found in the cupboards of my school-age friends' homes, and luncheon meat. By the time I went to college at UC Santa Cruz, I had come to love brown hippie food—but also Doritos and Budweiser.

As an adult living in Berkeley, California, I have long since dropped the Bud and Doritos and have developed a penchant for yuppie food. Like many others of my boomer generation, I first started drooling over restaurant menus in the 1980s and soon learned to love mesclun, or salad mix. In fact, my fascination with salad mix—then selling at fifteen dollars a pound—provoked the research that eventually became the subject of my first book, *Agrarian Dreams: The Paradox of Organic Farming in California*. *Agrarian Dreams*, which examines the production of organic food in California, shows how and why organic agriculture was unable to break away from the legacies of industrial farming in California. Much of it turned on California real estate, something I knew quite a lot about too, since many years ago my father shifted from health foods to the real estate business, another archetypal Southern California endeavor. Real estate figures in this book, too, because the kind of urban environments seen as *not* contributing to obesity tend to be extremely expensive places to live.

Today, as anyone who knows me will tell you, I'm one of those annoying San Francisco Bay Area foodies who shop at the farmers market once, twice, or sometimes thrice a week and get very excited about the deep yellow hues of egg yolks from pasture-raised hens, the sweetness of dry-farmed tomatoes, and the paradoxically relaxing work of shelling beans. I also read the food section of the newspaper diligently, spend a good deal of my disposable income on food and wine, and, worst of all, can barely conceal my distaste for food that doesn't meet my particular standards of quality, which for me turns on how it was farmed and processed. Still, as I continue to fluctuate between both ends of the "overweight" category about which you will learn, one of my doctors has invoked the "obesity epidemic" to warn me to watch my weight. As my blood glucose level has crept just above the "normal" range, another one of my doctors has told me to cut down on sugar. For the record, I never drink sodas of any kind and I would wager that my diet is as close to what the food guru Michael Pollan recommends as his own. In researching this book, I now have reason to believe that my body mass and blood glucose levels, along with the hypothyroidism I have developed, may have something to do with environmental toxins. Or maybe just middle age. Of course, I will never really know.

To continue my story: After receiving my PhD in geography at UC Berkeley, I had the good fortune to join the Community Studies Department at the University of California at Santa Cruz (UCSC). Established in 1969 as a way to provide students an academically rigorous understanding of social change efforts, the community studies major has been an outstanding and unique laboratory for examining the shifts in social movement objectives, strategies, topics, and institutional forms over the past several decades. Tellingly, the past decade has seen unprecedented student interest in food and agriculture as both site and means of social transformation.

This interest owes its intensity, in no small part, to the pervasiveness of foodie culture on California's central coast and in the San Francisco Bay Area. As I discuss in *Agrarian Dreams*, UCSC and the county of Santa Cruz were ground zero for the US alternative food and agriculture movement. Today students at UCSC can be rapt in their devotion to various permutations of local, organic, vegan, and so forth. Witnessing this interest, my department created a position in local/global political economy of food, and I was hired in 2003 to accommodate the many students who wanted to work in this area. Student interest has grown even more since then, buoyed by the sheer number of people and organizations involved in alternative food. I use the term *alternative food* as shorthand to describe institutions and practices that bring small-scale farmers, artisan food producers, and restaurant chefs together with consumers for the market exchange of what is characterized as fresh, local, seasonal, organic, and craft-produced food. These have taken hold mainly in certain coastal regions and university enclaves, whose rarified character can be measured by the degree to which my arguments will make more sense to those who live in or frequently visit those regions.

I tell you this because the insights my students bring from the community studies curriculum also figure in this book. To earn a community studies degree, a student is required to do field study with a social justice or social change organization full-time for six months. I have worked most closely with the students who work with organizations trying to transform food systems or otherwise address food- and environment-related inequities. How they first frame their social justice aspirations is telling. Many of my students want to enable people to make "healthy food choices" and even to "teach people how to eat." Typical statements to gain entry into the class include: "I would love to be a part of the food justice movement. . . . I would love to work with families that do not have the opportunity or proper education to live healthy and in harmony with the food they are living off of." Some have explicitly discussed obesity as evidence of the problem of inequity in the food system.

I refer to my students quite a bit in this book because I've come to see their comments as indicative of pervasive discourses in current food movements. My own research on food security and access to healthy food has shown me that my students' ideas are accurate reflections of how the alternative-food movement discusses social justice: namely, as a problem of lack of access to alternative food, with obesity as a consequence of this lack of access. In fact, what originally animated my interest in obesity as a research topic was that I observed activists invoking the obesity epidemic in support of programs to bring more fresh fruits and vegetables into the schools. I wondered how and why the alternative-food movement would latch on to this problem to which it could be a solution.

Meanwhile, I have watched my daughter make her way through the Berkeley public school system and, hence, exposed to the cooking and gardening curricula conceived by the chef-cum-activist Alice Waters. Although the goal of these programs is to connect children to nature and the taste of wholesome food, ideas about acceptable bodies have never been far off the agenda. In middle school, my daughter told me of how her cooking and gardening teachers discussed calorie counting. She also was asked to write a school essay on the value and ethics of student weigh-ins, and had been encouraged to watch cable television shows in which children policed their families' eating practices through various healthy eating initiatives. As a preteen she came to hear and know more about obesity, anorexia, and bulimia than I did at that age. As a teenager she has clearly internalized norms of body and good food—both for better and for worse.

At one point I noticed that all of the food writers who are rightful critics of the modern food system, including Michael Pollan, Marion Nestle, Raj Patel, Eric Schlosser, and Jane Goodall, were taking up the cause of obesity in epidemic fashion. Following in the footsteps of several generations of writers and activists who have criticized industrial food for both the environmental effects of producing it and the probable health effects of eating it, Pollan stands apart in bringing these ideas to what is likely the broadest audience ever. If Amazon.com commentary and various blogs are at all reasonable indicators, his best-selling books have convinced many people of the ecological irrationality of the conventional food system and transformed many diets to include much more local, seasonal, and organic produce—and much less processed food and conventionally raised meat. His 2008 letter to the president-elect and "farmer in chief" and his vocal activism on the 2008 farm bill have brought long-absent public attention to food and farm policy by showing how it matters for more than just farmers (Pollan 2008a). And in foodie enclaves, especially in the San Francisco Bay Area, he has achieved a godlike status. I constantly hear him invoked in conversations at farmers markets, upscale restaurants, and food-related conferences, meetings, and fundraisers. It is precisely because he is having such a visible effect on the shape of food politics that I feel compelled to engage some of his claims in this book.

Having stated that, I want to make something very clear at the outset: although I take issue with alternative food, for reasons that will be elucidated in this book, *I am not an apologist for the conventional food system and this book should not be read as a defense of it.* I rarely disagree with Pollan or these other authors regarding their critiques of industrial food production and corporate influence on food policy. If anything, I find that Pollan's critiques, especially, do not go far enough since they don't effectively challenge inequality in the food system. Eating local, organic, seasonal food that you prepared yourself may be pleasurable but it is not universally so, nor is it tantamount to effecting social justice. Of course, Pollan is echoing what many in the alternative-food movement for years have asked us to do: buy sustainably produced food, so that the market will respond and the food system will eventually transform to provide food that is grown with attention to agroecological principles. Not only is that logic highly aspirational but also, as I will argue in this book, the alternative-food movement's embrace of, well, alternatives that are in seeming opposition to what is bad in the food system works against broader transformation. This is because the creation of alternatives simultaneously produces places and people that for various reasons cannot be served by *an alternative* and therefore are put beyond consideration.

Obesity enters into this discussion because Pollan, more than any other food writer, has become carried away with linking growing girth to the US food system. In the *Omnivore's Dilemma*, for example, his primary narrative is that corn became the foundation of the national diet and made Americans fat. After *Zea mays* easily took hold in a variety of microclimatic conditions and outdid wheat in terms of its yield and easiness to grow, its strength turned into a weakness: corn was prone to systematic overproduction in US agriculture, so that even historically, surpluses ended up to no good, with corn liquor becoming the beverage of choice (and necessity) in pre-Prohibition drinking binges. Corn overproduction was later buttressed by a farm policy that subsidizes corn production to appease the farm lobby. Pollan then jumps to the omnipresence of corn in a fast-food meal: the high-fructose corn syrup that sweetens the soda, the feed of the steer that goes into the hamburger, often the oil that fries the potatoes, one of the many microingredients that stabilizes the bun. And he uses his own personal experiment to write about a broader "us" driving down the road and stuffing a McDonald's Happy Meal into our collective face, in a sort of daze of unnatural satiety. The narrative of corn is capped with what appears to be a simple fact. "When food is abundant and cheap, people will eat more of it and get fat" (p. 102).

One aim of this book is to make you question this claim—to show that it is not as simple as it appears. Why, for example, is food so cheap? Do people really eat it just because it is there? Do they eat more than they used to? Why isn't everyone fat? Simplified problems lead to simple solutions, and because local, organic, fresh, and seasonal food has been posed in opposition to all that is wrong with the food system, it is being posed as what is right for our bodies and health. So the solution has become education to encourage us to make a different set of choices. Never mind that the importance of organic, fresh, and local was constructed in advance of and independent of the obesity issue, so that this particular solution seems to have found a new problem. As a result of this articulation of problem and solution, we are being presented with a self-serving, self-congratulatory discourse that exalts certain ways of being and disparages others, and places blame in many of the wrong places. This is not only a superficial but also an unjust way to have this conversation. It may be time to put other things on the table in addition to that healthy, organic, local food and pay closer attention to the problem. But what *is* the problem? I hope this book gives you an answer other than obesity.

AN INTERESTING PARALLEL

In April 2009, researchers at the London School of Hygiene and Tropical Medicine released a study that "showed" that obese people add more greenhouse gases to the atmosphere than thin people. Assuming that obese people eat and drive more than thin people, they deduced that the extra fuel devoted to feeding and transporting the obese was exacerbating global warming. As one of the principal investigators, Phil Edwards, put it, "The main message is staying thin. It's good for you, and it's good for the planet" (Landau 2009).

This was not the first time obesity was linked to global warming, or environmental degradation and resource depletion more broadly. In a 2006 article titled "Luxus Consumption: Wasting Food Resources through Overeating" (Blair and Sobal 2006), the authors described several calculations they had made to ascertain "the impact of eating on the ecosystem" based on current estimates of obesity rates in the United States. They stated that the 4.5 kg of extra fat each person, on average, is carrying (a total of 9.9 trillion kcals in the national population) would be released as CO_2 at that person's death (p. 65). They also argued that the 600 calories per day per capita increase made available between 1983 and 2000, of which they estimated 400 calories were eaten and 200 wasted, was using an additional 0.36 hectares of land per capita, for a total of one hundred million hectares going to produce this excess food (p. 67). They concluded by pointing to the utility of "luxus consumption" as a concept that has great potential to motivate and offer students, in particular, a link between overconsumption and environmental degradation (p. 71). Using similar logic, another set of authors argued that more "temperate behavior" would lead to better environmental protection (Cafaro, Primack, and Zimdahl 2006).

In certain respects, these studies appear to be opportunities to link and amplify crises (e.g., obesity *and* global warming) rather than explain them. Casting individual consumption practices as the source of public health and environmental problems, even those as complex as global warming, is a coarse analysis at best. That they are linked at all demonstrates the persistence of

Malthusian thinking. Thomas Malthus's argument, first published in 1798, is that unchecked population growth would outstrip food production. The claims in these articles from 2006 and 2009, though, are more of the *neo-Malthusian* sort. Rather than too much reproduction, the problem is too much consumption; rather than too little food production, it is broader environmental degradation and resource shortage. Who is to blame? For Malthus, the responsibility for population outstripping resources lay most squarely with poor people, who, he believed, could not curb their sexual appetites because of their ignorance or negligence. For the authors of the recent studies, the problem lies with those who appear to be uneducated about or negligent of the impact their eating has on both their bodies and their carbon footprints.

There's much to critique in this line of argument, not the least of which are the ideas that appetite is a driving force of how food is produced and distributed and that insufficient food production causes hunger. I hope that by the end of this book you will be skeptical of these claims and others embedded in that argument, especially the idea that body size affects planetary health. But I begin here for another reason: to draw parallels between representations of the obesity epidemic and of the global warming crisis. I emphatically do not deny that the earth's atmosphere has warmed or that people in the United States have gotten bigger over the past thirty years. Rather, I want to point out how ways of looking at these phenomena shape our understanding of what might be done about them. Much of our knowledge of global warming is an artifact of computational models of global climate change that include certain biophysical phenomenon and not others and use computer simulation in lieu of observational measurements. That doesn't make them wrong, but it does make them partial (Demeritt 2001). The causes of global warming are complex and interactive, a convergence of a variety of human-induced activity and secular patterns in earth-sun relations, and yet the current scientific consensus is that reducing CO_2 emissions is what must be done. This prescription leads to a disproportionate focus on individual consumption choices about which people should be educated rather than, say, a focus on enacting policies that would enforce corporate accountability, or on mitigating the consequences for those most harmed (Forsyth 2003).

Analogous points can be made about obesity: although people have certainly gotten bigger since 1980, the "obesity epidemic" is an artifact of particular measurements and norms for assessing pathology. The causes of the rise in obesity are complex and interactive, and yet the current public health consensus is that reducing calorie intake, along with increasing calorie expenditure through exercise, is what must be done. Those who want to redress the problem put a great deal of effort into educating people to making better choices rather than into reforming the policies that allow bad food to be produced or mitigating the consequences for those most harmed. Yes, human bodies are different from the earth in the realm of the individually controllable, but perhaps not as much as you think.

Commonsense explanations of and solutions to both global warming and obesity are examples of what the environmental geographer Paul Robbins (2004) has called "apolitical ecologies," explanations of environmental degradation or resource depletion that do not account for social power in either *producing* environmental changes or *defining* them as problems. Instead, apolitical explanations posit that environmental degradation results from the aggregation of uninformed people making bad decisions, about which they should be educated. Political ecology, in contrast, subscribes to the idea that social, cultural, and political-economic relations profoundly affect both the materiality of the biophysical world and our understanding of it. So how might this apply to obesity?

TOWARD A POLITICAL ECOLOGY OF OBESITY

Obesity, I suggest, is an ecological condition that, like global warming, requires, if we are to understand it in a comprehensive way, that we pay attention to the broader political-economic and cultural context in which individual decisions affecting ecologies—even internal, bodily ecologies—are made (and human bodies do have ecologies). It also requires that we pay attention to the role of corporate behavior, state regulation, and the political economy more generally in producing or allowing pollution, degraded food, and problematic built environments, irrespective of the "choices" people make. At the same time, obesity being a condition that not all would agree is a problem, much less an illness, understanding it requires that we pay attention to how knowledge of obesity as a biological condition is constructed and interpreted. As it happens, the human-environment tradition in geography and cognate fields has much to offer on questions of health and illness, and many of the insights it has yielded in regard to the environment "out there" may be applicable to questions of bodily health "in here," and obesity in particular. In what follows, I draw on key insights from political ecology and science studies to suggest some of the ways we might consider obesity through these lenses.

Producing Ecological Problems

As a scholarly field, political ecology "combines the concerns of ecology and a broadly defined political economy" (Blaikie and Brookfield 1987: 17). It first developed in academic geography, anthropology, and rural sociology in response to once-standard explanations of human-induced environmental changes in the developing world, many of which were decidedly Malthusian. These explanations tended to attribute land degradation to direct resource users' lack of education or will to use resources wisely. Early political ecologists strove to show how seemingly destructive environmental behaviors needed to be understood in the context of broader political-economic forces. For example, a seminal work on soil erosion in developing countries discussed that Nepalese peasants who farmed on steep Himalayan hillsides were skilled land managers who built and tended terraces to prevent erosion. The extent to which they neglected sound practices often reflected their need to work away from their farms or produce more because of poor prices or the "rent-seeking" practices of an extractive state (Blaikie 1985). Political ecologists urged that individual behavior be understood within a "chain of explanation," referring to the entirety of interlinking forces beyond the direct resource user (Blaikie and Brookfield 1987).

The idea that broader political-economic forces shape the conditions in which overexploitation, degradation, or pollution of natural resources occurs is one of political ecology's most important theses (Robbins 2004). Surely, this can be seen in the case of the CO_2 emissions responsible for global warming, which political ecologists would attribute to corporate malfeasance or the necessity of unfettered economic growth rather than individual consumers' decisions to use incandescent light bulbs. Apropos of contemporary US agriculture, a farmer's decision to use toxic pesticides is often a matter of economic survival to ensure against crop loss since prices offered by buyers are notoriously low, with low prices often a result of state efforts to enhance farmers' productivity (see chapter 6). Yet, as we shall see, those pesticides may contribute to obesity. Similarly, consumers' choices may be highly constrained by forces far removed from their everyday lives, from the agricultural policies that have encouraged the substitution of high-fructose corn syrup for cane sugar to the economic development policies that have created urban environments that lack grocery stores with healthful food. To the extent that eating and exercise behaviors contribute to obesity, these behaviors don't happen in a vacuum of social possibility.

It is not only through individual decisions and behaviors that people may have become bigger, however. It appears that some of the growth in girth is environmentally caused in a more direct sense. This suggests a need to engage with environmental health and justice scholarship, which has considered the more immediate relationships between environment and health. This scholarship was begat by a social movement that arose in the US domestic context. The environmental health movement responded to mainstream environmentalism's long-standing dedication to wilderness preservation and relative neglect of urban, industrial environments' effects on health (Gottlieb 1993). Both the movement and supporting scholarship have also emphasized health inequalities: that different environments can produce differential life chances since groups marginalized by their race, class, gender, or citizenship status tend to be disproportionately exposed to health-depriving conditions in their jobs, neighborhoods, and home environments or have less access to health-giving environmental amenities (e.g., open space) (Pulido 2000; Shrader-Frechette 2005; Sze 2007). Interestingly, the newly emerged food justice movement has borrowed heavily from these ideas to frame the lack of access to healthy food and the prevalence of obesity in certain neighborhoods as an environmental injustice (Alkon and Agyeman 2011). Though important, such accounts effectively emphasize constrained choice rather than the more direct ways that the environment can affect health.

The probable role of environmental toxins in obesity (see chapter 5) would seem to require a more traditional reading of environmental justice perspectives that focuses on the effects of industrial processes and pollutants on bodily health, irrespective of behavior. It also calls for more engagement with the ecology of disease, specifically how environmental conditions work materially with bodies to debilitate them (Mayer 1996). Newer work on the ecology of health points to exciting ways forward. As put by Nancy Langston in her book *Toxic Bodies* (2010: 147), a separation between the body and the environment is impossible to sustain, since "the body is enmeshed in a web of relationships, not isolated in a castle." In her book *Inescapable Ecologies*, Linda Nash (2007) recites the multiple ways that the putative boundary of the body is permeated, through, for example, inhalation, ingestion, epidermal absorption, insect bites, suckling of breast milk, and open wounds. The work of the ecologist Sandra

Steingraber (1997) has been particularly exemplary in articulating some of the biological pathways between the ecologies of agricultural landscapes and of humans. By drawing attention to the effects of toxic exposures, both she and Langston highlight the social causes of cancer and developmental disorders far beyond individual decision making, and often attributable to a failure of environmental regulation. Their emphasis on prenatal exposures to toxins is especially significant for obesity, in light of the emerging evidence I will discuss.

Discovery of the possibility that environmental toxins are contributing to obesity offers the hope that attention will shift away from individual life-styles and the social scolding that accompanies that focus. As Phil Brown discusses in *Toxic Exposures* (2007), social movements have worked assiduously to reframe "contested illnesses" such as asthma, breast cancer, and Gulf War syndrome as caused by environmental exposures rather than lifestyle factors, precisely to draw more regulatory attention. Yet, it is equally important to consider why fat people (and others) might reject disease labels, even those that may be environmentally caused. Being pinned with a disease has consequences, which can include denial of health care or relegation to victim status (LeBesco 2004). In general, environmental health and justice approaches have been less concerned with the politics of disease knowledge and interpretation (Harper 2004: 298). It seems, though, that illnesses that are truly contested, such as obesity, beg for that sort of analysis.

Interpreting and Representing Ecological Problems

As it happens, political ecologists have been equally engaged in questions of knowledge production and interpretation of states of nature. This is because they were also responding to top-down evaluations of what constitutes "degradation." Many studies showed that ideas of degradation and overuse were inaccurate and infused with colonial or neocolonial ideas about land users' ignorance. For instance, in direct contradiction to narratives of deforestation promulgated by international development institutions, an investigation of forest cover in West Africa found that it was actually increasing, thanks to peasant practices (Fairhead and Leach 1995). Political ecologists also demonstrated that ideas of degradation were not only contested but also often used in the service of controlling and further marginalizing populations. For example, wildlife protection in Tanzania entailed the eviction and resettlement of native populations into increasingly smaller areas at the expense of traditional livelihood practices (Neumann 1998). These sorts of findings inspired broader concern with the politics of knowledge and representation in political ecology: for example, questions such as how we assess a degraded landscape and what purposes are served by calling an environmental problem a crisis (Robbins 2004). Given the tendencies to assess obesity in terms of illness and to apply crisis narratives (e.g., the obesity *epidemic*), such approaches are surely relevant.

Interpreting health "in here" is no less fraught than interpreting nature "out there." Both rely on ecological and biological sciences to render them understandable. Despite facile claims to the contrary, how we know nature, even through science, is always through human eyes, experience, passions, desires, and often competing rationalities (Williams 1980). If anything, health is even more complex since our own feelings, sensations, and observations of bodily processes allow us to report on, but also affect, our health. Significant cultural variations in the experience of childbirth pain, for example, suggest that pain cannot be reduced to the firing of synapses. As so wonderfully depicted in the book *The Spirit Catches You* (Fadiman 1998), the story of a Hmong child afflicted with epilepsy living in California, disease more generally is subject to interpretation. In this girl's case, doctors were continually frustrated by her parents' refusal not only to give the child medicine as directed but also to interpret the disease as life-threatening in the way the doctors did.

Still, scientific interpretation is not simply an issue of cultural relativism. (Few adhere to the "hard constructivism" or "cultural relativism" that denies the existence or knowability of a reality outside of language; Demeritt 1998.) The more germane point is that scientific discovery and reporting take place in social contexts, so knowledge of health and environmental problems necessarily reflects the manifold social relations that affect science: from grantor funding priorities to peer review to personal friendships (Hess 1997). For these reasons, it is important to scrutinize the practice of science as much as what it describes, for example, by tracing "the ways in which social interests, values, history, actions, institutions, networks, and so on shape, influence, structure, cause, explain, inform, characterize, or constitute the content of science and technology" (Hess 1997: 82). Funding and peer review have demonstrably affected obesity science, for example; perhaps practitioners' displeasure with fatness has, too. This suggests the usefulness of what some call a science studies approach, which examines how and for whom scientific knowledge is produced as a way to promote reflexivity about the scientific process (Reardon 2005).

Such an approach is particularly useful for engaging politically with biophysical factors that exist independent of explicit political-economic conflicts or outside of human experience, such as human physiological processes (Forsyth 2003: 7). What Forsyth calls a "critical political ecology" combines the insights of political ecology and science studies to allow for politicized explanation beyond the kind offered by political economy (p. 7). For him, the "aim is to highlight as far as possible the implicit social and political models built into statements of supposedly neutral explanation in order to increase both the social equity of science and its relevance to environmental problems experienced within diverse social settings" (p. 20). He suggests a number of tools toward this end, one of which is attention to metaphors and semiotics in representations of biophysical processes.

The use of metaphors to understand and explain bodily function is ubiquitous in matters of health. Yet medical experts often are not mindful of the metaphors they use to translate their findings to a broader public and, because those metaphors hold such cultural power, the public is usually not mindful of what messages they convey. Such mindfulness is important, though, since metaphors tell larger stories about what is ostensibly normal. Emily Martin's (1991) seminal work (pun intended) on the egg and the sperm tells of the inherent sexism of classic renditions of the active sperm penetrating the passive egg, even though some biologists have determined that the egg actively "selects" sperm. She also discusses how menstruation is often represented as waste from an unsuccessful fertilization rather than a regular cleansing of the uterus. Note that Martin uses metaphors, too; they are indeed unavoidable—and that is the point. How we know health depends on how we talk about it, and how we talk about it shapes how we think about it.

Scientific discussions of obesity employ all sorts of metaphors that paint the picture in generally unflattering ways. Fat cells are often portrayed in ways similar to fat people: they are described as yellow, bloated, greasy, flabby. This is despite research that shows that fat cells can play an important role in regulating appetite and metabolism. In that vein, the use of metaphors of pathology and adaptation bears scrutiny as well. Evolutionary biologists, for example, talk about the mismatch of our evolutionary heritage with our modern lifestyle and particularly the tendency to store fat, a tendency that was once adaptive and has become pathological (Power and Schulkin 2009). But what exactly makes it pathological—that it is debilitating or merely unsightly? More fundamentally, how do metaphors of adaptation and pathology more generally shape understandings of acceptable bodily change?

Forsyth (2003) also directs attention to the specific tools and techniques used to measure environmental—and thus health—problems. What others have called "artifactual constructivism" concerns the techniques, laboratory practices, conventions, observational methods, instrumentation, and measurements that produce scientific facts, an approach that, incidentally, has been applied to global climate change models (Demeritt 1998). Examining how tools and techniques shape scientific findings and thus knowledge is highly significant in medical science, which relies on hundreds, if not thousands, of such tools and techniques to experiment, measure, and diagnose. Imaging technology, biosampling, and patient questionnaires are just a few such techniques that are necessarily imperfect in what they can portray. As we shall see in chapter 2, tools developed from epidemiology to quantify the obesity epidemic favor the easily measurable or quantifiable, such as the body mass index, and draw inferences about pathology based on statistical conventions such as the bell curve.

Although much of the focus thus far has been on how the social shapes science, it is equally instructive to consider causality in the opposite direction: how new technologies and scientific findings shape and even create new social relationships (Hess 1997: 83). The notion of coproduction offers that reciprocity. Coproduction recognizes that the production of scientific knowledge is simultaneously the production of social order (Jasanoff 2004). Jenny Reardon's use of the term *coproduction* is particularly sensitive to the ways that scientific objects and phenomena are brought into being in the course of studying them. In her research on the Human Diversity Project, for example, Reardon (2005) found that efforts to study human origins independent of "race" tended to reinscribe racial categories because all attempts at defining populations to be sampled relied on various preconceived ideas about the category of race! Efforts to understand obesity as a scientific problem provide numerous examples of coproduction. As we shall see in chapter 4, studies that have attempted to show *that* (crucially, not *whether*) the built environment makes us fat are rife with already existing assumptions about the causes of obesity as mediated through the environment.

Perhaps the most important concept from science studies that applies to obesity is that of problem closure. Problem closure occurs when a specific definition of a problem is used to frame subsequent study of the problem's causes and consequences and thus precludes alternative conceptualizations of the problem (Hajer 1995: 22). Problem closure can entail defining the purpose of inquiry as, for example, determining the causes of a problem rather than mitigating its consequences, or even defining the problem in relation to socially acceptable solutions. In the case of climate change policy, problem closure is evident in the focus on reducing atmospheric gases rather than reducing vulnerability to climate change (Forsyth 2003: 79). Forsyth argues that it may be more important to focus on the effects of climate change rather than its causes, especially since the same changes can be produced by different causes. It is especially important to understanding how climate change is *experienced* since localized consequences are varied and still unknown. He draws this conclusion from a case that relates directly to obesity, that of HIV/AIDS. As recounted by Steven Epstein in *Impure Science* (1998), activists played a crucial role in reformulating the problem of AIDS from definitively identifying whether HIV is its cause to developing more antiviral drugs to treat its symptoms.

In the case of obesity, problem closure appears evident in the focus on getting people to eat more fresh fruits and vegetables, whether through health education, snack taxes, or changes to federally funded school meal programs. This is not to disparage fresh fruits and vegetables; it is to note that the solution in some sense wags the dog of the problem statement, for it assumes that obesity is caused by a lack of fruit and vegetable consumption. It also seems evident in the current emphasis on stopping and reversing the upward trend in obesity rates rather than investigating the ways in which bigger bodies affect biological functionality. In general, obesity seems a prime candidate for problem opening, especially in light of the social consequences of relegating vast numbers of people to having undesirable phenotypes. Like global warming, growth in girth represents a significant ecological change, but its dangers should be evaluated through engagement with those who are likely to be most affected by both the material condition and the discursive climate.

Following Forsyth, the point of a critical political ecology approach is not to falsify myths—or even necessarily to reveal another certain explanation. Rather it is to illuminate problems in new and meaningful ways that might lead to other types of policy interventions, if there are to be any at all. That's what this book aims to do. Yet, to do so requires not only a reconsideration of the problem definition but also a political analysis that orients attention to the broader policy and cultural environment that behavioral perspectives neglect. And that requires an engagement with the nature of capitalism in the early twenty-first century.

BRINGING CAPITALISM BACK IN

As suggested in the previous section, one of the ways problem closure takes place is through the creation of solutions that are politically feasible or reasonably practical, so the politically tenable solutions define the problem (see chapter 7). Educating people to eat more fresh fruits and vegetables is one example, since there are ample opportunities to fund such initiatives and powerful economic interests would be hard pressed to find fault or otherwise get in the way. And yet, as I will argue throughout this book, the problem for which obesity may be a weak proxy cannot be solved without challenging powerful economic interests. Furthermore, the limited menu of solutions to a deeply problematic food system reflects the cultural values and social power of those who have fared reasonably well under contemporary capitalism and thus are personally invested in particular ways of seeing the problem.

Here I want to introduce the concept of neoliberalism, since in many regards it is the defining principle of contemporary US capitalism since 1980 and has profoundly shaped how people think about their own duties and rights. As the eminent geographer David Harvey puts it in his *Brief History of Neoliberalism* (2005: 2), "Neoliberalism is in the first instance a theory of political economic practices that proposes that human well-being can best be advanced by liberating individual entrepreneurial freedoms and skills within an institutional framework characterized by strong private property rights, free markets, and free trade." It is, he argues, a particular twist on classic liberalism, which values individual liberties. Neoliberalism, in contrast, primarily values free enterprise, really a no-holds-barred approach to profit making in the name of the public good, despite its nods to broader liberties. As a practical political philosophy, neoliberalism has guided policy efforts to privatize public resources and spaces; minimize labor costs through, for example, defanging unions; reduce public expenditures on entitlements, subsidies, and other sorts of redistributive welfare (public health services, public education); eliminate regulations seen as unfriendly to business, especially health, labor, and other environmental protections; and reduce taxes in order to spur more private-sector investment (Jessop 2002; McCarthy and Prudham 2004; Peck and Tickell 2002).

Those who espouse neoliberalism have not been entirely successful—or consistent—in these efforts, since some state sectors, such as prisons, have grown significantly since 1980. And, importantly for this book, some policies that apply to the food and agriculture sector, such as the commodity subsidy program, are at odds with neoliberal philosophy. Nevertheless, as I will show in chapters 6 and 8, neoliberal policies have contributed to many of the food qualities, built environments, and chemical exposures associated with increased obesity. Equally if not more important, neoliberal economic policies have contributed to the heightened inequalities that have made cheap food a necessity and exacerbated the class and racial resentments that manifest in arguments about "good food."

In addition to particular economic policies, neoliberal philosophy has also generated ideas of self-governance and citizenship that further help the neoliberal political-economic project. The notion of "governmentality," originally coined by the philosopher Michel Foucault, refers to general strategies of rule that come into play at different times and places that encourage subjects to think and act in particular ways. While some "governmentalities" are directly coercive, those associated with liberalism tend to act through the will of individuals, who are educated to exercise rights and responsibilities (thus belying the idea that they are eminently free). In keeping with the idolatry of the market, neoliberal governmentality encourages subjects to make few demands on the state but rather to act through the market, or like the market, by exercising consumer choice, being entrepreneurial and self-interested, and striving for self-actualization and fulfillment (Rose 1999). Among other things, neoliberal governmentality shifts responsibility for care from public spheres (welfare) to personal spheres (self-help) (Burchell 1996; Dean 1999), and can depoliticize (or render futile) social struggles over resources and rights (Jessop 2002). As I will argue in chapter 3, neoliberalism has thus contributed to the idea that health is a personal responsibility more than a social one, which has allowed intensified social scolding of the obese. Likewise, neoliberalism has circumscribed the politics of the possible to that which can be obtained through "voting with your dollars," as discussed in chapter 7.

A FOOD SYSTEM PERSPECTIVE?

Many books and articles have been written about the so-called epidemic of obesity in terms of both its causes and its consequences. Alarmists treat it as the biggest public health threat (and more) of our time, with the potential to break the health care bank, exacerbate global warming, and send the country into economic collapse. Skeptics treat it as a discourse that serves to discipline and control, and in noting that fat people have always existed they come close to denying the abrupt change in body size seen in the past thirty years. Although I am sympathetic to the perspective that obesity is a disciplining discourse, this book will approach the topic from an angle different from either of those, reflecting, among other things, my scholarly interest in human-environmental relations. Taking the approach discussed here can show what's missing or perhaps mistaken about the alarmists' position while engaging with the ecological transformation in human bodies that the skeptics' position neglects.

I also approach this topic as a food studies scholar. As such, I am especially interested in the so-called food system perspective on obesity, a variant of the dominant alarmist position. Although the current conversation about obesity and good food includes medical professionals and researchers, health statisticians, city and regional planners, and public health practitioners, it is increasingly being shaped by nutritionists, alternative-food activists, farm and food policy advocates, food system researchers, and even food writers. And yet, those who share the idea that the food system is somehow responsible for the obesity epidemic tend to focus on food consumption more than food production, and tend to favor educational and consumerist approaches over food and farming policy as a means to transform food systems—and thus to affect obesity. Indeed, I will argue that their treatment of obesity exemplifies the strategic limitations of current ways of conceptualizing food system transformation.

To the extent that those who claim to take a food system perspective do focus on farm policy, they have been sold on the recently popularized idea that it is farm subsidies that drive the problem. Such an approach still does not engage how the food system—or the entire economy—produces the social inequalities and environmental exposures that are contributing to disparate health outcomes, whether or not they manifest as obesity. I hope to convince you that a food system perspective must go beyond the tremendous attention to lifestyles, eating behaviors, and even commodity subsidies that has recently preoccupied those in the food systems community. A food system perspective should incorporate the entire array of ideas, institutions, and policies that affect how food is produced, distributed, and consumed, including, for example, the roles of nutrition science, environmental regulation, the agricultural research and extension system, and international food aid and trade. (One of the reasons this book will focus primarily on the United States is to bring these policy issues to bear.)

OPENING UP THE CONVERSATION

In researching this book, I have attended several conferences and meetings where various actors from these epistemic communities came together to discuss how food and farming issues relate to obesity. I have also collected dozens of newspaper clippings and magazine articles on these topics and analyzed their content. I have looked at blogs and their often more important comment sections. I have listened very carefully to my students and others when they discussed these topics. My observations of these conversations provide a point of departure for the remainder of this book. What I have witnessed is a coalescence of a set of assumptions, which follows a more or less logical sequence:

- The rise in obesity is an "epidemic," and it is urgent that it be addressed.
- A set of tools from epidemiology, including body mass index, bell curves, and risk factors, adequately represent the pathology, distribution, and worsening of the condition of obesity.
- The broader public pays for obesity because the medical costs of obesity are great and socialized.
- Obesity results from an excess of calorie intake relative to calorie expenditure (the energy balance model).
- The built environment is largely responsible for obesity because of the ubiquity of fattening food and the dearth of opportunities for physical activity.
- Correlations between low socioeconomic status and obesity prevalence result from what people eat; specifically, low-income people are fat because they can afford to eat only cheap food, which gives more calories for the buck.
- Food is cheap and nutritionally inferior because of commodity subsidies.
- Obesity could be prevented with improved education and access to the right food, especially local, organic, fresh, and seasonal food.

Of course, there are minor points of disagreement over these assumptions in the various knowledge communities I have observed, or else there would be no room for discussion at all. Yet these disagreements rarely strike at the core assumption: that the rise in obesity is a huge problem and that there is an urgent need to do something about it directly, even in the absence of evidence that existing efforts to reduce obesity are effective (Campos et al. 2006).

In fact, researchers and advocates are so wedded to these assumptions that when they question one particular element—usually the one they know the most about from their own research—they do not question the other elements, which they take to be obvious. For example, on two different occasions I observed a prominent developmental biologist speak about the probable role of environmental toxins in causing obesity. In doing so, he explicitly refuted the notion that obesity results simply from an excess of calories taken in—a stance that portends a paradigmatic shift in obesity science. Yet, while presenting his own data with exquisite attention to the scientific methods by which they were obtained, he spoke of the other assumptions as if they were "common sense" and therefore needed no rigorous scrutiny. For instance, he stated that 8 percent of US medical costs are for obesity treatment, that low-income people tend toward obesity because of what they eat, and even that people in Europe are thinner because they eat more locally produced food (which is simply not the case).

In other words, discussions of obesity have engaged in a good deal of problem closure, which prevents other ways of thinking about it. If anything, the joining up of foodies with more traditional public health people has further delimited possible explanations, as well as solutions, if there are to be any. Of course there are minor points of disagreement. Foodies would have you opt for the full-fat yogurt as long as it was sustainably produced, because it is ultimately more satisfying, they would argue; nutritionists would encourage the nonfat version, or even the version with a synthetic sugar substitute, because it contains fewer calories. Nevertheless, both would tell you what to eat, despite the absence of evidence that dietary advice has done any good in mitigating the rise in obesity.

This book will challenge this problem closure by looking at some of the ways in which these presumptions do not hold up or lead to ethically problematic positions. I will not necessarily refute them with incontrovertible evidence. Rather, I will use a combination of countervailing evidence, political-economic and other social theoretical analysis, and ethical argumentation to suggest that all of these need rethinking. In response to these assumptions in particular, I will suggest that:

- The rise in obesity warrants explanation, but unexamined efforts to address it may do more harm than good.
- The emphasis on size and risk factors may not be the best way to think about pathology.
- The medical costs attributed to obesity are empirically suspect, and the emphasis placed on these costs reflects a shirking of social responsibility for well-being.
- Noncaloric pathways to obesity exist, as evidenced by new research on the role of environmental toxins and pharmaceuticals.
- The built environment reflects existing social relationships and political-economic dynamics, including racial and class patterns in size, more than it creates them.
- Low socioeconomic status can result from size as much as size can result from the behaviors associated with low socioeconomic status.
- Food is cheap because of deep-rooted geopolitical and political-economic interests that have encouraged overproduction and failed to regulate food production for health, safety, and welfare concerns.
- Eating behaviors are mediated by a more complex set of social factors than education and access; in any case, it is unlikely that the association of alternative food and thinness comes to be through individual diets of alternative food.

Undoubtedly, some will take my arguments as duplicating those of the early 1990s that, coincidentally, questioned global warming because of the limitations of global change models (Taylor and Buttel 1992). Among them would be Evelyn Kelly, the author of *Obesity* (2006), who is convinced that not enough is being done to stop obesity because people are suffering from "I-don't-care-itis." In this vein, it is worth considering that the climate change models were relatively new twenty years ago, but scientists have been trying to prove a mechanical relationship between, for example, overeating and obesity for more than 150 years with little success (Gard and Wright 2005). Again, my point is not to deny that people have gotten bigger but to suggest different ways of looking at the phenomenon.

In a nutshell, I will argue that the problem of obesity is an artifact of particular ways of measuring, studying, and redressing the phenomenon so that existing assumptions about its causes, consequences, and solutions are built into existing efforts to assess it independently as a problem. Not only does the problem definition leave out other possible explanations of both obesity's causes and its effects; some of the consequences of these explanations and proposed solutions work against social justice, whether or not that is the intention. Mainly, the conversation is very limiting, since it averts our gaze from what's really gone awry.

This, however, is not the only reason I subtitle the book "Obesity, Food Justice, and the Limits of Capitalism." This book is about limits in many senses of the word: the limits of industrial food production, the limits of the body to absorb what the food system produces, the limits of alternative-food movements to transform industrial food production. It is also about the limits of personal choice and so, I suppose, the limits of dietary limits. Ultimately, though, it is about the limits of capitalism.

CHAPTER 2

How Do We Know Obesity Is a Problem?

In the opening paragraphs of *The Fat of the Land: Our Health Crisis and How Overweight Americans Can Help Themselves* (Fumento 1997: xv–xvi), one of a raft of popular books that have fed hysteria about America's obesity problem, Michael Fumento recites a series of claims. First, he asserts that obesity "is the most common chronic health problem in America" and "its incidence is skyrocketing and the number of illnesses it appears to cause is increasing." He adds, "It boggles my mind to know that in the two years I took to write the book 600,000 of my fellow countrymen have had their lives cut short by this disease." The next paragraph begins with the claim that "a third of American adults are now classified as obese, defined as being at least 20 percent fatter than they should be" (a tautology if there ever was one). Paragraph three begins, "Worst of all, there is no end in sight to this epidemic. . . . But there is no natural constraint on obesity. It is the one disease that can just be getting worse and worse." Then he uses a trope that has become de rigueur in obesity discussions: he recounts that his travels in Europe, where Americans could be identified by their bigger body sizes and less stylish clothing, led to a set of epiphanies about the lifestyle-related roots of American fatness.

It is incontrovertible that Americans on average have gotten bigger over the past thirty years. But have they necessarily become fatter? Or more prone to illness? And is the trend so inexorable that everyone will soon be fat? One of the problems with Fumento's presentation—and others like it—is that it is difficult to separate the wheat of argument from the chaff of moral panic (Campos et al. 2006; Gard and Wright 2005). The presentation is also striking for its tautological definition of obesity and the seeming contradiction that no natural constraints exist for a condition that also causes death. Indeed, Fumento is quite loose with his definitions of disease and attributions of causality. Substantively, however, the claims are quite typical. But are they right?

This chapter will show that the "obesity epidemic" is an artifact of particular measures, statistical conventions, epidemiological associations, and rhetorical moves. The point is not that they are wrong; rather, it is that they paint the picture in ways that tend to overdramatize some elements and underspecify others, especially those that might lead to different conceptualizations of the problem. In general, existing ways of measuring and representing obesity show more concern with phenotype than with pathology—they are more interested in size than in disease. Thus, the visibility of fatness and the fact that many find it aesthetically displeasing seem to influence scientific and public understandings of it. Furthermore, statistical associations of obesity and death are treated as causal certainties, rather than tools of knowledge, which also distorts the ways we understand obesity as a health issue. As one consequence of these treatments, the discourse on obesity tends to pathologize fat bodies and neglect the pathways to impaired functionality, whether or not they manifest as fat. Indeed, this is evident in the very ways we define and deploy the term *obesity*.

DEFINING OBESITY

The term *obesity* reflects a medicalization of fatness. To medicalize is to treat particular behaviors or conditions as diseases or disorders. These can then be measured, monitored, and presumably cured (Sobal 1995). These days many states of being are medicalized, from attention deficit disorder to chronic fatigue syndrome to anxiety, shyness, and depression. Importantly, many medicalized conditions aren't necessarily life threatening, although they can interfere with well-being.

Medicalization is thus a double-edged sword. It can provide access to resources to treat unwanted conditions, and for some people having an official diagnosis and a possibility of treatment brings relief (Barker 2005). Medicalization also seems to introduce civility into discussions of bodily and behavioral difference. The more neutral, scientific-sounding names typically given to people with medicalized conditions, such as *obese patient, homosexual,* or *alcoholic,* replace more pejorative terms, such as *fatty, fag,* or *drunk.* At the same time, medicalization can turn nonnormative conditions and behaviors into problems in need of biomedical solution, and subject people to medical scrutiny regardless of their desires (Saguy and Riley 2005). Surely, the hysteria about the obesity epidemic belies the pretense that medical conditions are not judged. The term *morbidly obese* seems especially designed to elicit revulsion. In addition, as Kathleen LeBesco (2004) points out, medicalization diminishes the subjectivity of fat people, making them victims, not agents, of their own embodiment. For these reasons, fat activists prefer *fat*, just as "homosexuals" have adopted *queer*. Out of respect for these conventions of self-identification, I use *obesity* when representing the public health discourse; I use *fat, big,* or *large* when describing people in my own voice.

So in exactly what ways has fatness been medicalized? The World Health Organization (WHO) defines obesity as having "abnormal or excessive fat accumulation that presents a risk to health" (World Health Organization 2011). Note that the definition is about adiposity, not weight or size. This is appropriate since adipose tissue does play a role in regulating bodily function, as we will see in chapter 5. Abnormal and excessive are very different concepts, however, and that's where the definition gets slippery. *Abnormal* implies unusual form, so the problem resides simply in difference, whereas *excessive* implies a negative effect on functionality. Without reference to what exactly is impaired by this excess fat, such definitions give rise to tautological reasoning like Fumento's: you are obese if you are fatter than you should be. Alas, this slippage between condition and disease, between indicator and pathology, is the tip of the iceberg of the obesity epidemic's construction, so that a nonnormative (i.e., undesirable) body size that is no longer abnormal (i.e., unusual) stands in for much more than it can conceptually hold.

MEASURING OBESITY THROUGH BMI

The first statistical studies derived from national health examinations (the National Health and Nutrition Examination Survey) showed little change in age-adjusted mean body mass index (BMI) between 1960 and 1980, hovering around 25 for both men and women. Then, measurements taken between 1988 and 1994 showed a shift upward in mean BMI to 26.8 for men and 26.6 for women, and measurements taken between 1999 and 2002 showed another increase to 27.9 and 28.2 for men and women, respectively (Flegal et al. 2002; Kuczmarski et al. 1994). To translate, a change in women's BMI from 25 to 28.2 is a 13 percent increase in body mass, equivalent to about twenty pounds for a woman who is five feet five inches tall. Refuting the claim that trends in obesity are inexorable, growth in mean BMI between 1999 and 2008 slowed or leveled off for all population groups (Flegal, Carroll, et al. 2010). Specifying further, the moderate growth in mean BMI from 1960 to 1980 was a function of *height* as well as weight (see below); the marked rise in mean BMI after 1980 was a function of weight only (Power and Schulkin 2009: 24).

Since the BMI is the basis of calculation for the obesity epidemic, it makes sense to begin by looking more closely at this standard measure for determining who is too fat. The BMI is actually one of several proxy measures for obesity. Various other ways exist to measure "excess" body fat. They include skin-fold measurements, underwater weighing, computerized tomography (in-body visualization), and the widely used but rarely admitted "eyeball test" (Kelly 2006). Few are used in epidemiological settings because it would be prohibitively expensive to collect data on them from large enough samples. The BMI, in contrast, can be calculated from self-reports of height and weight obtained from health surveys, and from body measurements taken by health professionals in clinical settings. So it is primarily for epidemiological ease that the BMI has become the preferred way to approximate the prevalence of obesity. In effect, however, the use of the BMI has redefined obesity away from a question of impaired functionality and toward one of form.

The BMI is supposed to measure the relationship of body fat or adipose tissue to lean body mass in a way that can determine excessive adiposity. In fact, however, the BMI is merely a ratio of weight to height, specifically a calculation of a person's weight (in kilos) divided by the square of the height in meters (kg/m^2). So how did it come about that a weight to height ratio could measure adiposity, much less describe (or prescribe) optimal body size? Changing techniques of body measurements have generally reflected changing cultural ideas of optimal size as well as new scientific ideas (among other things, making historical comparisons of fatness difficult) (Hamin 1999). What is interesting about the BMI, though, is that it derived not from clinical assessments of health as it relates to body size, but from an observed mathematical pattern in body size. Specifically, through clinical observations a nineteenth-century physician named Adolphe Quetelet noted that weight tends to vary with the square of height. As discussed later in this chapter, this was just one of Quetelet's contributions to the use of statistical averaging to define the normal (Hacking 1990).

Quetelet's findings on weight/height ratios were largely ignored until the 1940s, when a statistician at the Metropolitan Life Insurance Company charted the death rates of its policy holders using this ratio (Oliver 2006: 19). Eventually, the resulting actuarial tables were deemed unreliable because the data were collected from self-reports of people purchasing insurance policies. Undoubtedly, in an earlier era of poor nutrition and lean bodies, people overstated their weight to suggest vigor and health in order to obtain the best price for insurance. Nevertheless, the ratio lived on as the standard way to determine normal and abnormal weights. Separately, self-reporting lived on to remain the primary way to collect data on height and weight. Well into the 1990s, men still tended to overstate their weight while women consistently understated it (Villanueva 2001).

Besides issues of data reliability, the BMI is actually a very crude measure of adiposity. The BMI makes no allowances for variations in bone mass and density, or somatic difference more generally. The earlier Metropolitan Life tables once categorized people according to small, medium, and large frames, but the BMI establishes one norm only. Moreover, the BMI cannot differentiate between lean body mass (muscle and bone) and fat body mass. Someone with ample muscle and bone, such as a body builder, would have a relatively high BMI, especially because muscle and bone have higher weight densities than body fat (Campos 2004). This is also how increasing heights, from better (or different) nutrition, have also contributed to increasing BMIs. Similarly, BMI values will be higher for someone with a long torso and short legs, because of the mass of the torso relative to limbs.

In addition, BMI doesn't account for recognizable and accepted variation across populations according to sex and "race," variations that actually present some critical puzzles for existing explanations of obesity. For now, note that both men and women are measured by the same index, even though women have evolved to store more adipose tissue for pregnancy and nursing, and women more generally show more marked variation in BMI across different sociological categories. Racial differences are even more confounding, since biological race is a problematic concept, with the establishment of racial differences being a product, not a basis, of racism (Hall 1992). Nevertheless, an important study found that black girls do not have more body fat than their white counterparts, despite their higher mean BMI; higher proportions of muscle tissue account for these higher BMIs (Flegal, Ogden, et al. 2010). The study used a new technology involving X-rays to ascertain total body fat and lean soft tissue. African Americans also tend to have relatively dense bones, which can account for higher BMIs (Ettinger et al. 1997). In general,

BMI is not a reliable measure of body fatness. Some estimate that at best it accounts for 60 to 75 percent of the variation in body fat content in adults (Ross 2005: 92).

More important, as an indicator of health status BMI doesn't capture much that is relevant to the functionality of fat. Since muscle, bone, and fat play very different roles in the body, using BMI as an indicator of an underlying health issue can create a significant diagnostic problem. For instance, established correlations between BMI and high blood pressure suggest an association, if not a clear causal link, between adiposity and high blood pressure. Correlations between skin-fold measurements (a measure of adipose tissue) and high blood pressure have not been established, however. This could mean that the association is between lean muscle and high blood pressure (Gaesser 2002). Someone with high BMI and high blood pressure might thus be misled to reduce his or her fatty tissue in ways that could worsen the problem. Among other things, this issue renders BMI inappropriate for clinical settings where it might be used to check and prescribe individual behaviors.

Furthermore, the character and placement of fat deposition seems to matter tremendously in terms of health outcomes. A number of studies have demonstrated that those who have substantial fat deposition on their torsos—so-called apples—are at higher risk for cardiovascular illnesses than "pears," who carry fat on their hips. Similarly, subcutaneous fat (fat right below the skin) is generally harmless, whereas visceral fat (fat surrounding the internal organs) is associated with diabetes, stroke, and cardiovascular disease (Montague and O'Rahilly 2000). According to the evolutionary biologists Michael Power and Jay Schulkin (2009), subcutaneous fat is an evolutionary adaptation. Groups that lived for long periods in high-latitude regions developed the ability to metabolize high-fat food substances that were available in cold climates, whereas those who were habituated to regions closer to the equator were less able to metabolize fat when exposed to more abundance and tended to deposit it viscerally. The BMI standard cannot possibly measure this variation in fat disposition.

CONSTRUCTING AN EPIDEMIC WITH BMI

In 2006, scientists from the Centers for Disease Control and Prevention (CDC) reported that obesity prevalence had nearly tripled between 1960 and 2003–4, from 12.8 percent of the population to 32.2 percent (Ogden et al. 2006). In the same study discussed earlier, CDC scientists also reported that as of 2007–8, 68.0 percent of adults in the United States were either overweight or obese; of those, 33.8 percent were obese, and 5.7 percent were extremely obese (Flegal, Carroll, et al. 2010). In the earlier discussion, I flagged increases in mean BMI; here I point to changes in the *rates* of overweight and obesity. Rates of overweight and obesity, often invoked in reports of an obesity epidemic, are based on BMI values, yet they depend on an additional calculation that determines the *proportion* of people in a population considered obese. Determining proportion, though, depends on categorization of different BMI values.

As an index, the BMI compares weight-to-height ratios across a population. It relates only a relative value; a 19 or a 27 or a 33 has no intrinsic meaning. The crucial step is in classifying the index: in other words, assigning categories and determining into which category a given BMI value should go. Naming those categories establishes their meaning and thus what is normal and what is not. The classifications were first determined by scientific panels at the National Institutes of Health (NIH) and WHO, based on numerous observational and epidemiological studies that generally relate BMI to mortality and morbidity (Hamilton and Filardo 2006). Still, assigning a range of indexes into one category rather than another makes them absolute rather than relative measures and, as Hamilton and Filardo argue, wrongly suggests an established relationship between a category and particular outcome. Today, the ranges and their names are as follows:

BMI	Weight Status
Below 18.5	Underweight
18.5—24.9	Normal
25.0—29.9	Overweight
30.0—39.9	Obese
Above 40	Morbidly Obese

According to these ranges, a six-foot person heavier than 183 pounds would be overweight; a five-foot four-inch person heavier than 173 pounds would be obese. Rates of overweight are based on the percentage of people with BMIs of 25 and above (a combination of the overweight, obese, and morbidly obese ranges); rates of obesity are based on the percentage of people with BMIs of 30 and above; and rates of morbid obesity are based on the percentage of people with BMIs of 40 and above. Thus, an individual with a BMI of 40 is counted in all three categories (overweight, obese, and morbidly obese).

The problem with these cutoffs is not just that they are arbitrary. By forcing indexes into specific categories, the cutoffs imbue small shifts with great meaning. For example, consider the cutoff of 30 that currently separates overweight from obese. The difference between a BMI of 29 and 30 represents between five and eight pounds of weight depending on height, and many people, of course, will have BMIs slightly below the higher cutoff. So, if actual weight gain in the last, say, ten years was on average about seven pounds per person, much of the rise in obesity could be a consequence of those people who happened to have been on the high end of the overweight category moving into the next category. With a specific cutoff, that is, rates of obesity incidence can increase dramatically when average weight gain is quite minor (Whitley-Putz 2004). Rates of prevalence, which represent the percentage change of those marked with a condition from one time period to another, can appear dramatic for the same reason. A tripling of obesity prevalence from, say 0.1 to 0.3 percent of the population does not an epidemic make.

Even as these statistical conventions can overdramatize the magnitude of the change, they underspecify its dimensions. It is not entirely clear from these numbers whether many people have become a little larger or if a few people have become much larger, since both phenomena can increase mean BMI. As it turns out, mean BMI is not uniformly getting higher. Rather, the distribution of BMIs is becoming skewed, meaning that large people are becoming larger and pulling up mean BMI. Represented on a bell curve, this change would show a slight shift to the right at the top of the curve, with the right tail of the curve further above the x axis than the left tail (Flegal et al. 2002). Although the bell curve is a contestable way to define a pathological problem, as I will discuss later, this skewing does point to a phenomenon that deserves attention, for it points to possible environmental and medical causes of obesity that are somewhat neglected (see chapter 5).

Yet, it is not only statistical conventions that have contributed to the sense of a dramatic increase in obesity. In addition, obesity rates have been affected by changes in the guidelines for these ranges. In June 1998, the NIH released new guidelines that reduced the lower BMI limit of the overweight category from 27 to 25. Because of that change, several million Americans became overweight overnight (Kuczmarski and Flegal 2000). Since then, the WHO has recommended that the cutoff for overweight be reduced to a BMI of 23 for people of Asian origin, based on evidence that Asian populations have different associations between BMI, percentage of body fat, and health risks than European populations do (World Health Organization Expert Consultation 2004). The change was then rejected because the data didn't support a unitary BMI cutoff point. The observed risk for different groups varied quite significantly, notwithstanding that these variations can be an effect of differential health treatment. The good news is that these proposed and completed changes suggest that scientists are paying attention to health risks and how they vary, details that are effaced in the highly reductive discussions of obesity. The less-than-good news is that, had the changes gone through, rates of overweight would have changed without anyone gaining weight, and many might not have noticed.

For these reasons and more, the question of whether the upward movement of BMI in the past thirty years should be characterized as an epidemic bears scrutiny. The term *epidemic* is far from neutral. For many, the term connotes contagion and disease that one gets from close contact, inhospitable living and working conditions, or filth, squalor, and decay. The disease is generally precipitated by a vector, whether bacterium, virus, or parasite. Yet, there is not even agreement that obesity is a disease, much less a vector-borne one. At best it is a symptom of a disease—or a condition associated with a disease. By the same token, an epidemic can simply mean a rapid spread or increase in the occurrence of something. This latter definition is obviously less inflammatory, but it is imprecise and somewhat hysterical when applied to growth in girth. Commenting specifically on obesity as an epidemic, the CDC scientist Katherine Flegal (2006) usefully differentiates the more delimited uses of the term from the more metaphorical ones. Even in a more metaphorical sense, the term is generally intended to connote an unexpected rise in occurrence with sudden and widespread death or destruction—an event, not a trend. Yet the rise in BMI is just that: a trend. Besides, the epidemic language is somewhat cruel, simultaneously minimizing the violence of serious plagues and overstating the association of corpulence with death.

ASSOCIATING OBESITY AND MORTALITY

In 2004 the CDC released a study that claimed that poor diet and lack of exercise was nearing tobacco as a primary cause of death, having contributed to 400,000 deaths in the year 2000 (Mokdad et al. 2004). This study received a great deal of media attention, as did an earlier study that had attempted to measure deaths attributable to obesity (Allison et al. 1999). Fumento's claim that 600,000 people died in the two years in which he wrote *Fat of the Land* was based on the latter study, which concluded that about 300,000 people per year die from obesity, depending on how you adjust for smoking. This raises the question of the methods employed to establish that people die earlier from being fat.

The Allison study took rates of mortality associated with "elevated BMI" in various epidemiological cohort studies (in which a group of people and their health conditions are followed over time) and applied them to the number of actual deaths in the year under study: 1991 (based on what epidemiologists call the attributable fraction method). This was a relatively straightforward calculation that projected "excess" deaths attributable to obesity by comparing them with rates of mortality for nonobese people. Where it might have erred is in how it accounted for confounding risks such as age and smoking (Katherine Flegal, personal communication, July 20, 2010). The aim of the Mokdad study was more ambitious: it was to identify "major external (nongenetic) modifiable factors that contribute to death." Generally, statistics on causes of death are based on vital statistics the CDC collects from the states, which report annual number of deaths by cause of death. Leading causes of death are usually categorized by diseases (e.g., heart disease, cancer, stroke), or injuries in the case of accidental deaths. This study, however, attempted to establish the number of deaths that were behaviorally caused (e.g., tobacco use, poor diet and insufficient exercise, sexual behavior, use of firearms). This entailed deriving the number of "extra" deaths by attributing a certain number of deaths to a range of risk factors established through epidemiological cohort studies. In other words, if an epidemiological study established that smokers had higher rates of mortality than nonsmokers, a certain percentage of the total deaths would be attributed to smoking, irrespective of the cause of death noted in the vital statistics.

In addition to attributing cause of death based on probability factors rather than on what was listed in death certificates (as happens in all studies using attributable fractions), the treatment of obesity in this study was particularly circular. Aiming to name behavioral causes, researchers used rates of obesity as a proxy calculation of deaths from poor diet and insufficient exercise, adding a trivial number of deaths attributed to these behaviors among those not obese. They thus assumed that obesity results from poor diet and insufficient physical activity, letting the condition stand in for the behavior. This latter aspect is a classic case of coproduction such that the investigation of a phenomenon uses tools or techniques that already presume much about the nature of the phenomenon, which then brings it into sharper existence (Reardon 2005). The conflation of behavior and condition didn't really matter though, as most news sources attributed the "excess deaths" to obesity anyway.

As it turned out, that figure of 400,000 deaths was revised markedly downward to 112,000 deaths, based on another study, also by CDC scientists, who reanalyzed the same evidence (Flegal et al. 2005). The later study, while using the same method of applying attributable fractions to excess deaths, was more precise in that it adjusted for differences in mortality rates at different ages, in effect acknowledging that fat varies in its functionality at different ages and can be protective as people grow old (Flegal et al. 2004). These adjustments revealed that people who are modestly overweight have a lower risk of death than those who are of "normal" weight, and showed no "excess mortality" for mildly obese people (those with BMIs between 30 and 35). As such, this study also challenged the correlation of lower BMI with lower mortality. Flegal and her colleagues have since reviewed a good number of existing studies that attempt to measure excess mortality related to overweight and have found that virtually all of them show that adults in the 25–29.9 BMI category have no higher risk of dying than those in the normal range (Flegal et al. 2007b). This is one of the reasons that more recent reports of obesity prevalence no longer refer to the overweight category.

In keeping with these findings, graphic representations of documented associations between BMI and mortality tend to follow more of a U or J curve rather than a unidirectional trend line. For example, a plot graph of mortality rates among Norwegian men and women of middle age showed high mortality on both the low and high end of BMI values, and slope quite clearly steepening at a BMI of below 21 and above 31 (Ross 2005). In other words, extreme thinness is associated with increased mortality, too, and the range of BMIs not significantly correlated with increased mortality is much wider than the narrow "normal" range of BMI. Of course, that still begs the question of the nature of the association of very high or low BMI with increased mortality.

Remarkably, up until 2007, the association of body mass index (BMI) with cause-specific mortality had not been reported for the US population. This provoked the CDC to study "cause-specific" deaths before drawing conclusions about excess deaths related to obesity. In this study, researchers linked data on cause of death and vital statistics with BMI ranges and risk factors drawn from health surveys. What they found is that obesity and overweight correlated with higher mortality from cardiovascular diseases and certain cancers, but lower mortality from other causes, whereas underweight and normal weight were associated with higher mortality from some cancers and noncardiovascular diseases such as acute and chronic respiratory illnesses and infectious diseases (Flegal et al. 2007a).

Even then, the fact that obesity and extreme thinness are *associated* with higher mortality from certain diseases is not to say that obesity or underweight *cause* these diseases, or that adiposity itself is a cause of illness and death. Epidemiology, as the health policy expert Gary Taubes (2007) discusses, is based on observed associations, not controlled clinical studies, and only the latter can determine "cause." Nevertheless, the field of public health does have standards for when it is legitimate to infer cause from correlation. A set of tests to establish causation of illness includes the strength, specificity, and consistency of the explanation as well as the ability to determine a specific biological mechanism (for an excellent overview, see Ross 2005: 102–5).[1] Yet, unlike lung cancer and skin cancer, for which clear causal agents have been identified, thus far obesity per se has failed to pass muster as a clear identifiable cause of any chronic illness (Ross 2005; Taubes 2007). Even in the association of visceral fat and heart disease, the epidemiological links are robust but the biological pathways have been difficult to establish (Montague and O'Rahilly 2000).

The relationship between type 2 diabetes and mortality is particularly complex and may not involve obesity directly. Type 2 diabetes is defined as impaired ability to respond to insulin (i.e., insulin resistance) such that glucose is not absorbed into cells and instead stays in the blood. Excessive glucose circulation can lead to complications such as kidney failure that may eventually cause death. However, type 2 diabetes itself is not counted as a cause of death in vital statistics (Ross 2005). Studies showing that diabetes symptoms improve because of changes in diet and exercise regardless of weight loss suggest that type 2 diabetes may be caused by poor diet and lack of exercise, regardless of the presence of obesity (Gaesser 2002). Moreover, the established epidemiological association between adiposity and diabetes can reflect a protective relationship. Sequestering blood glucose into fat tissue is an adaptive response that prevents the excessive circulation of glucose in the blood (Power and Schulkin 2009). In addition, fat cells can secrete hormones that protect against insulin resistance (Kershaw and Flier 2004). When fat contributes to insulin resistance, it has to do with the excess production of inflammatory molecules (Power and Schulkin 2009). Even then, to the extent that obesity is associated with inflammation, it may be that both type 2 diabetes and obesity are symptoms of other diseases or results of other biological agents not identified or established (Clement and Langin 2007). In short, the *causal* relationship between adiposity and insulin resistance is neither straightforward nor unidirectional.

Further confounding the issue, strong associations between morbidity or mortality and obesity may be due to disease treatments. Such "iatrogenic" weight gain is a common side effect of the use of steroids to treat life-threatening illnesses such as systemic lupus, asthma, and rheumatoid arthritis (Pijl and Meinders 1996). Importantly, it is also an effect of insulin therapy to treat diabetes, which can then contribute to cardiovascular disorders (David and Rehman 2007). In these cases, the cause of death cannot really be attributed to obesity. I will return to the contribution of pharmaceuticals to obesity in chapter 5.

If pressed, many public health professionals would have little argument with what I have presented thus far; they, more than anyone, are aware of the limitations of epidemiological evidence. Yet, as Taubes (2007) points out, their logic is different. From a medical perspective, epidemiological studies may be incapable of distinguishing a cause and an effect. But from a public health perspective, even a minute effect is good because, when applied over a large population, minor results multiply to establish significance. So, the logic goes, if public health practitioners can encourage, say, a reduction of one hundred calories a day over a large population, perhaps their efforts to prevent obesity will have statistical success. The problem, though, is that these epidemiological tools are being deployed as both medical and moral prescription. Tellingly, after the CDC revised downward the findings about the 400,000 deaths per year related to obesity, Dixie Snider, the chief CDC scientist, stated that he hoped the findings would not take away from the importance of focusing on obesity as a major public health problem and contributor to death (Stein 2004). Such proclamations call for more sensitivity to the notion of "at risk" and how it relates to pathology—and death.

ESTABLISHING RISK FACTORS

In a separate article from the one that reported these 400,000 deaths, Mokdad et al. (2003) reported that overweight and obesity were significantly associated with diabetes, high blood pressure, high cholesterol, asthma, arthritis, and poor health status. This was based on phone surveys collected in 2001 through the national Behavioral Risk Factor Surveillance System, in which subjects reported their own BMI and health status in response to questions of whether a medical professional had ever told them they have one of those conditions and diseases. The researchers then used statistical programs to generate "odds ratios" for the association of BMI and these medical conditions, to conclude that obesity is strongly associated with several major health risk factors. A perusal of much of the medical literature reveals that much of the "established" relationship between obesity and certain diseases is one of risk, not certain biological pathway.

The risk factor is a key artifact of epidemiological method. Risk factors are generally not diseases themselves but symptoms, behaviors, or biological dispositions that are associated with higher rates of disease contraction. Specifically, they are "predictors," or probabilities. In the case of obesity, a risk factor reflects the relationship between the incidence of obesity and the incidence of the disease in question. To say, then, that people with a particular condition (such as BMI above a certain threshold) are "at risk" for a particular disease speaks to their greater likelihood of getting the disease.

Establishing risk factors is not straightforward. One reason is that these probabilistic relationships are established through real-life observations that are not medically neutral. BMIs are reported in both clinical and survey settings. But diseases are generally established only in clinical settings by sick people seeking out treatment. Therefore, clinical settings are unlikely to see fat people who are otherwise healthy, especially because a visit to the doctor can elicit unwanted advice. Cohort studies are specious for the opposite reason: those willing to be monitored over a long period tend to exhibit a wide range of behaviors and characteristics that predict healthiness (wealth, education, interest in exercise, etc.) (Taubes 2007). In either case, the sample may not be representative of the population.

Furthermore, changes in the threshold ratio of what constitutes "at risk" can significantly affect the apparent severity of the problem, just as changes in acceptable BMI ranges did. For instance, using new clinical evidence, in 2004 a panel that develops cholesterol guidelines for adults lowered their recommended target level of LDL cholesterols from less than 130 mg/dL to less than 100mg/dL (Grundy, Cleeman, and Bairey Merz 2004). Assuming that LDL cholesterol levels themselves had not changed much, effectively a much larger group became at risk for a cardiac event. It is easy to see the fallacies of these approaches when you look at the limit. In any given population, however construed, some proportion will contract a given disease. With a low enough threshold, everyone in that population would be rendered "at risk." The classic example that drinking milk puts you at risk for alcoholism (since you've established a drinking behavior) pokes fun at that logic, yet it is not that far from a position currently being taken that we must fight being overweight because that puts us at risk for obesity. Is it even possible to be obese without having been overweight at some point, or to be seven feet tall having avoided being five feet tall? The basic idea cannot be taken lightly, though. The increasingly popular use of genomics to produce means of "early detection," as the social theorist Nikolas Rose (2007) points out, probably will have the effect that nearly everyone will become "at risk" or a "pre-patient" for something. Similarly, rather than sick or not sick, with risk factors everyone's health becomes precarious (Armstrong 1996). And aging puts you at risk for just about all disease-related death.

In the main, the problem with the risk factor is that it subsumes a welter of symptoms, indicators, and diseases, all of which may relate to one another, but often with little clarity about what exactly is pathological. "No longer the symptom or sign pointing tantalizingly at the hidden pathological truth of the disease," one illness becomes a risk for another. "Symptom, sign, investigation and disease thereby become conflated into an infinite chain of risks" (Armstrong 1996: 400). The so-called metabolic syndrome is one classic example. *Metabolic syndrome* refers to a set of conditions involving high blood pressure, high triglyceride levels, bad cholesterol ratios, elevated blood glucose, and "central obesity," referring to large waist circumference, which puts people at risk for heart disease and diabetes. Since many of these risk factors tend to cluster together, naming the condition has generated significant controversy about whether it is any more than a sum of its parts (Matfin 2008).

This is particularly the case with obesity since obesity per se is rarely the cause of death. To be sure, obesity is but one condition among a multidirectional network of external indicators, biomarkers (indicators taken from biological samples), conditions, and diseases. First, there are risk factors for obesity: these include a broad range of behaviors, conditions, and inheritances such as poor diet, race, genetic factors, and hypothyroidism. Hypothyroidism is itself a condition that may or may not lead to problems, diagnosed through the biomarker of insufficient thyroid hormone in blood samples. Then there are the diseases for which obesity is a risk factor. One is type 2 diabetes, but type 2 diabetes can equally be a risk factor for obesity. Type 2 diabetes is associated with other conditions, not all of which lead to diabetes, such as insulin resistance. The presence of type 2 diabetes is often diagnosed by biomarkers such as fasting blood glucose levels, with levels over 125 mg/dl signifying prediabetes and over 150 mg/dl signifying diabetes. It is also worth noting that blood glucose levels rise with age, so that in an aging population just about everyone will receive a diagnosis of type 2 diabetes if the threshold is set low enough (Petersen et al. 2003). Blood glucose levels, though, are not equivalent to the symptoms of diabetes such as thirst, frequent urination, and extreme fatigue, which can occur for many possible reasons. And these are not equivalent to the discomforts that signal debilitated bodily function from the impaired ability to absorb glucose into cells: worsening vision, kidney damage, overtaxing of the pancreas, and hardening of the arteries, some of which can lead to death. Nor are social factors absent from risk factor discussions. For instance, poverty is one of the risk factors for obesity. But, alas, obesity is also a risk factor for poverty.

Because of the overabundance and multidirectionality of risk factors, some use the term *independent risk factor*, suggesting a factor strong enough to suggest an underlying cause of the disease. Independence, however, refers to a statistical convention that merely shows that a variable makes a significant contribution to a statistical model that includes already established risk factors; it does not establish cause (Brotman et al. 2005).

None of this is to say that obesity doesn't impair function or make one susceptible to certain diseases—or that certain death is the only way to legitimately name a disease. At some level, having to identify a cause of death is part of the problem construction, for it medicalizes what is the most inevitable thing biological beings do (Armstrong 1996). Rather, it is to note that several degrees of separation exist between obesity as an indicator of a medical problem and the manifestation of a pathological condition. The use of risk factors makes it particularly difficult to pinpoint where the pathology lies. That gives space to the possibility that obesity is a weak proxy for some underlying pathology (Campos et al. 2006). This possibility is particularly salient since obesity the risk factor is determined by measurements of non-normative (undesirable), albeit increasingly normal (as in usual), body size.

CONFLATING THE OUTLIER WITH THE PATHOLOGICAL

As I have characterized them thus far, many of the conventions used to describe the obesity epidemic necessarily focus on normality rather than pathology. This is because they derive from the field of public health and its reliance on epidemiological statistics. Epidemiological techniques developed for good reason, as ways to spot trends in and provide prevention for communicable diseases, for example. However, in allowing trend-spotting to be conflated with medical diagnosis, they entered into more troubling territory.

As the medical sociologist David Armstrong (1996) discusses, different medical models have different sites and mechanisms for diagnosing illness. Bedsides, hospitals, laboratories, and libraries are spaces differentially suited to register symptoms (patient's complaints), signs (doctor's observations), and disease pathology, but all require some contact with the patient. What he calls surveillance medicine, in contrast, can be extracorporeal, involving virtually no contact with an individual patient. The doctor, in other words, can use a risk factor, established through a health survey in which various statistical methods are used to analyze the problem, to make recommendations to a patient. Since in almost all cases, the patient would not even have participated in the health survey, surveillance medicine completely detaches diagnosis from the body of the patient.

The aim of many of the statistical methods used to analyze health data is to establish bases of comparison, for it is extremely difficult to determine acceptable, good, or even optimal values other than through comparison, especially in the absence of patient contact. The convention of standard deviation, used to verify descriptive statistics of large samples, such as BMI values from health surveys, is a prime example of a comparison-oriented technique. As discussed earlier, its graphic representation in the bell curve helps visualize BMI values for a population or a sample, with the top of the curve around the mean representing BMIs that most would have and the tails of the curve representing outliers. But is this an appropriate use of standard deviation? The standard deviation was originally conceived to establish *mathematical* probability based on a mean. Unknown physical quantities, such as astronomical distances, would be measured many times over. To determine which ones were more reliable, scientists would plot those measurements. They assumed those around the mean to be accurate and threw away those deviant as inaccurate (Fendler and Muzaffar 2008). The standard deviation—the measurement that expresses the dispersal of values away from the mean—was thus supposed to represent error. Too high a standard deviation and perhaps the statistical mean was not robust enough.

It was our friend Quetelet who extended bell curve thinking to medical and human sciences and redefined its use to establish a norm (cited in Fendler and Muzaffar 2008; Hacking 1990). Quetelet transformed the theory of measuring unknown physical quantities into the theory of measuring ideal or abstract properties of a human population. Subsequently, bell curve thinking "began to turn statistical laws that were merely descriptive of large-scale regularities into laws of nature and society that dealt in underlying truths and causes" (Hacking 1990: 108). The extension of bell curve thinking to the human sciences produced a crucial and profound shift in the meaning of *normal*. Normal, as in usual, became normative, as in socially desirable or moral. The height/weight tables—and thus the BMI—are classic in this regard. Rather than merely describing a regularity, a typical weight/height ratio, BMI is now used normatively, to say what weight/height ratios ought to be.

Fendler and Muzaffar discuss an additional consequence of bell curve thinking: making nonnormality tantamount to pathology.

> Before 1800 [when the bell curve was primarily used in medical discourse, not social science] pathology was the central and specified term; anything that was not pathological was assumed to be healthy. The desirable condition, then, was not specified, not circumscribed, and the possibilities for ways of being healthy were theoretically unlimited. After 1800 . . . the term *normal* became the central and specified term. Moreover, the specifications for the term were constituted in a measurable population—either in terms of an average or in terms of a socially defined virtue. In this definition, anything that could not be specifically defined as normal/average was then regarded as pathological/not-normal. In this newer sense, then, the possibilities for being normal are effectively circumscribed as those characteristics that are average or common, and the possibilities for being not normal are limitless. (Fendler and Muzaffar 2008: 75)

As they note, Quetelet's conception of the "average man" was particularly telling in its circularity. To compare characteristics such as height, sexual identities, intelligence, and so forth across populations, you had to note differences, outliers, by which the mean would make sense (Fendler and Muzaffar 2008: 73). Since it takes abnormality to determine normality, difference itself became the problem.

Clearly, bell curve thinking has helped shape the problem of obesity. Normal has become the goal, regardless of whether the outliers of too much or too little fat are pathological. That said, the "obesity epidemic" represents a problem for bell curve thinking, since mean BMIs have crept upward, in effect creating a new normal. Specifically, as mean BMIs have inched up to 28, the "normal" is no longer equivalent to the normative of 20–25. To reconcile this issue, many turn to historical norms, and say that present-day embodiments are a deviation from the natural.

CONFLATING THE CHANGE WITH THE UNNATURAL

Since much of the increase in BMI has occurred since 1980—irrefutably, an abrupt change—another way in which representations have shaped understandings of obesity is through the rhetoric of the natural. Appeals to the natural borrow heavily from evolutionary biology, which as a field tends to claim that people are fat because they evolved to store fat in times of scarcity, but these times are no longer (e.g., Power and Schulkin 2009). Without dismissing the science that investigates how body morphology and functionality evolves in accordance with living conditions, this line of argument nevertheless suggests that human's natural state is one of hunting and gathering, rendering modernity in all of its forms a problem. Broadly such claims raise important philosophical questions about human knowledge of nature and specifically how interpretations of nature are often put in the service of social power (Haraway 1991; Williams 1980). With regard to the topic at hand, they raise a critical question about which moment in evolutionary time was the pristine one from which human embodiment has since deviated.

Along related lines, a relatively recent study that has attempted to identify more secular trends in US BMIs, by aligning data that are not easily commensurable, identifies that BMIs began to increase in the early part of the twentieth century. The authors thus conclude that the "obesity pandemic" has much earlier origins and that the "transition to post-industrial weights was a gradual process and began considerably earlier than hitherto supposed" (Komlos and Brabec 2010: 1). This suggests that nonnormality began considerably later than the Paleolithic age. Together, both arguments suggest the existence and knowability of a body form outside of history and geography to which all can or should conform.

Both sorts of claims also reveal an aesthetic preference for the thin and tall. People have grown significantly taller in evolutionary time and particularly over the course of the twentieth century. Far fewer pages have been given over to agonizing about that. As Kathleen LeBesco (2004: 85) writes, we seem to feel compelled to explain fatness, just as we do homosexuality, while thinness (and tallness), like heterosexuality, is generally taken for granted. In this vein, it is worth keeping in mind that gains in both girth and height also indicate improvements in health and nutrition—and longer lifespans. More people are susceptible to the chronic diseases associated with size because public health measures have reduced early mortality from contagious ones. My point is that explanations of increased size, girth especially, cannot assume that one kind of embodiment is more natural or more probable than another. Therefore the massive hand-wringing about girth alone is getting in the way of knowledge.

BEYOND SIZE

Optimal size cannot be known because it cannot be ascertained outside of social contexts that necessarily favor different embodiments or outside of comparisons of sizes that were themselves produced by socionatural entanglements. Using size to predict health outcomes is particularly fraught. They are weakly associated, especially when age and height are factored in. Attempts to reconcile these weak associations, through, for example, expanding the range of normal sizes or controlling for age, are an improvement over existing ways of thinking about the health issues surrounding obesity. A more radical approach is to reject both probabilistic and natural notions of normativity and embrace human variation instead.

At least we might decenter thinness as the norm to which all should aspire. To that end, some people, particularly in fat activist communities, subscribe to Health at Every Size (HAES). HAES is an alternative framing of fatness, the organizing principle of which is to decenter size but otherwise to encourage good eating and exercise behavior (Saguy and Riley 2005). Others read the HAES approach as an alternative, gentler form of weight loss program, which gives in to healthism (chapter 3), making HAES controversial within the fat activist community. It nevertheless suggests that size may not be the best way to think about pathology, and, furthermore, that concern with it may be averting our collective gaze from the nature of the problem and where it lies (Campos et al. 2006). To be sure, the *visibility* of obesity seems to be affecting our thinking.

And there are consequences for letting it continue to do so. For it is precisely in the circumscription of problem populations and the medicalization of difference that social justice begins to be compromised. Susan Craddock (2000b) among others, has shown that associations of disease with specific communities or populations can do great violence indeed. As she discusses, HIV/AIDS helped produce the category of at-risk lifestyles among gay men; smallpox helped racialize "the Chinese" (Craddock 2000a). Moreover, she notes, linking diseases with deviance or places with diseases can legitimize marginalization of various "populations" and in that way can actually further structural inequality. Those associated with a disease may have a more difficult time finding employment or even care for the very thing that ails them. The *visibility* of the "problem" population makes it easier for all this to happen.

Crucially, Craddock's critique speaks to the violence of neglect as well as that of intervention. Linking specific disease attributes with particular identifiable populations runs the risk of excluding from care those who do not fit the category of "at risk" and subjects those who do fit to unnecessary surveillance. Early public health interventions in HIV/AIDS worked to pathologize gay men as a population at the same time that it suggested to others that they were not at risk. Analogously, fat people are cajoled to eat differently because of their proneness to diabetes, irrespective of their health profiles—or diets, while thin people can eat junk food to their hearts' content and not be called to account (LeBesco 2004). The use of size as an indicator of risk appears blunt at best, and possibly much more damaging.

To sum up, the obesity-disease connection has been established by reductive measurements, correlative reasoning rather than causal determination, and rhetorical devices that leave out as much as they tell. Stripped of absolute categories such as overweight and obesity, the language of "epidemic," and the often misleading equation of thinness with better mortality outcomes, the recent increase in body mass relative to height does not cry out for redress quite as loudly. Still, despite the many issues in measuring and interpreting obesity, to deny that people have gotten fatter over the past thirty years would be foolish. The "obesity epidemic," although an artifact of certain measurements, statistical tools, and scientific understandings (like global warming), does not exist only through language. The issue is how we interpret these changes, how we treat them, and the consequences of both.

Finally, it is worth considering that not everyone has gotten bigger in America: some were always big, some have gotten thinner, and some were always thin and stayed that way. And there is substantial variation in BMI in relation to demography, geography, and class. Understanding the parameters of these changes and variations matters, not only for determining causes of obesity but also with regard to the appropriateness, urgency, and kind of public health interventions—if there are to be any at all—and the psychic damage that obesity talk does to people who consider themselves too fat. Yet, these variations and multiple causalities collapse in the language of the obesity epidemic and its inextricable aesthetic and moral concerns (Gard and Wright 2005). It is therefore important to consider why many people are so apoplectic about obesity, and how that affects the way we look at the problem.

CHAPTER 3

Whose Problem Is Obesity?

It's weird but I've never realized obesity was such an emotional issue. It is so political—but not just for fat people. . . . I mean most of the people in this class that have strong viewpoints aren't themselves fat, but I get the feeling that they are anti-fat. But why do fat people make people mad?

—Student's observation

I open this chapter with a student's journal entry from a course on the Politics of Obesity I first taught in 2005. I developed this class to supplement a course I regularly teach on food and social justice that prepares students for full-time field studies in related fields. Noting that many of my students aspired to "teach people how to eat" or "increase access to healthy food," I was especially keen to push students to be more reflective about bodily difference and missionary-like interventions. Truth be told, I also wanted to work through many of the ideas that would eventually become part of this book. I thus planned to address the politics of obesity from many angles, including the sociology of science, feminist body image, and my own specialty, the political economy of food. Oddly and perhaps naively, I expected to find a sympathetic audience; students at my university are strongly anticorporate, which made me assume they would find much more fault with the food industry than with fat people. And an abiding feminist tradition at the university led me to think that students would be at least a little circumspect about naming nonnormative bodies as problems.

To my surprise, the course material was not so well received, at least at first, and in fact provoked some intense negative reactions. Students were particularly discomfited by much of the material at the beginning of the course, including that discussed in the previous chapter, a guest lecture by the fat activist Marilyn Wann, author of *FatSo?*, and another guest lecture on media representations of fat people. Even critiques of the food system discussed in later chapters of this book—and later in the course—produced unease. After the first few lectures, some students became very angry and disruptive while others were quieter in their discomfort. (Still others were quite sympathetic to the course material.) Although the disruptive students turned out to be very useful pedagogically—and analytically—for their willingness to express what others might only think about fat people, I still wondered: Why did the course make students so mad? Why *do* fat people make (nonfat) people so mad?

It seems to me that reflecting on these questions can tell us a great deal about why the obesity epidemic as a social concern has gained such traction among those apparently not afflicted by it, as well as shed light on the consequences of this concern. Of course fat people have long been subject to a great variety of pejorative characterizations. Contemporary ideas about fatness are different, however—often cloaked in the language of health. At some level, this seems perfectly reasonable, given the way that the "obesity epidemic" has been represented in the media. But this association is not just a reflection of particular ways of defining and constructing the problem, as I discussed in the last chapter. These ways of seeing obesity have taken hold through the proliferation of ideas about personal responsibility, health care, and citizenship that are endemic to neoliberalism. As Mitchell Dean (1999) suggests, neoliberalism's conceit is its encouragement of self-actualizing, choice-making individuals under the banner of "freedom" and in lieu of more socialized means to provide health and welfare. In keeping with these ideas, many people view obesity as a huge economic cost to the public, especially as it affects the cost of health care.

More generally, obesity seems to violate a set of norms of self-efficacy that some call *healthism*, norms that are strongly related to neoliberal notions of governance. These norms are not universally legible, much less universally shared. And yet, healthism seems to give cover for distaste for, if not outright revulsion against, fatness. Moreover, it allows neglect of those not enrolled in such ethics and exaltation of those who are. Therefore I argue that invoking health to talk about obesity can work against social justice. I will be drawing on comments written in student journals to make some of these points.[1] The vehemence—and lack of empathy—with which some students expressed these comments will illustrate some of the ethical lapses in this thinking and the extent to which healthism may not be equivalent to concern about well-being.

WHY FAT PEOPLE MAKE OTHER PEOPLE MAD

At the most basic level, what seems to agitate people about obesity is the cost of health care for the obese. The media has played a substantial role in promulgating the message that the obesity epidemic is costly, beginning with the 2001 *Surgeon General's Call to Action to Prevent and Decrease Overweight and Obesity*, which reported that health care costs associated with overweight had grown from an estimated $39 billion in 1986 to $117 billion in 2000 (US Department of Health and Human Services 2001). In 2008, estimates came to $147 billion a year (Finkelstein et al. 2009). Since these numbers were released, many an editorial has warned of the obesity "epidemic" as a major threat to the US economy, in terms of both expenditures on health care and decreases in worker productivity.

Of course, there's much to question in these figures. Rising health care costs ostensibly associated with obesity may be a consequence of rising obesity, but they also may be a consequence of the price-gouging practices of private insurance, prescription drug, and medical testing companies, as well as medical doctors themselves. More subtly, calculations of health care costs associated with obesity may result from changes in how medical science conceptualizes the relationship between obesity and diseases or even changing measures of obesity, as discussed in chapter 2. For example, in developing these statistics is the cost of treating diabetes attributed to obesity? Was it attributed to obesity decades ago? Is the cost of treating diabetes different for someone who falls below the range of BMIs considered obese? The claims are also rife with errors of omission. Missing in those statistics are the costs of dieting or other attempts to be thin or the mental health costs of poor body image resulting from the incessant drumbeat demanding perfect body size and shape. The extraeconomic mental health costs just in frustration, guilt, and self-hatred are incalculable.

Nevertheless, the apparent consensus is that the costs of dealing with obesity are substantial and that the broader public pays for obesity because medical costs are pooled, so that the healthy pay for the unhealthy. Medical professionals have certainly signed on to this perspective. In researching this book, I listened to many complaints about the costs—and inconveniences—of treating obese patients from doctors and nurses. Many public health professionals and food system advocates share this view, as well. A great number of published articles and conference talks begin with a quick nod to the growing public burden of obesity-related health expenditures. And now public officials at the highest level do, too. The second paragraph of the 124-page report issued by the White House Task Force on Childhood Obesity (2010) discusses the economic costs of obesity and particularly the claim that obese adults incur $1,429 more in medical expenses annually than their normal-weight peers.

Economists have thus painted obesity as a classic free-rider problem, claiming that pooled health care insurance creates the "wrong" incentives (Bhattacharya and Sood n.d.; Finkelstein et al. 2009). Since obese people have higher lifetime health care costs but live fairly long lives, others are paying for them. Smokers, in contrast, die early, so they are not such a public burden; over their lifetimes they contribute more to the social safety net system than they take. The bright side, as Bhattacharya pointed out at a talk I attended, is that since obese people are poorer, on average, than nonobese people, the fact that the rich pay for the health care of the obese can be seen as a progressive tax such that the wealth pay proportionately more.

So engrained are these ideas that Michael Pollan has chimed in on this too, with an editorial in the *New York Times* (Pollan 2009a) in which he used the platform of rising health care costs to link obesity and type 2 diabetes to "big food." Remarkably, the piece was expressing skepticism of Obama's early proposal for health care reform because it focused too much on regulating the insurance industry and not on diet. As Pollan put it,

> to listen to President Obama's speech on Wednesday night, or to just about anyone else in the health care debate, you would think that the biggest problem with health care in America is the system itself—perverse incentives, inefficiencies, unnecessary tests and procedures, lack of competition, and greed. . . . No one disputes that the $2.3 trillion we devote to the health care industry is often spent unwisely, but the fact that the United States spends twice as much per person as most European countries on health care can be substantially explained . . . by our being fatter.

This came not too long after Pollan defended the natural food supermarket Whole Foods against a proposed boycott. The boycott was initiated in response to the *Wall Street Journal* editorial by Whole Foods' CEO, John Mackey, in which he attacked the "public option" under the supposition that "health care is not a right." On the blog spot *New Majority*, Pollan wrote that "Mackey is wrong on health care, but Whole Foods is often right about food, and their support for the farmers matters more to me than the political views of their founder" (Goldstein 2009).

Certainly, some of my students had signed on to the notion that they pay for others' health care—and that health care is not a right. This was one of the journal comments written after Marilyn Wann came to give her lecture:

> I will admit, Wann was a good public speaker, but her message was *not* something I was buying into. Not a bit. And by the end of her presentation, I felt like the most conservative person in that room, when in reality, I'm LIBERAL. So this morbidly obese woman gets up in front of class and begins giving her very biased explanation of why being fat is OK. Now I know that her message included many other points also, but when you come down to it, she was full-on supporting FAT America.... I don't understand why Wann was surprised at obese children being taken from their parents by CPS—those parents are slowly *killing* their kids! ... And what makes Wann think she should be able to have health insurance when she is going to give herself a heart attack if she doesn't fix her health? ... Being fat is a choice, not a damn excuse for those lacking self-control. (f) [all emphases in original]

As you see, though, this woman's entry is about much more than health care costs. Ideas of choice, control, self-improvement, responsibility, and revulsion are woven into that quotation too. Furthermore, the nods to choice in this quotation and the ones that follow are not to a choice between two moral equivalents, but between the right and wrong ones, shedding some light on the hidden morality of choice. What is additionally striking about that quotation is the cognitive dissonance about where her perspective places her on the political spectrum. This is an issue that surfaced many times in that class, actually, and reflects some difficulty students had in reconciling what they thought and how they felt. To be sure, some combination of these affects emerged as students reflected on a number of different issues, as the following demonstrates.

CORPORATE BEHAVIOR

> There is almost no accounting for personal responsibility. People should be (and I believe they are) capable of not consuming everything the market throws their way. (m)

> It would be so easy if we could just blame the food industry for all our weight issues.... I am wondering when we are really going to talk about personal responsibility in this class. (f)

> I think the people who eat the fast food are to blame. It is *their* choice to pull up to the drive-through, or to "supersize" their meal.... Although I agree that advertising and the food industry is partly at fault for advertising snack foods, I still feel that it is ultimately an individual choice to eat these foods. It basically comes down to

will power. There are always temptations in life, but that doesn't mean we have to go after those temptations. (f)

SELF-IMPROVEMENT

By age 13 I was like 5'2' and 200 lbs of all fat and no muscle. . . . At that moment I made the decision to change my life and become who I had always felt was the real me. I always knew that being fat was always temporary and it was a lifestyle choice. . . . By the time sophomore year began girls began to notice me. I had the choice to date any single girl in the school—seniors included. . . . Having worked hard to change my body type gave me confidence and made me realize that I am in complete control of my destiny. (m)

Let's just say for a second that there are no health risks associated with obesity and its all about, as Campos [author of one of the course readings] says, about not getting a date or being called "fatso" or other social limitations. Isn't that enough of a reason to lose weight? I think so. I used to be fat. I lost about 50 pounds in high school. I was called fat. I couldn't get dates. I know exactly what that is like. And let me tell you, now that I'm thin, I feel fucking fantastic. I eat right. In fact now I'm a vegetarian. . . . Campos can kiss my formerly fat vegetarian ass. . . . So throw out the BMI. Along with it throw out your bathroom scale. Buy a full-length mirror. Stand in front of it naked and you'll know exactly where the problem is if you have one. (m)

I respect [Marilyn Wann] for doing that and believe you should accept yourself, but why not work out and lose weight to make yourself healthier? It just seemed like she was all about accepting yourself, but not about improving yourself. (m)

HEALTH ITSELF

I believe in this day and age, people know exactly what they are eating. . . . [M]y argument is that people do know, many times they simply choose not to live healthy lifestyles, and *this* is the major cause of obesity. (f)

I am in no way saying that fat people should lose weight to look skinny, but they should do it to be healthier. . . . I realize that not all overly fat (obese) people develop health problems, but I know a majority of them do. . . . Basically I have no problem with people who choose to be overweight, but I don't think that people who choose to be "obese" and have the risk of major health problems have the right idea in celebrating their weight. (f)

Alongside the anger, or even to temper it, students expressed much earnestness about health. In fact, the more students became unmoored in this course, the more they drew on foundational notions of health to anchor these challenges. Many who were quite ready to concede the dangers of dieting invoked the language of "healthy lifestyle" as a sort of middle-ground position. Even some of the more contentious people eventually came to the conclusion that the issue wasn't size per se but that of a "healthy lifestyle."

My initial reading was that the use of health cloaked their displeasure with the aesthetics of fat bodies. To be sure, one reason that Health has gained traction, much to the chagrin of Beauty, is precisely that it is a caring as well as "scientific" way to converse about nonnormative bodies. And yet, the conflation of health and beauty cannot be denied. We know that health is often defined in terms of a person's appearance (e.g., she looks healthy), irrespective of the actual physical state of the body. Those of us who lived through a period when the suntanned skin of white people was sure to elicit positive comments on the state of one's health surely see the point. More pointedly, health gives cover for practices that may not be very healthy. For example, interventionist cosmetic surgeries, which themselves can be dangerous, are increasingly done under the aegis of mental health (Metzl 2010).

Still, I continued to struggle to understand how the notion of a healthy lifestyle could seem unassailable to many of my students, and how a group of students that generally pride themselves on being liberal-minded and often overtly anticorporate could be so dismissive of political-economic explanations. What I did not foresee was the extent to which students were already enrolled in ideas that conflate self-care and particular embodiments with personal responsibility and good citizenship.[2] The course made them mad, in other words, because they had a horse in the race. They had been educated in healthism, a key idea that was born about a decade before they were.

FROM HEALTHISM TO BIOLOGICAL CITIZENSHIP

The term *healthism* was first coined by the sociologist Robert Crawford in 1980 to "describe a striking moralization of health among middle-class Americans," so that health became a "super value" that trumps other social concerns (Crawford 2006: 410). Health, as Crawford noted, is not simply the absence of illness, which can possibly be achieved through various cures—biomedical and otherwise. Health has a "positive" connotation that relies on various ideas and assumptions about what constitutes a healthy body and then demands obtainment (Klein 2010). Since health can never be achieved once and for all, it requires constant vigilance in monitoring and constant effort in enhancing.

When Crawford first coined the term, he was referring to a new health consciousness, influenced by the emergence of the modern environmental movement and its concern with toxins, as well as the women's health movement, which rejected the authority of the medical establishment. Healthism, he noted, drew from existing cultural trends toward holistic medicine, self-help, a "new temperance," and other "life-affirming" ways of being in the world. In keeping with much New Left thinking of the 1970s, these movements displayed a healthy skepticism of government for its intrusiveness in personal freedoms. They were also significantly anticorporate in their sensibilities and tended to applaud populist, grassroots, and cooperative efforts as models of alternative ways of providing goods and services.

Eventually, though, as Crawford tells it, this sensibility became increasingly self-absorbed and less collectivist. In part, these cultural changes accompanied shifts in the political economy. Good health became a means to prove self-worth and flexibility in the increasingly competitive political economy. This point is made by Emily Martin, who in *Flexible Bodies* (1994) posited that changes in notions of body functionality seemed to parallel changes in the 1980s economy. Specifically, she argued that new metaphors of immunity, which imagine bodies to be pure and functional until seriously compromised, seemed to become the dominant way to conceptualize human health at about the same time that flexibility was heralded as the new way to manage the dynamics of capitalism. More generally, the 1980s ushered in a distinct cultural shift that emphasized financial success and me-ism, notwithstanding the attribution of the 1970s as the "me decade."

As neoliberalism matured as a set of cultural values, its social Darwinist underpinnings, which make individual achievement, entrepreneurial prowess, and competitive spirit markers of worth, became more explicit. As they relate to the care of the self, bodily practices that seem to indicate self-efficacy and self-control were readily associated with personal qualities that lead to both individual and collective success. That is one way that a thin, fit body became an indicator of health, regardless of the effort required to make it so (LeBesco 2004). Cultures of the body that emphasize its malleability and centrality in displaying "identity" also played into the association of self-efficacy with fitness and thinness. Thus, through its association with capability and self-control, thinness took on a valence under neoliberalism beyond its enduring post-Victorian, American aesthetic values (cf. Bordo 1993). We can see this conflation of fitness and success-oriented behavior in "reality" television shows such as *Survivor*, in which competition often involves both individual and team play. Often, that is, the individual winner is the person who manages to provide for the social body but is nevertheless the most competitive. We see an even more pointed coupling of body improvement and personal empowerment in *The Biggest Loser*, where contestants compete to lose the most weight (about which much could be said), with the help of personal trainers and lifestyle coaches. As viewers will most certainly concede, reality television is reflecting back strong messages about how we should be and encourages us to judge harshly the shirkers and less able.

Yet, healthism has obtained its largest boost because of the way it articulates with health care management, especially in the United States. For, as with many other New Left ideas, healthism unfolded alongside the rise of the New Right, which was equally distrustful of the state, although in its case because of the government's powers to "tax and spend" (Rose 1999). The Right especially derided programs of public welfare that seemed to foster dependency, and therefore sought to place health responsibility onto individuals in the name of reducing big government. Rather than furthering modernist state intervention, that is, neoliberalism devolved the task of improvement to the individual, who was expected to exercise choice and to become responsible for his or her risks (Dean 1999: 146).

The ideology of healthism, as Crawford puts it, thus aided the devolution of health responsibility from the public sphere to individual action. In the United Kingdom, this reversion was incomplete. To reduce health care costs, the British government sponsored an all-out educational effort to teach people to make "right" choices—to make it a duty of individual citizens to monitor their own sexuality, eating, and drinking—but continued to provide national health care. In the United States, by contrast, healthism helped legitimize a much more serious decommitment to state-mandated health services, taking the form of the "managed care" system, which, among other things, can exclude from care those with preexisting conditions, including obesity. The logic of managed care, as has now become evident, is to avoid unprofitable patients and/or shift costs back to patients, and thus to provide health care mainly to the healthy and wealthy, belying the idea that the public pays for obesity.

In any case, seeing care for certain groups as an excessive cost reflects an arguably perverse way of thinking about health care in terms of human need. You can see the moral hazard when you apply the same logic to education— for example, arguing that slow learners are a burden to the education system. It also neglects the role that the health care system plays in economy stability. The health care system provides an enormous number of jobs, particularly in labor-intensive primary care. In other words, care for the sick is an economic burden only in health care systems where profit is the bottom line and public services are underfunded and politically unsupported—that is, systems in which only market logic is considered legitimate. Nevertheless, the internalization of this logic helps explain the broad acceptance of the idea that obesity is the biggest economic health problem facing the United States.

As I have suggested, it is not only the cost of health care but also the idea that those who are not healthy hurt the nation that has made obesity seem such a social problem. Consider this quotation from a student that recites what much of the media has said about obesity's costs to national economic output:

> People need to take more self agency in being healthy. The fact is we do live in a country where capitalism rules all. How can fatties be expected to perform in a work related area if they can't be productive? (m)

People have also written that obesity thwarts military readiness. Invoking anxieties about productivity and readiness in regard to obesity exemplifies the notion of biopower that the philosopher Michel Foucault first formulated (Foucault 1985). For Foucault, the question of how states became increasingly involved in medical surveillance was a critical one. He was particularly concerned with the origins of the welfare state (Cooper 2008). He coined the term *biopower* to refer to state concern with the health, vigor, and longevity of its population (population health) to secure nationhood and capitalist productivity.

As demonstrated in that quotation from a student, biopower has taken on a particular flavor in the neoliberal era, distinct from that associated with the welfare state. The welfare state, as Melinda Cooper (2008: 8) puts it, "protects life by redistributing the fruits of national wealth to all its citizens, even those who cannot work, but in exchange it imposes a reciprocal obligation: its contractors must in turn give their life to the nation." In other words, the welfare state's interest and involvement in health, in "life itself," is a sort of social contract that involved the socialization of risk in the reproductive sphere in return for duty to the productive sphere. The neoliberal state, in sharp contrast, subjects both the productive and reproductive spheres to economic calculation (p. 9). This takes the lid off social protection and guarantees, and redefines good citizenship as being a minimal consumer of state health and welfare services. This provides an additional explanation of how the cost of treating obesity has come to be seen as such a public burden.

Finally, healthism has become salient because of the changing nature of disease itself (Crawford 2006). Unlike, germ-induced illness, many diseases of more modern etiology, such as breast cancer and heart disease, do not manifest symptoms for years. Preventative strategies do not turn on traditional public health practices such as quarantine, vaccination, or antibiotic control, but rather on influencing particular behaviors, predispositions, and conditions. Therefore, establishing particular risk factors and probabilities and using them, along with health promotion and health education, to shape individual behavior—to adopt "healthy lifestyles"—has become the paradigmatic public health intervention (Petersen and Lupton 1996).

As one consequence of much of this, epidemiology is no longer the coin of just medical scientists trying to further knowledge about disease etiology and prevalence. Rather, the public dissemination of information on norms, deviations, and risk factors for illness ("the new public health") has become the dominant strategy to encourage the general public to manage themselves in ways that are supposed to maximize their own life chances (Petersen and Lupton 1996). Epidemiological knowledge has thus become a critical tool in recent efforts to instill what the philosopher Nikolas Rose (2007: 13) has called biological citizenship, referring to the adoption of "active, informed, positive and prudent relations to the future" with regard to practices of the self.

In short, thanks to its confluence with the neoliberal economic project, healthism morphed from a critical perspective on both the biomedical establishment and industrial toxins, to an embrace of self-care, to an utter devolution of health responsibility to the individual in the interest of both reducing the health care costs of the body politic and performing fitness. As put by Nikolas Rose in a celebratory way, "health, understood as a maximization of the vital forces and potentialities of the living body, has become desire, a right and an obligation—a key element in contemporary ethical regimes" (Rose 2007: 11). But does that mean it is good for you?

IS HEALTHISM GOOD FOR YOU?

As Richard Klein (2010), a cultural historian and the author of *Eat Fat* and *Cigarettes Are Sublime*, remarks, health has come to have such a positive value that it is simply unthinkable not to choose it. Some have argued that it is precisely the amorphous character of health that allows degrees of admonishment, surveillance, and control that would likely be considered utterly intrusive in other spheres of life. One such critic was Peter Skrabanek (1994), a forensic toxicologist who located healthism in historical trends very similar to those Crawford did. He saw a world of difference between efforts to "maximize health" and "minimize suffering." He was especially critical of "lifestylism," which he defined as the emergent mix of dietary obsessions, prescribed exercise regimes, avoidance of risk behaviors, and regular self surveillance" (Skrabanek 1994: 58). According to Skrabanek, these are "unhealthy obsessions" that impose discipline at the expense of freedom. He and others have elaborated why this is so.

First, as the Australian food scholar Gyorgy Scrinis (2008) has argued, much of this self-surveillance depends on nutritional and medical advice that is profoundly reductionist. Bodily health, Scrinis notes, is often reduced to a set of diet-related and quantifiable biomarkers, biochemical processes, and bodily functions. He references many of the indicators discussed in this book, including the BMI, rates of disease incidence, risk factors, and caloric intake and output as enshrined in the energy balance model. He refers in addition to measurable indicators of bodily function such as LDL and HDL cholesterol levels, blood sugar levels, and the glycemic index (GI). All of these may render the body legible, but they divorce health from the broader social and ecological context of the body (p. 42). As such, they may not capture wellbeing at all. He takes special note of nutritionism, by which he means the understanding of, marketing of, and decision making about food in terms of the role constituent nutrients and substances play in human health. Emphases on vitamin content, reduced caloric or carbohydrate content, and the inclusion of antioxidants, probiotics, and fiber do more than just cultivate what he calls "nutrition confusion" and promote questionable dietary advice. "The reductive focus on nutrients has overridden and concealed the important question of the type and quality of foods and ingredients that are consumed. Nutritionism has also undermined other ways of engaging with and understanding foods, including traditional, cultural, sensual, and ecological approaches" (p. 57).

Second, the way that epidemiological knowledge induces vigilance is by warning the "normal" by using the others as examples. This can be gleaned from the writings of Geoffrey Rose, an eminent figure in the field of public health. In his famous 1985 article on sick individuals and sick populations, he effectively made the case that public health interventions should not be directed to the 20 percent or so considered at high risk for disease; the purpose of interventions, instead, should be to change societal norms of behavior, to intervene at the level of the population. What he was suggesting, in effect, was that the 20 percent at risk are examples for the rest but not themselves targets for treatment. Mitchell Dean (1999: 100), writing on neoliberal notions of self-governance, has subsequently written that the very idea of dividing populations into subgroups, some of whom are seen to retard the general welfare of the population, is to prevent, contain, or eliminate the abnormal. This tactical use of risk factors is especially apt for diseases and conditions, such as obesity, that we are told cannot be cured, only prevented, in light of diet failure (Germov and Williams 1999; Sobal 1999). Many of the obesity statistics discussed throughout this book work in this vein: to warn the relatively thin. The extent to which you, the reader, find yourself drawn in by them (as apparently my students did) speaks to the effectiveness of this strategy. But they also create categories of people beyond repair.

Third, healthism tends to negate the role of pleasure in human well-being. As both Skrabanek and Crawford note, healthism shares much with early temperance movements, which associated denial with goodness. Richard Klein (2010) reminds us that pleasure can be healthy, including the risks that inhere in adult pleasure. For, he asks, what is longevity without pleasure? Others reject the simple instrumental logics and notions of perfection enshrined in "health." Cuomo (1998: 79) writes, "Although physiological considerations must be part of what it means to flourish, human flourishing cannot be solely understood as the fulfillment of biological needs, and when biological criteria are used we must remember that these are always conceived and filtered in and through social and cultural lenses."

Fourth, healthism is oddly conflated with longevity, which is why the icons of healthism, from Paul Bragg to Jack LaLanne, obtain credibility from having reached old age (although in Bragg's case, his actual birth date and thus age at death remains controversial). Yet, one fact on which there is very broad consensus is that no one lives forever and that death is most definitively "normal." Therefore, in any effort to achieve health, we are effectively endeavoring to substitute one kind of dying for another. To say this is not to excuse avoidable violent and painful forms of death, be they from war, murder, or toxic exposure, but to acknowledge that quests for health in a crucial sense fight the inevitable. We know that in modern industrialized countries chronic diseases have substituted for communicable and pathogen-induced diseases. If we avoid accidental death and manage to live a cancer-free and heart-disease-free life, there's a good chance we'll die from the slow deterioration of our bodies and minds. Yet, there are people who will pursue this path most stridently, which, depending on your perspective, can be a healthy or an unhealthy obsession.

Fifth, the equation of healthism with empowerment is suspect. As Scrinis (2008) argues in regard to nutritionism, it can create ambiguous tendencies. On the one hand, knowing the nutritional qualities of food can enable an active, empowered, and critically informed individual or, on the other, it can create a disempowered, confused, and dependent individual. How empowering is it, he seems to ask, to be dependent on scientific expertise and advice, susceptible to food marketing claims, and anxious about "what to eat"? Empowerment writ large is a contradictory project. This is because to "empower someone" suggests already existing imbalances in power relations. Empowerment often takes the form of expert therapy, behavior modification, nutritional and exercise advice, and other sorts of training to produce these feelings of freedom and empowerment (Dean 1999; Rose 1999). And, of course, those who feel empowered through weight loss or maintenance are showing remarkable subjectification to messages about fat, beauty, and health.

Together, these point to the disciplinary aspects of health discourses generally and that of obesity specifically. Comments from the course I taught demonstrate these disciplinary effects:

> As a result of studying the inactivity of Americans as a whole I have started to go back to the gym and started working out again. (m)

> In fact, this class is a great motivation for good nutrition and exercise [week 1]. I've started analyzing my diet and exercising more, so I guess this is a positive thing, but my overall self image may be worsened [later in course]. (f)

> This class has been affecting me negatively. Although it seems as though I should feel better about myself after hearing the lectures, I end up feeling really conscious of what I eat and my size. . . . I found myself taking tips from pro-ana [anorexia] websites, which is not what I intended by looking at them for class. (f)

> Enough with the social theory . . . here's what's happening to me right now—I've become incredibly attentive to what, exactly, I've been eating lately. [After writing a media analysis of low-carb diets]: Even though I approached each article with a critical eye, knowing well the suspicious nature of mediated information, I still become extremely attentive to the carbs that were part of my life, trying to limit them (against my best intentions). . . . [Toward the end of the course]: And even sillier, the guilt then become two-fold because I feel guilty and angry at myself for caring about what I eat. . . . I wonder how to halt that cycle. (f)

> A very interesting point that seemed to be shared by all of us [project group] was how much more aware of our bodies and more self-conscious this class made us.

We are all normal size, average fitness level women. We discussed how this class, more than any "societal pressures"—ads, etc. made us more aware and less inclined to eat things we thought of as fattening. (f)

Reading about fatness is really triggering my own suppressed fear of becoming fat. It's interesting because I've always thought of myself outside societal norms with respect to thinness because of my bisexuality/queer identity. . . . It helps that I shut out most visual media and try to intellectualize my insecurities, but it's hard in this class because we're looking at so much media. It's doubly frustrating because I intellectually realize that we are all neurotic with health and body image, but emotionally I feel stung personally when reading *Fat Land* [another obesity-anxious popular book] and looking at commercials. (f)

As Paul Campos, author of the *Obesity Myth* (2004), has argued in relation to obesity, those most inclined to diet or engage in what he calls "chronically restrained eating" are those within ten pounds of "normal" range. This certainly seemed to be the case for my students whose fears of fat the course seemed to unleash. What these comments demonstrate is that even critical discussions of health can incite self-discipline.[3]

Most crucially, these comments seem to indicate that healthism speaks to those who are already reasonably healthy (Crawford 2006; Skrabanek 1994). Healthism, in other words, seems to appeal to those who are already self-efficacious, believe that they both deserve and can obtain health (beyond freedom from disease), and otherwise have the resources and inclination to take on the project of health—qualities, I suspect, that are probably shared by many of my readers, my students, and, to be honest, my own friends, family, and self. As such, good health may well be more an effect of success than a prerequisite of it (Berlant 2007). What about those not moved by healthism?

IS HEALTHISM (GOOD) FOR OTHERS?

Despite that they are taken for granted, norms of healthism are not universally shared, legible, or obtainable. Some do not participate in the ethics associated with healthism and biological citizenship simply because they do not want to. Whether they indulge in "unhealthy" practices as somewhat mindless self-medication (Berlant 2007) or as deliberate resistance to discipline (Lupton 1997) may be irrelevant. The question is whether, by rejecting healthism, they become deserving of whatever befalls them. Since that is the conclusion healthism leads to, the fat resignification advocate Kathleen LeBesco (2004) has written against participating in norms—or claiming victimhood—as a way to retain biological citizenship. She critiques the Health at Every Size approach because it does not decenter health as well as size and is arguably complicit in extending moral obligation around eating, exercise, and "healthy lifestyles." For similar reasons, she critiques the fat acceptance movement for accepting victimhood. Why should active participation in health be the standard by which we judge citizenship?

Some, in addition, may not believe possible the disease-free—even pain-free—life, with maximum longevity, that health promises. In Karen Barker's *Fibromyalgia Story* (2005), the author explores the condition of fibromyalgia, diagnosed by the expression of a set of painful symptoms associated with the condition, yet without an identifiable causal agent. According to Barker, white women suffer disproportionately from fibromyalgia and are relieved to receive a medical diagnoses; the prevalence of the condition among African American women is considerably less, in part because they do not seek diagnosis and treatment for a rather unspecified set of aches and pains. Perhaps, Barker suggests, African American women do not carry cultural expectations that life should be free of suffering. She thus intimates that the cultural differences in health practices may have a good deal to do with legibility. To what extent are healthy lifestyle norms culturally specific?

And some simply can't obtain health, as defined in these ways. Profound structural inequalities give rise to disparate health outcomes, which are denied by healthism's focus on "lifestyle" (Skrabanek 1994). The geographer Bruce Braun's (2007: 12) critique of Nikolas Rose is most apt here. He notes that "we are faced with growing populations—undocumented workers, the working poor—who are excluded from this ethopolitical order; that is those who are denied the political right to health, or lack the resources that might enable them to 'choose'—in short, who cannot be the neo-liberal subjects that Rose presupposes." Expressed this way, the issue is more than one of health care access and affordability or even health knowledge. Who has the choice to have choices? Who has the right to have rights?

Despite healthism's cultural and social specificity, those taken by healthism can display significant lack of tolerance for those who are not. Consider these indicators of healthism's less salubrious qualities:

> It is not only a physical issue, but a mental issue. For the most part, the higher percentage of obese people is because of uncontrollable eating habits. . . . [Later] People don't want to make their own meals and don't want to exercise. No wonder

why America is getting fatter. . . . [Even later] What I don't understand is that if they are poor, they can't afford to eat out or to buy video games, which the middle/ rich class can. So, I would think that poorer kids would get more home-cooked meals and more exercise. (f)

Every time I go to the gym it makes me really sad because there are never over-weight people. In fact, most of the time there are skinny people and people who don't need the gym. (f)

Let's face it, a big portion of this country is lazy and needs some guidance. But, I do believe that if you take someone who is overweight and given them guidelines to be healthy, they can do it. [Later] I hate to say this but it's partially true. Since they are poor and may come from different countries, they don't have the education to help them make the right choices when it comes to food/health. Instead they try to assimilate themselves to American culture by watching our ads and eating our food. This isn't to say that this doesn't happen to (some) white people. I'm sure they deal with some of the same problems as minorities. (f)

Even the people on welfare live amazingly healthy and safe lives . . . basically everyone in America is wealthy, priviledged [sic] and relatively well-fed. . . . I try not to go to the south so I don't know much but there seem to be a lot of fat asses literally in the south. They are uneducated, remote, unhealthy humans that need help. Is the Fat Acceptance movement going to help them or their kids? (m)

I have trouble accepting that I shouldn't discriminate against someone who is knowingly fucking up their health. (f)

As these quotations show, appeals to health seem to allow a great deal of moral judgment of those who do not appear to adopt practices associated with healthy lifestyles.

Therein lies the problem: by coupling health efficacy with notions of rights, responsibilities, and good citizenship, those not captured by its purse seines are afforded little basis on which to make claims for health care and other resources. Healthism thus provides a protective veneer for neglect or exclu-sion. As I will discuss in later chapters, those who embrace market-based approaches to food system change are complicit in this neglect.

Reciprocally, healthism elevates the status of those who do participate in its norms. As put by the sociologist Alice Julier (2008: 484), "When fatness is conflated with bad nutrition, bad health, and sedentary lifestyles, those who are not fat gain status through that association." Healthism thus allows bodies to be signs of individual character, and, hence, deservingness (Crawford 2006; Dean 1999; Petersen 1997; Rose 2007).

More pointedly, healthism gives cover for—and perhaps even dignifies—obsessions that might otherwise seem narcissistic or self-serving. The feminist legal scholar Anna Kirkland (2010: 474) argues that one reason that feminists, for example, have embraced the environmental account of obesity (to be discussed in chapter 4) is that they are part of the cultural subgroup with the most investment in both the personal appearance norms and cultural practices that mark elite status. "What if it is the case," she asks, "that many elites find the terms of the environmental account to be simply a more palatable way to express their disgust at fat people and the tacky, low-class foods they eat?" Those who adopt a food system perspective that conflates good eating with doing good also stand on the slippery slope she identifies.

AGAINST HEALTHISM

Obesity, as the health condition that seems most amenable to self-induced transformations, stands apart as the litmus test of biological citizenship. In response, this chapter has argued that the cloak of health that covers distaste for obesity is not so healthy. Fat people are subject to all manner of discriminatory health care practices besides the denial of insurance for preexisting conditions. Many studies have shown, for example, that medical practitioners are uncomfortable with treating the obese and therefore obese people often avoid seeking medical treatment for serious problems (National Task Force on the Prevention and Treatment of Obesity 2002; Puhl and Brownell 2001). That fat people are treated poorly in the health care system in many ways belies the idea that concern with fat is about concern with health. If health were valued as it is purported to be, it would be unthinkable to deny coverage for fat people, much less scold them for having nonnormative bodies. Instead, the way we talk about health and obesity reflects a neoliberal perspective that subjects care and well-being to economic calculation, exalts those who demonstrate their deservingness through self-care, and justifies neglect for those who don't.

That said, much of what has come under the aegis of public health historically has rarely been neutral with regard to race, gender, and class difference and has sometimes been explicitly eugenic (Crawford 2006). For instance, in response to a typhus scare in the United States that yielded forty-seven cases and four deaths, more than 871,000 Mexicans were subjected to intense health inspections when crossing the border between 1910 and 1930. These inspections included some combination of vinegar and kerosene delousing, a mass shower of kerosene, soap, and water, a smallpox vaccination, and a lengthy psychological and medical exam (Stern 1999). Craddock's (2000a) rich history of the public health battles in San Francisco in the late nineteenth and early twentieth centuries shows that public health campaigns were inseparable from the social agendas of dominant social groups. She takes particular note of the way elites supported spatial segregation of the Chinese into Chinatown to thwart the spread of smallpox. Even current healthy city initiatives, with their emphasis on social context and prevention, have racial consequences, since inscribing some places as unhealthy and in need of intervention can lead to enhanced surveillance and possible economic disinvestment (Brown and Duncan 2002). There are certainly class consequences of naming places as obesogenic, as I will discuss in chapter 4.

For that matter, if obesity is a health problem, we really do have to question the many solutions promoted on behalf of obesity reduction. Obesity is the justification for some highly invasive therapies. Between 1973, when it first came on the market, and 1997, dexfenfluramine (Redux) was an FDA-approved appetite suppressant used to manage obesity, withdrawn only when the FDA began to receive overwhelming clinical evidence that the use of "fen-phen" was causing heart valve disease. There is some evidence that bariatric surgery is effective in reducing mortality for the morbidly obese; nonetheless, this needs to be balanced against the fact that operative mortality is more than 1 percent for certain procedures and those who receive the surgery face other complications (Buchwald et al. 2004). Broadly speaking, many treatments are designed for weight loss (and some size loss), irrespective of the effect on disease or mortality. Questions of efficacy are important as well. Weight loss programs are notoriously ineffective at producing substantial, long-term weight loss. Commonly, dramatic weight loss tends to be followed by equally dramatic weight gain. "Yo-yo" dieting causes illness as well, most notably gall bladder disease, and some starvation diets have led to such severe metabolic problems that dieters have ended up morbidly obese (Campos et al. 2006).

To question healthism is not to dismiss concerns about illness or disease, however. Few would welcome the return of typhoid or yellow fever, diseases that have been eradicated thanks to public health measures. (We should note that typhoid and yellow fever, as communicable diseases, were far more threatening than obesity is.) Nor, for that matter, should we gloss over the serious structural inequalities that prevent some groups from getting access to the health care they need or expose them to proportionately more disease-causing agents, including environmental toxins. As the geographer Ruth Gilmore (2002) has so succinctly put it, early death among racialized populations is one of the clearest signs of still-existent racism. The point is that health cannot be allowed to trump other concerns, precisely because it has never been wholly innocent of class, race, and other social projects (Roberts 1998). This, then, requires us to think differently about health and where blame lies for health inequalities, whether or not they manifest in fatness. I hope the next few chapters convince you that it is untenable to see much of what does manifest as fatness as a matter of personal responsibility.

CHAPTER 4

Does Your Neighborhood Make You Fat?

"Data Show Manhattan Is Svelte and the Bronx Is Chubby, Chubby" read a headline in a July 2009 edition of the *New York Times*. The story reported on a study that had just been released that had compared obesity rates in the Bronx and Manhattan boroughs of New York City (Chan 2009). As might be expected, Manhattan's rates of overweight and obesity were far lower than those in the Bronx, and "the prosperous swath of Manhattan from the Upper East Side down to Gramercy Park had the lowest obesity rate (less than 15 percent) in the city." As reported by the *Times*, the head researcher, Andrew Rundle, noted that at the neighborhood level, socioeconomic and demographic factors were the strongest predictors of obesity rates. He then equivocated, stating that even when adjusting for poverty and race, at least three factors are associated with reduced obesity: proximity to supermarkets and groceries where fresh produce is sold; proximity to parks; and access to public transportation, which reduces reliance on cars. The article thus concluded that increasing the number of produce markets and making neighborhoods easier to walk in might reduce obesity rates.

This study is one of dozens, and possibly hundreds, of studies completed in the past decade or so that test the thesis that people are fat because they are surrounded by cheap, fast, nutritionally inferior food and a built environment that discourages physical activity. This theory was first formalized in the academic literature as the "obesogenic environment" (Swinburn, Egger, and Raza 1999; Hill and Peters 1998). According to Hill and Peters (1998: 1371), "our current environment is characterized by an essentially unlimited supply of convenient, relatively inexpensive, highly palatable, energy-dense foods, coupled with a lifestyle requiring only low levels of physical activity for subsistence. Such an environment promotes high energy intake and low

66

energy expenditure." Importantly, the part of the thesis that speaks to the food environment articulates with a major approach in food systems research which has focused on questions of spatial access to healthy food and the way food retailing practices entice people to buy the wrong food (Winson 2004).

Along with generating research, the thesis has animated various planning, advocacy, and educational interventions to address these obesogenic qualities of the built environment. These have included creating outlets for fresh fruits and vegetables in urban "food deserts," redesigning (or remarketing) public spaces to encourage walking and bicycle riding, or city-sponsored educational campaigns to achieve obesity reduction (Herrick 2007). The last has been a favorite of cities pinned as being some of the country's fattest, such as Houston, which topped a list created by *Men's Fitness* magazine several years in a row.

The focus on the built environment in explaining and attempting to prevent obesity is in many ways salutary. Deemphasizing individual behaviors would seem to diminish the moral scrutiny and invocations of personal responsibility that typically accompany discussions of obesity's causes. Moreover, it brings some needed focus to food industry and regional planning practices, which potentially assigns culpability to powerful and malignant actors. So I don't want to dismiss this line of argument altogether. However, these so-called environmental explanations of obesity are flawed in a number of respects. A key one is that the studies designed to test the thesis are based on entrenched assumptions about the causes of obesity, leading to the kind of equivocation mentioned earlier. Apropos to the Bronx-Manhattan study, the existing assumptions also neglect, or at least downplay, the salience of race and class in explaining spatial patterning of obesity and defining what constitutes a healthy environment. As such, the obesogenic environment thesis and efforts to study and fix it tend to reinforce healthism, ironically so. That is because environments that are characterized as obesogenic tend to have features that, when juxtaposed to ideal, let's call them "leptogenic" (after the Latin for thinness) environments, reveal important, unstated preferences for certain types of places and their attendant lifestyles. And these preferences may, ironically, worsen wealth disparities among different environments.

This chapter will discuss these arguments in detail. In addition, it will introduce findings from a study I conducted that did not presuppose how built environments affect obesity. On the contrary, unlike the deductive approach of the quantitative spatial studies I discuss, this study was entirely inductive, designed to explore how people who live in so-called obesogenic environments mediate these environments in their own terms. First, though, I want to introduce the more typical ways researchers approach the obesogenic environment.

COPRODUCING THE OBESOGENIC ENVIRONMENT

To the extent that the Bronx-Manhattan study found that lack of proximity to grocery stores and parks and lack of access to public transportation "predict" obesity, researchers were testing those as variables in the models they used. This approach to formulating and studying the obesogenic environment exemplifies what those in science studies call coproduction. Coproduction refers to assumptions about a scientific object's causes and character being built into models of examining it (Jasanoff 2004). The obesogenic environment thesis internalizes two critical presumptions, only one of which is explicit. *Explicitly*, it assumes the energy balance model, which holds that obesity results from an excess of calories in relative to those expended. To the extent to which it black boxes questions about human behavior, specifically how humans negotiate their environments, it *implicitly* assumes that the environment simply acts on people, so that people are objects, not agents, in these environments.

The energy balance model is taken for granted in virtually all discussions of obesity, yet, as I will discuss in chapter 5, it is not indubitable. Nevertheless, rather than testing this assumption, studies of the obesogenic environment embed it in ways that can render these studies circular. For a particularly marked example of this, consider how *Men's Fitness* calculates America's fattest cities. In making their calculation, they do not even begin with those cities with the highest BMI per capita. Rather, they use a range of indicators, not all of which are controllable, including statistics on total number of clubs, gyms, and sporting goods stores; fruit and vegetable consumption; alcohol and tobacco use; air and water quality; and parks and recreation facilities. (In determining the worst cities they give good grades to cities that have qualities associated with good health and give poor grades to cities that have qualities associated with bad health, such as bad air quality.) In other words, they include measures that they *assume cause* obesity in measures *of* obesity—a clear instance of coproduction.[1]

The concept of coproduction is also meant to elucidate how science helps produce the social worlds it is intended to explain. The obesogenic environment thesis does this in multiple ways. First, the idea that the environment acts on people in unmediated ways is in some sense a by-product of the thesis itself, yet it leaves the impression of unthinking behavior in regard to these environments. Second, by making judgments about what constitutes a lepto-genic environment (e.g., air quality in the *Men's Fitness* study), it contributes to the economic and cultural valuation of the places it describes. Third, by incorporating factors such as proximity to grocery stores and parks in its mea-surements, it effectively validates a policy approach that emphasizes supply-oriented issues of availability and proximity rather than demand-oriented ones of, say, affordability and need.

The Bronx-Manhattan study nevertheless differs in emphasis from many others. First, it nods to the importance of studying thinness as well as fatness (i.e., to make any claims about neighborhood effects on obesity we have to show neighborhood effects on thinness). Second, it acknowledges that class and race have a role in explaining neighborhood differences in obesity rates. This point, alone, does not negate the assumptions of the thesis; indeed, it is perfectly compatible with the supposition that race and class differences in BMI are a consequence of differences in energy intake and expenditure. But it does suggest the existence of factors independent of the built environment and even leaves open the possibility that race and class variations in obesity rates are unrelated to energy balance. Where it falls into the same trap as the *Men's Fitness* study is in assuming that the problem features of the built environment are independent of who lives there. I argue, instead, that the relationship among the built environment, spatial variation of obesity, and spatial variation in race and class are all of a piece that cannot be dissected and made amenable to various supply-oriented interventions. Gentrified urban cores such as Gramercy Park are thin and wealthy, and it is unclear which begets which. Conversely, features associated with obesogeneity are precisely what make the Bronx affordable and thus available to those whose class status may exist by virtue of their being big. Yet, the quantitative spatial research that attempts to demonstrate the relationship between the built environment and obesity cannot account for this inseparability, leading to the reductionist—and simplistic—conclusion that more grocery stores will reduce obesity.

OBESOGENIC ENVIRONMENTS: STUDYING THE STUDIES

It is worth considering how researchers might go about trying to prove a relationship between obesity and features of the built environment. Some might simply observe that people seem fat in a particular place and then look around and try to ascertain what's different about that environment. Those who assert that Europeans are thinner because they walk a lot are basically relying on this sort of casual observation. But if they tried to publish these "findings" in a scholarly journal, they might not be taken seriously. So instead they turn to more established scientific methods for establishing relationships between health outcomes and place: geographic information systems (GIS) and spatial analysis. Basically, these involve the use of spatial statistics and mapping to demonstrate correlative relationships between places with higher obesity prevalence and environmental features that might contribute to obesity. Fair enough. But what assumptions go into the data selection? What data are available to make these correlations and what kind of explanations might be left out because of lack of data? And what does statistical analysis imply about human behavior? My argument here is that it is in the effort to operationalize the thesis that the simplifications become manifest.

First, researchers would need to ascertain variations in prevalence of obesity across space to establish that some neighborhoods, places, or regions have higher obesity prevalence than others. They would tend to use BMI as a measure of obesity, since height and weight are the size measurements collected for large numbers of people. At the national level these are collected through the National Health and Nutrition Examination Survey (NHANES) and the Behavioral Risk Factor Surveillance System (BFRSS). BFRSS samples many more people, but NHANES is considered more accurate because it includes in-person interviews and medical examinations—and collects more detailed (and longitudinal) data about socioeconomic status and behaviors that can be used as variables in an analysis. Thus, the choice of which survey to use would influence the depth and breadth of findings. To show that BMI values vary across space, researchers would need to sort individual BMI values by geocodes—codes that identify the individual with a particular state, county, zip code, or census tract. To measure neighborhood environmental influences, researchers would want these codes to be available at fine-grained scales, but they might find that due to sampling issues in health surveys (especially detailed ones such as NHANES), it is difficult to obtain statistically reliable measures of BMI at finer-grained scales than the state, metropolitan area, or county.

They might then map this variation to identify pockets of high obesity prevalence. The maps put out by the CDC that show obesity rates by state

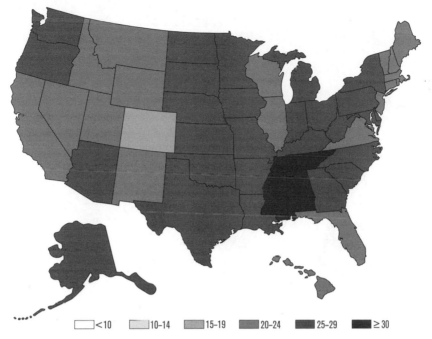

FIGURE I. Obesity rates by state, 2007 (*percentage of adults with BMI ≥30*)
Source: Behavioral Risk Factor Surveillance System, CDC.

and county illustrate the differences in what the scale of analysis—as well as researcher assumptions—may lead the researcher to hypothesize. The state map (figure 1) might draw your attention to the "thin" Rocky Mountain west and suggest that obesity has something to do with exercise and spending time outdoors. Alternatively, you might look at the map that selects for whites only (figure 2) and see that West Virginia is the fattest state, and consider that obesity has something to do with economic decline. The more fine-grained county map (figure 3) might draw your attention to lower rates of obesity around cosmopolitan coastal cities and university towns—or higher rates of obesity in areas with high populations of African Americans and Native Americans. Whether by state or by county, these maps, which visualize *rates* of obesity per geocode rather than, say, *average BMI* per geocode, might give the impression of dramatic differences among different regions. Using the latter would tend to produce finer gradations of difference among places and might lead you to question whether obesity "clusters" much. Of course, how the maps were color-coded would also affect the visualization, since colors close

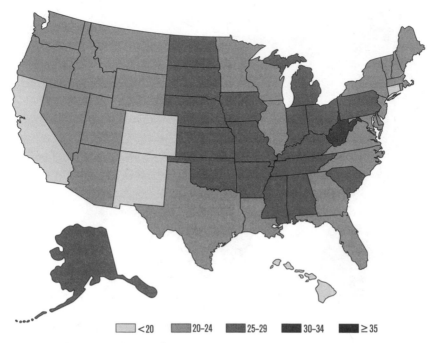

<< 20   20–24   25–29   30–34   ≥ 35

FIGURE 2. Obesity rates by state for non-Hispanic white adults, 2006–2008 (*age-adjusted percentage of adults ≥20 years old who are obese*)
Source: Behavioral Risk Factor Surveillance System, CDC.

in tone suggest more graded difference than colors different in hue. And red almost always calls out for alarm.

Thus far, however, the analysis would only have identified geographic variation in obesity—or, perhaps, clusters of obesity. In any case, many researchers do not start with the map; instead, they identify a place or region they wish to study for its obesogeneity—or compare two places in close proximity, as in the New York study. Either way, the next step would be to identify statistical associations between higher obesity rates and environmental features. Naturally, to show that these statistics are robust as geographic phenomena, they would want their models to incorporate spatial dimensions such as proximity to or density of various features, regardless of whether or in what way proximity or density is a deciding factor in peoples' decisions.

To demonstrate relationships between features of the built environment and BMI variation, the researchers would need to hypothesize what features might actually contribute to obesity and turn them into variables. If they

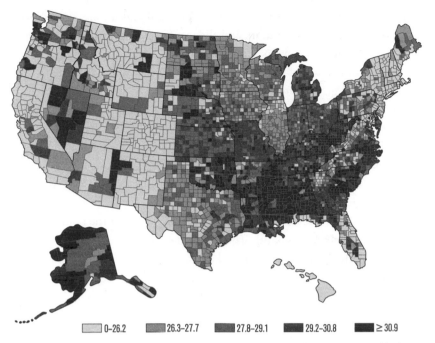

FIGURE 3. Obesity rates by county, 2007 (*age-adjusted percentage of adults ≥20 years old who are obese*)
Source: Behavioral Risk Factor Surveillance System, CDC.

were testing the obesogenic environment thesis, they would want to ascertain differences in (junk) food availability and opportunities for or obstacles to physical activity. On the food side, researchers might be interested in the availability and mix of grocery stores, fast-food restaurants, big-box stores, and so forth. Interestingly, though, researchers might assume different things about the roles these play. For instance, many might assume that big-box stores are a feature of the obesogenic environment based on the supposition that they encourage people to buy more food than they need for the week. One research team went against the grain, however, to hypothesize that big-box stores allow people to purchase more fruits and vegetables at lower cost (Courtemanche and Carden 2010). On the physical activity side, researchers would most definitely consider suburban sprawl, which figures prominently in notions of obesogeneity. One research team, Plantinga and Bernell (2005), suggested several ways in which low-density residential areas have contributed to obesity: the poor connectivity of street networks that increases trip distances, suburban layouts that make walking and cycling impractical and unsafe, the reduced viability of public transportation, and the insufficiency of park development. And although many seem to agree that low-income urban neighborhoods are a problem because of their density of convenience and liquor stores and dearth of good grocery stores (so-called food deserts), researchers' suppositions are more mixed about the impact of these neighborhoods on physical activity. Some have hypothesized that low-income, dense, urban neighborhoods inhibit physical activity, based on the supposition that people might fear walking in their neighborhoods (Lee 2006). Others have suggested that the fear of walking might be offset by the necessity of walking among carless residents (Poortinga 2006).

But it would not be enough to conceptualize features of the built environment that contribute to obesity. The researchers would need to find data to approximate those features. But what kinds of data are available? They would likely turn to business censuses to obtain data on things such as the number of restaurants, gyms, and big-box stores found in a geocode, remote-sensing technologies to find operational measures of urban density, and health surveys to obtain data on drive-to-work times. Researchers might also do their own surveying, perhaps walking and driving to estimate travel times to different sorts of businesses. These are typically the sources of data most published studies have used to measure variables such as housing density, vehicle miles traveled, distance to grocery stores, density of fast-food restaurants and convenience stores, and the presence of big-box retailers (Papas et al. 2007). Some have tried to be more creative: one study looked at the number of interstate highway exits in a county as an "instrumental variable" for fast-food availability (Dunn 2008), but a second study directly challenged these conclusions on methodological grounds (Anderson and Matsa 2009).

Finding data would not be the only challenge researchers face. They would also have to make their data geographically commensurate, which might entail aggregating all of their data, including their BMI data, to the largest geographic scale used. Too coarse a scale, though, provides very little information. A demonstrated relationship between the density of fast-food restaurants per square mile and rates of obesity on statewide levels (Maddock 2004) doesn't seem all that convincing. To get that finer-grained analysis, researchers might make compromises in other dimensions of the research. For example, the North American Industry Classification System used in the business census does not differentiate fine dining from family-oriented chain restaurants in the "full-service restaurant" category. Whether that restaurant is Denny's or upscale Charlie Trotter's in Chicago would seem to matter greatly. A study in Erie County, New York, which found a statistically positive relationship between women's BMI and diverse land use, especially when restaurants dominated nonresidential land use, was not able to identify the type of restaurant that predicted higher BMIs (Raja et al. 2010). In the absence of fine-grained data, researchers might be tempted to assume the relationship between features of the built environment and obesity based on a third factor. One study, for example, attempted to look at the relationship between convenient access to fast food and the prevalence of obesity among black and low-income populations focusing on Orleans Parish, Louisiana (Block, Scribner, and DeSalvo 2004). The researchers found that fast-food restaurants were associated with predominately black and low-income neighborhoods, but without equivalent ecologic measures of obesity, they were only able to assert the relationship.

These are just some of the constraints of quantitative models, and it appears that data availability has driven much of the research. Yet, as a result of these constraints, many possible explanations of geographic variation in obesity are not explored, whether cultural, economic, or environmental. Data on, say, cultural attitudes toward appropriate body sizes are hard to quantify, much less collect on a zip code basis. Conversely, data that *are* available at the ecologic level go underutilized in these studies, perhaps because they don't fit existing assumptions about what causes obesity. To my knowledge, no studies have looked at, for example, unemployment rates, housing prices, proximity to cultural centers and institutions of higher learning, or, for that matter, proximity to toxic waste dumps and exposure to pesticide drift. To what extent does this exclusive focus on the supply side of food and physical activity also incorporate existing assumptions about how the problem could be solved?

While the data are in part constrained by existing assumptions about the biological causes of obesity, the method helps reproduce assumptions about the behavioral causes of obesity. Spatial analysis, like epidemiology, can only demonstrate association. These studies pay scant attention to human behavior, because they are methodologically incapable of doing so (Brown and Duncan 2002; Kearns and Moon 2002). In leaving questions of behavior untouched, however, they can easily give the impression that the environment simply acts on people in unmediated ways, as if once you find yourself living in the sprawling suburbs the fat will pile on. Surely, the idea that merely the presence of bad food makes people fat is well circulated. It is fairly explicit in Michael Pollan's

(2006: 102) claim, "When food is abundant and cheap, people will eat more of it and get fat." Jane Goodall, Gary McAvoy, and Gail Hudson (1995: 240) make a similar leap when they write, "there is no mechanism that turns off the desire—instinct, really—to eat food when it is available." Since not everyone is in fact fat, and since these writers make great efforts to educate people to the quality of food to encourage informed decisions, they are in effect betraying their healthist sensibilities, suggesting that those who manage to exercise restraint in such environments (or avoid them altogether) must have greater disciplinary powers, taste, and knowledge.

Some researchers let their own interpretations stand in for these unexamined behavioral explanations. Lopez (2004), for example, asked whether some people might choose to live in areas of sprawl in order to avoid walking, but then dismissed that possibility as being unreasonable. Plantinga and Bernell (2005: 490) suggested that consumers make a tradeoff between weight gain and low-price housing. Specifically, they claimed that people who choose low-density suburbs do so to maximize price utility, whereas those who "have a stronger aversion to weight" seek out "healthier locations" (p. 490). And Rosenberger, Sneh, and Phipps (2005) wondered if areas rich in natural amenities and recreation would attract what they call "healthier migrating populations." So whereas in some spatial analytic studies, subjects are simply treated as objects; in others, people are treated as rational, utility-maximizing actors, with little constraints on their decisions other than, perhaps, income.

As a whole, the results of these studies have been fairly inconclusive. Studies of food environments yield particularly mixed results. The most robust results seem to be in the association of sprawl and obesity. Lopez, for example, used individual-level data from BFRSS with an index of urban sprawl for various metropolitan areas and found modest but significant correlations between sprawl and overweight/obesity after controlling for variables such as gender, age, race or ethnicity, income, education, and diet. Yet, another variant of the physical activity argument produced less robust results. Rosenberger, Sneh, and Phipps (2005) examined the relationship between recreation supply and obesity in West Virginia (one of the fattest states in the country) and found no statistically significant relationship between the quantity of recreation opportunities and rates of obesity across various counties, although they did find a relationship between the quantity of recreation opportunities and rates of physical activity—which they then *presumed* would triangulate to rates of obesity. Notably, however, a study of parks in New York City was able to link access to safe parks, physical activity, and lower BMI (Quinn et al. 2007).

Alas, though, the same questions remain begged: is it really *access* to parks that predicts obesity or is it class/race clustering and segregation across New York City that makes these correlations robust? Likewise, is it really about the *layout* of the suburbs or the situations and characteristics of people who live in the suburbs? And is it really about all suburbs or particular kinds of suburbs?

A DIFFERENT APPROACH

With these concerns and questions in mind, I set out to ask people who live in so-called obesogenic environments about how their daily practices are affected by their surroundings in ways that most research presumes to affect body size. I was particularly interested in white women, in light of well-documented inverse correlations between socioeconomic status and BMI among this particular group (Chang and Christakis 2005; Lee 2006; Zhang and Wang 2004). Let me be clear on this point: women in all racial groups vary much more in BMI than men do, and white women show greater variation in BMI than any other racial group. So it seemed to me if there was something to be discovered about how the built environment affects obesity, it would be among those whose bodies seem most prone to social influences.

I conducted a small study in 2009–2010 in two different former farming towns in California: Tracy and Fresno. Tracy is located in San Joaquin County, which, as shown in table 1, has high rates of obesity in comparison with both statewide figures and California's thinnest counties, Marin and San Francisco, which are arguably "leptogenic" environments. Although Tracy is a relatively old town in California's Central Valley, it has grown quickly in the past twenty years, primarily because it is within commuting distance of the San Francisco Bay Area, and the high-tech industries of Silicon Valley in particular. It has many of the characteristics that are typically quantified in studies of obesogenic environments: long commute times, sprawling residential housing without walking linkages to public spaces, a dearth of nearby sites for outdoor recreation, and new, auto-oriented retail districts of big-box stores, malls, and fast-food and chain restaurants. Fresno, in Fresno County (which also has comparatively high rates of obesity), is an older and larger valley town that has become a city in the past thirty or so years. The most significant difference with Tracy is that residents tend to work in the area rather than commute.

TABLE I   PERCENTAGE OF ADULTS OBESE OR OVERWEIGHT BY
COUNTY, 2007

	San Joaquin	Fresno	Marin	San Francisco	Statewide
Percentage of adults obese	28.9	28.7	13.6	11.8	22.7
Percentage of adults overweight or obese	65.0	63.6	41.9	42.9	57.1
Percentage of white women obese	21.1	19.6	11.8	9.5	18.4
Percentage of white women overweight or obese	58.4	46.2	30.3	30.4	45.4
Median home price (in dollars), Dec. 2008	253,500[a]	157,499	704,545	638,888	

[a] For town of Tracy only.

SOURCES: Overweight and obesity rates: California Health Interview Survey (2007), http://www.chis.ucla
.edu/. Median home prices: California Association of Realtors, http://www.car.org/3550/pdf/econpdfs/
County_Sales___Price_Statis8.pdf; Median Price of Existing Single-Family Homes; California Association
of Realtors, December 2008 Median Prices, http://www.car.org/marketdata/historicalprices/2008medianp
rices/dec2008medianprices/.

Still, it is known for large strips of retail stores and fast-food restaurants. And
although the oldest parts of the city are built on a grid with shady streets and
sidewalks (typical of older valley towns), the vast majority of space in Fresno is
sprawl. For recreational amenities, residents look to the nearby Sierra Nevada
foothills for boating and the famous national parks—Yosemite, King's Canyon,
and Sequoia—for hiking, climbing, and skiing—all of which are at least a 1.5
hour drive away.

The study involved intensive interviews with middle-aged (35–60) white
women, the population with BMIs that vary the most in relation to class
and, apparently, location.[2] The percentages of white women considered obese
in these two towns are nearly double those in the two thinnest counties,
Marin and San Francisco, as shown in table 1. Not incidentally, these latter
counties are two of the wealthiest, here demonstrated through median home
prices, which were the two highest in the state at the county level in 2008. In
selecting twelve women for intensive interviews, I was aiming for maximum
variation (in their size and socioeconomic status), in keeping with recommendations of methodologists of small-sample qualitative research (Seidman 2006).
Frequency is not a goal of this sort of qualitative research, but depth
and cohesion are, and saturation is reached when you find the gem that puts

everything in perspective (Morse 1995). Interviews were conducted by my graduate research assistant, who made a best (eyeball) guess whether interviewees fell into "normal," "overweight," "obese," or "morbidly obese" ranges of BMI. (Several interviewees volunteered that information without prompts.)

These interviews revealed quite a bit about the obesogenic environment thesis, namely, that the ideas embedded in the thesis are well enough circulated to have affected how these women felt about where they live. It appears, however, that other aspects of their lives were more salient in affecting their behavior. And, in defiance of the energy balance model, their behavior did not easily map onto their body sizes. In what follows, I draw on interviews to demonstrate these claims. Interviewees' names are fictionalized to protect confidentiality.

The women interviewed were well aware of the ways that their environments are supposed to—and sometimes do—affect behavior. Several interviewees complained about the ubiquity of chain and fast-food restaurants, although women in Fresno, which housed a Whole Foods supermarket and Trader Joe's, were generally more satisfied with options for grocery shopping. (Remarkably, both stores were uniformly associated with healthful eating, as was vegetarianism, despite that much of what is carried at Trader Joe's is snack food and ready-made meals, glorified by labels of "natural" and "organic.") They also spoke approvingly of the farmers markets in each town. Regarding opportunities for physical activity, women in Fresno spoke about traffic and heat as obstacles to walking, while those in Tracy focused on commute times that cut into exercise opportunities. In both places, women mentioned the need to drive long distances to take advantage of outdoor recreation amenities but also noted the existence of plenty of gyms in town, for those who *like* to use them.

Cynthia, an obese, moderate-income woman in her late forties, discussed how several aspects of the obesogenic environment concatenate in Tracy:

> The problem with Tracy is that it's primarily a commuter community. We have a lot of people in Tracy that have moved here to try and get away from high prices and find family life. But they commute. So they leave at 4, 5:30, or 6 in the morning and they don't get home until 6:30, 7 o'clock at night so there's lots of picking up food on the way home. Their kids are involved in sports so they're helping their kids chasing all their sports but a lot of times that involves late . . . eating fast food . . . eating Taco Bell, that kind of stuff on the way to the game, on the way to practice, or whatever else is going on. So unless you really live and work in Tracy, it's hard to stay in a healthy regime because of your lifestyle.

Beth, a middle-class (moderate-income, homeowner) "obese" woman in her early fifties from Fresno, made an explicit comparison with a "healthier" environment, in this case, Lake Tahoe. According to Beth, who had grown up in the Central Valley, but had also lived in Lake Tahoe,

> The food options in Fresno suck. They totally suck. Like in Tahoe if you stopped off at the coffee place you could get a healthy something to eat. Even their cookie was healthy and then in Fresno you drive back and it's all fast food, it's all processed. You can't even get anything good to eat here. It's all chains. It's sad. It really is sad.

Beth also compared Fresno to Tahoe in terms of walkability. She said she used to walk in Tahoe, but didn't like to walk in Fresno because she gets "hot, sweaty and ugly."

Indeed, almost all of the women disliked where they lived—and thought they'd be different, thinner, if they lived elsewhere. Those in Tracy complained about the lack of proximity to places they wanted to go and the disappearance or absence of community. People in both towns looked to other places—often the coast or mountains—as places where they could live the lives they really wanted and, for that matter, enjoy the food and exercise opportunities that these towns lack. Despite her professed love for Fresno, including the smells and "the earthy feel of the farm community," Susan, who was mildly obese and who had been big as a child, preferred to eat out on the coast, and also commented that she did more walking on the coast, which she visited regularly. Janine, who was very big (and had always been so) even though she belonged to a community-supported agriculture program and was delighted to cook homemade meals with the local, fresh produce, spoke wistfully about her days living in Santa Rosa, where there was nice scenery for walking and biking and not just the mall or gyms. Most strikingly, Rachel, who had become morbidly obese in her adult life, had traveled a lot and lived in Sweden and associated her time in Sweden with better health, even though the food was fatty ("mayo and cheese") and even though she couldn't exercise in the cold winters. Living there was "more inspiring to her artistic side," while Fresno made her feel "dull and bored and frustrated." Then she stated quite explicitly that she'd be thinner if she lived elsewhere—not only because she'd eat healthier food but also because she'd lead a more enchanted, less stressed-out life.

By the same token, several women expressed relief that these places allowed them an opportunity to let go of difficult-to-attain bodily norms. This sense of comfort reflects a variant of the obesogenic environment thesis, albeit one that is often applied to African Americans. To wit, studies that have sought to test whether BMI values are higher in African American communities hypothesize that shared norms, values, and beliefs shape notions of acceptable body sizes (Boardman et al. 2005; Robert and Reither 2004). Several of these women stated that they felt comfortable in Fresno or Tracy precisely because of the way they looked relative to those around them. Beth noted that she felt better about her body than she did when she was eighteen and stuck out for being fat; now, "I feel like a lot of people look like me so yeah it's much easier." Susan also noted a climate of body acceptability in Fresno, as demonstrated by the lack of high-end stores and the prevalence of what she called "industrial clothes." Janine's fond remembrances of Santa Rosa were tempered by having "to worry about size 00 walking by you." As she said about Fresno, "Yeah we're just not like a couture area. We're just not on that cutting edge of Fashion Week and this and that and it's just not, you're not on display here; it's not like, oh the beautiful people live in LA or they live in NY or in Hawaii or whatever." In other words, there was something about the social context of Fresno and Tracy that allowed for bigger bodies—and they noticed it.

The Experience of Class

To the extent that interviewees felt their lives constrained by their environments, in discussing their daily lives, it appears that other aspects, particularly those related to class, were much more salient in affecting their eating and exercise behaviors. Many women mentioned the cost of Whole Foods, and the less financially secure women most definitely shopped at discount grocers and stores where they could buy generic food in bulk. A couple claimed they sought out cheap fast food because they could get a lot for little money. One of the thinnest women interviewed, by the way, was also the least financially secure. Cathy had lived in Fresno her entire life and because of her limited budget ate from fast-food restaurants, big-box stores, and wholesale groceries, and always bought the cheapest food, careful not to buy name brands because of the extra cost. Even then, the cost of food was not necessarily the most determinate factor in affecting what and how they ate; some did not have partners to help shop for and prepare food. And some noted that it was their male partners who preferred buying at the cheaper places and cooking with more meat. Strikingly, a couple of the larger women talked about their lack of interest and talent in preparing food, one to the point of rancor. They would buy fresh vegetables that "would just rot in the fridge." For Rachel, it came down to a matter of time.

> I would have a chef who would make healthy meals. Like, I like healthy meals, when I go eat, like, vegetarian (I was a vegetarian for a year, I just wasn't able to sustain it). You know I love healthy stuff when it's cooked well; I just don't want to do it myself. It just takes too much time and I'm not that interested in food preparation. But I can appreciate it, you know, and I love to eat a good healthy meal when someone else makes it. Maybe that's laziness but again, time.

Not only time, but also issues with child care, and especially stress, made a couple of interviewees quite adamant. Beth, for example, who detested the Fresno environment, attributed having reached two hundred pounds by the time she was eighteen, not to the environment per se, but to stress:

> I would start off every year, school year, lost weight during the summer (would really focus on it) and then would always gain ten or so pounds during the year because I was so stressed out raising my daughter by myself. Her dad only took her two weekends a month so I took her the rest, I had all the responsibility. And then starting the teaching career there's so much stress on being wonderful. And I don't know, there was a point when I hit like pre-menopause about 40, where I just put on 20 pounds and couldn't wear any of my clothes so I'd wear the same crappy things, like 5 things. I don't know, I went through this weird period where I just put on a lot of weight and got really stressed out and pulled back. And I don't know if I ever really came out of it. . . . I used to just say, just flat out, "I'm bitter. I'm very bitter."

And Jackie, a single mom whose former husband had died and who was in a pretty tenuous economic situation, noted several ways in which her situation affected her ability to maintain supposedly healthy practices. For example, she didn't particularly like fast food but her son loved it. She also said she couldn't afford Whole Foods. She reported having hardly any time to herself and sleeping three hours a night. She didn't use the weight room in her apartment building because she couldn't bring her son. She wouldn't have minded walking but had no one to take care of her son while she was out. Basically, she was at her wit's end:

> I'm obviously obese. I need to lose weight. I know that I should. Yeah so, I mean, it's funny because in college I was a runner and I was half my size, you know, so I know what it's like to be thin and feeling good and being buff. But, especially since

I've moved to Fresno, I've had a lot, a lot of stress, and when I am stressed I eat. And I've had more stress than you can even imagine.

It is worth noting here that several recent studies have found connections between stress and obesity, specifically the kind of stress that affects those whose work situations afford them little control or autonomy. And it is not necessarily stress eating that accounts for increased weight, suggesting that other biological mechanisms are at work (cf. Berlant 2007). Rather, elevated cortisol, the stress hormone, is strongly associated with visceral fat accumulation and metabolic syndrome (Björntorp 2001; Rosmond 2005). To the extent that these aspects of class do potentially affect size, they are not incorporated into models of obesogenic environments that focus on proximity and affordability.

Nevertheless, it *is* class that appears to prevent these women from living where they might want. Virtually all of the interviewees lived in Fresno and Tracy because of affordability, where, as shown in table 1, median housing prices are far below those in the more desirable places of Marin and San Francisco. Either they never had the opportunity to leave or they moved there, especially Tracy, because they could afford to buy a home. Cynthia, a Tracy interviewee, moved to Tracy when "prices in San Jose went off the charts." But when asked where she'd most like to live, she said Santa Cruz, where she had grown up. Likewise, Mary moved to Tracy expecting to stay there for only five years. Rachel was quite explicit that she never intended to stay in Fresno but that finances had gotten in the way of moving. With class so salient in their clearly constrained choices to live in these places, it wouldn't seem farfetched to argue that it is class that explains the prevalence of obesity rates in these towns, more than the built environment per se. Consider the following.

The Place of Class

Contemporary geographers emphasize that spatial patterns in housing, commercial development, and public-land access are a reflection of social relations of race and class rather than a producer of them (Schein 2006). These spatialized patterns of race and class have accentuated in an era when many economic development opportunities stem from the buying power and taxability of local residents (Massey and Denton 1998). Consider the origins of two of the kinds of urban environments associated with obesogeneity. One is the so-called food desert, a term used to describe low-income urban neighborhoods, generally inhabited by people of color, with a paucity of supermarkets and other venues to purchase healthful fruits, vegetables, meats, and grain products, often coupled with an abundance of liquor and convenience stores where only snack food and highly processed ready-to-eat meals can be purchased (Cummins and Macintyre 2002). The existence of such neighborhoods is rooted in racist insurance and lending practices (redlining), which have historically made it difficult to develop and sustain businesses in certain areas (Eisenhauer 2001). Importantly, the food desert phenomenon is also attributed to white flight and the net loss of supermarkets to suburbs with larger sites, fewer zoning impediments, and customers with greater purchasing power (Alwitt and Donley 1997; Cotterill and Franklin 1995). These are the urban ghettos conceived as too scary for walking.

Juxtaposed with the investment-starved urban ghetto and landscapes of dearth, the other problem landscape is one of new investment and excess, albeit the cheap kind. These expansive working- and middle-class suburbs owe much to new waves of regional economic development in the form of big-box stores, malls, and outlet centers—as well as the white flight that created food deserts in the urban cores. Much of this was driven by localities starved for tax revenue that encouraged such retail development to generate sales tax revenue. As the foreclosure crisis has taught, much contemporary suburban sprawl has also been driven by developers and mortgage bankers encouraging a struggling, debt-ridden middle class to move far from the urban core to take advantage of cheap housing in areas with lower land values. In other words, to the extent that some places have many features that are supposedly obesogenic, it reflects the financial resources of those who inhabit such places and the waves of investment and disinvestment that have produced such environments. Therefore, what may be "predicting" the prevalence of obesity in certain places is, in fact, race and class (putting aside for now what produces variation in size relative to race and class), with features of the built environment being an effect of that spatial patterning rather than a cause.

That brings me to Diane from Fresno, the exception that possibly proves the rule. Diane was an educated, solidly middle-class woman with a long marriage and adult children. Although she claimed she had a "weight problem" as a teenager, she was thin at the time of the interview, possibly below the normal range of BMI. Diane admitted to being price conscious, especially since her family had hit some hard times. For example, she said she had a hard time

justifying buying apples at Whole Foods for her own family. Diane also recognized that living in Fresno limited her exercise opportunities because "the
air quality sucks" and it is intensely hot in the summer—both of which, she
acknowledged, got in the way of outdoor activity, as does the long drive to the
national parks. Diane never imagined she would have stayed in Fresno. And
yet, Diane attributed the family's staying in Fresno precisely to their financial
situation. When discussing the air quality, she said: "That's one of the weird
things about Fresno. We live here. Obviously you financially can't just pick up
and move. We deal with it."

Still, Diane managed to negotiate much of this environment, which
for her depended on time possibly even more than money. Rather than
worrying too much about food, she managed to run two miles a day, despite
the heat and smog, or work out at the gym, noting at several junctures "the
privilege of time."

> I realize I have to take personal responsibility for me, knowing that I don't have
> the freedom to walk in a climate that's limiting. Like I said, transitional months
> (fall and spring) are great. I realize that I have the luxury of being able to run in
> the morning. I'm not a single mom. I don't have to get on the bus to go to a job.
> We have the luxury of belonging to this little health club, you know, where we can
> stop in there and swim if we want or use the weights. That's a luxury. I realize that.
> If I was working full-time, single mom, had to come home and do the second shift
> with my children. If I was on a limited income and your question before, "*When
> you go shopping are you cost conscious?*" hell no, I wouldn't be, we wouldn't be able
> to really eat the way we do now.

Yet, it was Diane's remarks on her love-hate relationship with Fresno that
was the gem that put everything in perspective. She was quite excited about
the emerging arts scene in Fresno and how that was affecting the cultural
value of Fresno:

> Well, it's interesting that Fresno has always been the butt of a lot of jokes culturally
> when I was growing up but it's really gone through a lot of cool changes. I told you
> we were coming from downtown art hop open studio night. There's a great theater
> here. There's a lot of interesting revitalization downtown. There's the university has
> great things to do as well.

This quotation, along with several nods to "personal responsibility," suggests
that Diane had taken on norms of body management that are associated with
higher-status people—and higher-status places. As she put it, "So for me and

my needs to stay healthy, I'd have to not blame it on Fresno and I'd have to just be creative."

OBESOGENIC SPACES AND IDEAL PLACES

Diane's comments, along with those of several other interviewees, suggest a perceived disjuncture between healthy lifestyles and places like Fresno. If Fresno's environment is so problematic, what does a healthy, or leptogenic, environment look like and, more important, who can afford to live there? What I am suggesting is that the concept of the obesogenic environment reveals unstated preferences for places with the amenities often associated with urbane, privileged environments, including university towns, artsy enclaves, gentrified urban cores, and even older well-heeled suburbs. By lauding environments unobtainable to most, we begin to see how the obesogenic environment thesis might help produce a social geography.

On the food side, it is surely striking that the distinction between food deserts and food cornucopia is confusing. Is the problem dearth or ubiquity? When you separate the wheat from the chaff of the claims, it becomes clear that the critique is really not about ubiquity and more about the availability of too much of the wrong food (fast and junky) relative to the right food (fresh and wholesome). The case in point is an emerging discourse that characterizes endless strip malls of chain restaurants and fast-food joints as food deserts because they lack "real food" (Breitbach 2007). Those who tout the obesogenic environment thesis would hardly characterize ubiquitous farmers markets and gourmet market halls, upscale restaurants, and natural food stores as a problem.

The distinction between the damned and the preferred is even odder but equally pronounced on the physical activity side. The problem of suburban sprawl is not only the absence of sidewalks and the presence of freeways but, it seems, the absence of unique character or interesting form (Ritzer 1993). Curiously, though, since some suburbs are not known or tested as obesogenic, they seem to escape this critique. This would include the elite older suburbs of New York, Boston, Philadelphia, and Chicago, or, here in California, the exurbs of Marin County, again one of the thinnest places in the state. Marin County, for instance, would by several measures count as an obesogenic environment, with its low housing density, long commute times, and large malls and strips replete with fast food, although some would note the upscale restaurants and markets and the beautiful recreational amenities alongside those "obesogenic" features (but again, would a spatial model capture this mix?). Equally confusing is the finding that mixed-use areas have lower rates of obesity than residential ones (Lopez 2004). This would not be surprising to anyone who has traipsed through the Upper West Side of Manhattan or San Francisco's Noe Valley. And yet, the Bronx and South Side of Chicago are also "mixed use" but are apparently obesogenic nevertheless. Studies that speak to fear of walking (Lee 2006) or lack of "safe" parks (Quinn et al. 2007) raise further doubts that the issue is really just a matter of spatial layout.

Furthermore, for a thesis that aspires to name structural and environmental causes it actually returns a great deal of responsibility—or lack thereof—to individuals (Kirkland 2010). Too much food and too little sidewalk translate into too much eating and too little exercise, where the environment plays a mediating role, at best. And yet, since the thesis doesn't allow much for the agency of people who inhabit these environments, it reinforces the idea that they are unthinking dupes, without personal responsibility. Only those who manage to escape these environments or mediate them well, such as Diane, are endowed with agency. So the thesis also reveals unstated preferences for certain lifestyles associated with self-efficacy, personal responsibility, and, apparently, a good deal of time and money to take advantage of the amenities the favored environments offer.

In short, the thesis takes the tenets of healthism and lifestylism and projects them onto the built environment. Just as healthism tends to laud the lifestyles of those with class and race privilege, this spatialized healthism tends to laud spaces made by class and race privilege. The problem is that if the idealized "leptogenic" environment is one of privilege, there are limits to how much we can redress the obesogenic environment without confronting class and racial inequality.

BEYOND THE BUILT ENVIRONMENT AND THE SUPPLY SIDE

The obesogenic environment thesis, with its focus on access and proximity to grocery stores, restaurants, parks, gyms, and public transportation, leads to the conclusion that if these conditions are changed, behaviors will follow. It thus draws forth a set of interventions that are strongly supply-sided. Arguably, that is the reason that public health professionals and food system advocates have embraced the thesis. Supply-side interventions are reasonably palatable politically and provide clarity about what to do. Accordingly, public health advocates have put a good deal of effort into soda bans in schools or good neighbor agreements that ask corner liquor stores to sell fruits and vegetables, or even creating more walkable public space in new suburbs.

And those who endorse such efforts often do so in the name of combating racial and class inequality. Yet, if these obesogenic environments are as inseparable from race and class as I contend they are, picking out particular features of the built environment and making them more leptogenic isn't likely to cut it as a body-size-altering strategy—and may have unintended consequences. It effaces the problem that the very conditions and amenities that make certain places sites of "the good life" make them unobtainable to most. It must be remembered that elite suburbs themselves came into being in escape from the "dangerous classes" of the city in an earlier historical period (Szasz 2007). And these gentrified urban cores that allow rarified eating and walking in public space are themselves products of particular economic development strategies to attract capital, which in doing so displace those with fewer means (Smith 1996).

Towns and cities with artistic, independent, and healthful restaurants, beautiful outdoor amenities, vibrant public spaces, and unique character are "leptogenic," to be sure. But they are leptogenic not only because of the food choices and physical activity opportunities they offer. They are leptogenic because wealth has made them into even more pleasant (but costly places). That is because places with wealth both attract businesses to meet the food tastes of residents and generate the taxes to improve and maintain those enjoyable public spaces. Yet the more wealth they attract, the more they become inaccessible to many, as home prices follow. Thin real estate is expensive.

On that note, I have continued to skirt the question of the relationship between socioeconomic status and body size. Most people assume that it derives directly from energy intake relative to expenditure, and therefore that the wealthy white women who differ from their poorer peers must eat much less and exercise much more. Chang and Christakis (2005) suggest that the importance of thinness as a means to maintain and display class status makes high-income white women work harder at it. Others have argued that body size is a cause of class status rather than the inverse (Julier 2008;

Kirkland 2010). This is based on the many studies that have demonstrated how weight bias affects people across the course of their lives, including student-teacher relations, college admissions, marital prospects, and job advancement. Kirkland and Julier's point is not that thinness guarantees you high status, although a thin body and a beautiful face do seem to be a vehicle for upward mobility for some women (through, for example, marriage, the beauty professions, and to some extent the sex trade); it is that fatness pretty much guarantees that you will not have high status. The question of what begets which is far from settled, and I will complicate it further in chapter 5. Suffice it to say that just as living in Fresno and Tracy relaxes pressures to be thin, living in wealthy areas seems to intensify pressures to be thin. By the same token, the features and resources available in thin and fat places affect the possibilities for self-management in such places, so the relationship between size and place seems profoundly iterative.

No matter what, to replicate features of the leptogenic environment to make people thin is unlikely to be efficacious. Kirkland (2010) likens efforts to get people to lose weight in order to make them higher status to programs to promote marriage among the poor because married people are healthier and wealthier. Such programs miss the point. Analogously, so might programs to make people thin by replicating the environments of wealthy people. But these programs are not just missing the point. Trying to make environments more like those of the wealthy upholds an economic differentiation of urban landscape that could have perverse social justice ramifications. Already efforts to redress the supply-side problems, such as community gardens, farmers markets, and spruced-up parks, have led to gentrification, which is why people in low-income areas are beginning to reject such projects (Quastel 2009).

So when the food and health writers glorify certain places for the qualities they have (e.g., gentrified urban cores) and devalue others for their dearth (e.g., food deserts), they actually contribute to the problem. It is precisely this simultaneously cultural and economic valuation process that George Lipsitz describes in *The Possessive Investment in Whiteness* (1998), in which he shows how the legacies of racist housing policy actually produced wealth for whites in the suburbs in inverse relationship to African Americans in the inner cities. Bringing wealth and investment to certain places and leaving others behind are causally linked processes (Szasz 2007). So even if you could prove that the built environment matters in terms of contributing to obesity through practices of the self that they encourage or discourage, you can't address the problem without addressing class cultures, class inequalities, and the policies that continue to heighten or exacerbate them. And yet, as the next chapter will discuss, it is not so clear that it is only self-practices that are contributing to changes and variation in size, which, among other things, further complicates the presumed relationship between class and socioeconomic status.

CHAPTER 5

Does Eating (Too Much) Make You Fat?

In 2003, I attended a symposium at UC Berkeley called "The Politics of Obesity: A National Eating Disorder." It was organized and hosted by Michael Pollan, and Marion Nestle, Kelly Brownell, and Joan Dye Gussow, all highly respected figures, were the featured speakers, chosen because, as Nestle put it that day, they were "the only ones addressing the obesity issue from a food system perspective." Early in the presentation, she paused to punctuate a point: "It's simple," she said, "obesity results from too many calories in and too few calories out." I've heard this repeated many times at the conferences and talks I've attended on this topic. This includes a 2010 conference on food/farm policy and obesity at which a spokesperson from the US Department of Agriculture (USDA) said that the reasons for obesity are that "people eat too much too often, too much of the wrong things, and exercise too little. . . . [I]t's pretty simple." At the same conference, another highly regarded nutritionist pointed out that since fat people have fat dogs and cats, the increase in obesity can't be because of genetics.

Is it simple? Ask a chronic dieter and you might not get the same answer. Some people are fat no matter what they do, and some are thin no matter what they do. Of course this isn't a huge surprise, and scientists on all sides of the obesity debate would concede this point, even if the popular writers tend to efface it. There have always been very fat people—and thin people—and all sizes in between.

Nevertheless, individual exceptions do not invalidate trend data (Krimsky 2000: 37), and the trend data show something that warrants explanation: moderate growth in mean BMI since 1960, and then a marked rise in mean BMI beginning around 1980, with changes in height flattening out (Power and Schulkin 2009). As noted in chapter 2, the rise in mean BMI of about three points since 1980 represents about a twenty-pound weight gain across the American adult population. This has been accompanied by the amply noted rise in childhood obesity. From 1980 to 2008, the prevalence of overweight in children ages two to five increased from 5.0 percent to 10.4 percent; for those ages six to eleven, from 6.5 percent to 19.6 percent; and for those ages twelve to nineteen, from 5.0 percent to 19.1 percent (Ogden et al. 2010; Ogden et al. 2002).[1] What has precipitated this abrupt population-level shift since 1980?

Furthermore, during this same period, significant differences in BMI have become evident across race, class, and gender. In the most recent national study, 53 percent of non-Hispanic black women and 51 percent of Mexican American women in the 40–59 age group were deemed obese, compared to 39 percent of non-Hispanic white women, but differences in obesity rates by race or ethnicity were not as dramatic among men (Flegal, Carroll, et al. 2010). A major analysis of health data collected in California found significant differences in rates of obesity by socioeconomic status (Lee 2006), although much more for whites (and especially white women) and, to a lesser extent, Latinos than for African Americans and Asian Americans. What accounts for this variation?

Just about everyone assumes that both the increase and the variation relate to energy balance (too many calories consumed relative to expenditure), with some adjustments for genetic predisposition. Childhood obesity, in particular, is presumed to result from the increase in snacking and junk food eating on the food side, and television watching and video game playing, relative to outside play and sports, on the physical activity side (Brownell and Horgen 2004). Class and racial differences are presumed to result from the cheapness of high-caloric food, which encourages those with less income to buy and eat it. As I will discuss in this chapter, however, the evidence is just not there that people eat more calories than they did a generation ago or that different socioeconomic groups eat different amounts of calories. And traditional genetics cannot explain the observed changes and differences.

Holes in the energy balance model, both empirical and conceptual, thus lead to two questions: (1) If changes in caloric intake do not satisfactorily explain the increase in size, what does? (2) Why is the conversation so focused on calories? This chapter primarily focuses on the first question. I will discuss the probable role of environmental toxins, food inputs, and a few other non-calorie-related factors in contributing to obesity. Crucially, some of the substances I will discuss not only affect appetite, satiety, and metabolism, but also can directly spur the growth of adipose tissue. In addition, many of these are used in agriculture and food processing, suggesting something missing in the food system perspective. To be sure, the slow and sometimes hostile reactions to this emerging science suggest a good deal of investment in the energy balance model, especially among those touting a food system perspective, and present a clear instance in which already existing assumptions about the problem are foreclosing or stalling other possible explanations. In the conclusion of the chapter I entertain why this might be so, thus touching on the second question.

To the extent that environmental factors truly beyond individual control, as well as the nonnutritional aspects of food, are contributing to the increase in size, this implicates a different set of actors from those who are said to make bad food decisions—or take less heroic approaches to their body management. In presenting this evidence, I hope to begin to shift the conversation from how much is eaten to the way food is produced, from the emphasis on individual choice to the need for stronger regulation. First, though, I want to show why prevailing explanations don't suffice.

TIPPING THE ENERGY BALANCE MODEL

Are people bigger?
Oh yeah, absolutely. Even my children. I mean. We are not, uh, garbage eaters, for the most part my children would rather have fruits and vegetables than garbage, well, more so my older son than my younger, but still they like fruits and vegetables and that kind of stuff. And both of my children are big, and it's like, I know what my children eat, and I think they should not be as big as they are.

—Tracy interviewee

As already noted, typical explanations of population-level changes and variation in BMI look to some combination of energy expenditure and genetics: one representing behavior and the other biological disposition. As we shall see, neither satisfactorily explains these phenomena. The woman from Tracy thus makes a good point.

Empirically, the presumption that since 1980 people have been taking in more calories relative to those they expend has simply not been demonstrated. In a thorough review of the literature on caloric intake and expenditure, Michael Gard and Jan Wright (2005) found no real proof that food intake in industrialized countries has risen and activity levels have declined, particularly in the years since 1980, but plenty of presumptions based on "common sense." As they reported, the literature on food intake is quite contradictory, with some studies suggesting even a reduction in energy intake over the past several decades. More to the point, the degree and direction of such changes are just not known, especially in the absence of good longitudinal data. Epidemiological data are based on recollection and food diaries, which tend to underreport food intake. Supply measures, such as food availability indexes, rely on estimates of farm production, adjusted for exports and imports, nonfood uses, and food wastage (the amount of food never eaten but tossed) (US Department of Agriculture 2002). These are gross estimates at best. Nor has the putative decline in physical activity been convincingly demonstrated. Studies of physical activity are also notoriously unreliable, based on self-reporting (Baillie-Hamilton 2002a; Gard and Wright 2005).

Intuitively, it is not hard to see how the energy balance model might be a little suspect. Americans have been eating processed food, high in simple carbohydrates (e.g., white bread and Betty Crocker mixes) and lots of fats for most of the twentieth century. In many respects, less fattening foods have become more available since 1980. Thanks to the global food trade, there are more fresh fruits and vegetables available year round; thanks to engineering and breeding, there are more lean meats than fatty ones; and thanks to food science, there are more low- or zero-calorie food substances than were once imaginable. As for the idea that contemporary jobs involve less toil, Gard and Wright remind us that toil is hardly a thing of the past for many people. Notably, work in the construction industry, house-cleaning, restaurant service, and farming—all physically arduous—tends to be done by the very population groups in America that are getting bigger: working-class Latinos and whites. Plus, the shift to office jobs occurred long before the leap in BMI in 1980. Nor are sedentary lifestyles particularly new, although a couple of generations ago people were listening to their radios rather than checking email upon returning home from work.

Interestingly, more readily available cross-sectional data (studies that compare behaviors across populations) utterly debunk assumptions that certain groups eat more than others. Data published by the USDA on "What We Eat in America," based on national health surveys, show similarity among racial groups in daily caloric intake in 2007–8: 2,198 calories for whites, 2,095 for African Americans, and 2,109 for Mexican Americans (cited in Kirkland

2010; US Department of Agriculture 2010). Furthermore, and remarkably, the same USDA study did not show that caloric intake differs by income. Those earning less than $25,000 per year reported consuming 2,104 calories per day while those earning more than $75,000 per year reported consuming 2,238 per day. These surprising data may be written off as self-reporting. Yet, to write off such comparative data would assume that certain groups are more prone to underreport food intake than others; the extent to which we make those mental adjustments demonstrates our own stake in preexisting ideas.

Empirically, then, the evidence just doesn't exist to attribute differing obesity rates on population and subpopulation levels to energy balance, and some scientists of human biology are concluding that diet and physical activity cannot account for these changes anyway, since a good deal of energy expenditure is devoted to metabolism and other physiological processes (Hatch et al. 2010). If it's not the calories, where else can we look for an explanation?

THE GENETIC BLACK BOX

In current ways of thinking about obesity, the only other way to account for change and variation in BMI is through genetics. The problem with genetic explanations is that they are unspecified and can be nonsensical in explaining change (Power and Schulkin 2009: 292). This is because genetic sequences are established evolutionarily. The glacial pace of evolutionary change simply does not square with an abrupt rise in obesity since 1980 (Baillie-Hamilton 2002a; Crossley 2004; Power and Schulkin 2009). Therefore, only a genetic mutation could explain this abrupt change—or, as I will explain later, what is now called an "epigenetic" effect.

Scientists have been able to pin some extreme cases of obesity on a gene mutation that restricts production of the hormone leptin. Leptin, after the Greek word *leptos* for thin, is secreted in proportion to adipose tissue. Scientists have theorized that leptin regulates food intake in relation to fat stores, thus serving as a sort of "lipostat" (Power and Schulkin 2009: 179). Bodies without leptin "think" they are in a state of starvation and thus will eat more (Pool 2001: 4). In general, though, the occurrence of single-gene mutations is low, and less than 5 percent of obese people have been shown to have identifiable hormonal, physiological, or molecular genetic abnormalities (Power and Schulkin 2009: 38). Gene mutation theories also tend to employ genetic reductionism, as if a single gene expressed a trait. The so-called thrifty gene, which might have evolved to encourage fat storage to withstand periods of famine, has not been located through genetic mapping, despite forty years of effort (Fee 2006). No singular gene has been established to predict obesity at all; genetic pathways to obesity appear multiple and interactive (Power and Schulkin 2009). In any case, without evidence of mutation these genetic pathways could explain only variation in rates of obesity, not a trend.

Explaining variation in biological function through genetic coding raises its own set of issues. Through their exhaustive review of literature on genetic contribution to obesity (often through twin studies), Gard and Wright (2005) found that variation among individuals attributed to genetic factors ranged from 50 percent to 90 percent. Because of the lack of specificity regarding the genetic piece, Gard and Wright conclude that genetic arguments have become a red herring or, as they put it, a "black box," employed to hold the energy balance model together.

Trend explanations are thus left with an argument that borrows on evolutionary theory but really amounts to the energy balance model. And that is that we are fat because our current environment of food availability, particularly the prevalence of fats and sugars, is mismatched to our evolutionary heritage (Popkin 2008; Power and Schulkin 2009). The evolutionary biologists Michael Power and Jay Schulkin describe it this way: As early hunter-gatherers, humans evolved to store fat. Fat was particularly important for reproductive success, probably more important than being able to withstand famine. Fat was also critical to feed large and thus metabolically "expensive" brains. In addition, humans evolved to desire energy-rich food, since they also expended so much energy in obtaining it. Although generally scarce, starches and sugars figured prominently because they were easy to digest and in some cases tasty. Such foods favor fat disposition because they raise blood glucose, which is an important source of energy but can be toxic if left in the blood supply. Sequestering fat in adipose tissue thus developed as an adaptive response that would prevent too much blood glucose and fat circulation in nonadipose tissue. The problem now, as they put it, is that these mechanisms are "overtaxed" and pathological rather than adaptive. In support of this argument, much has been made of the Pima Indians, who when living in an isolated part of Mexico were thin, but when exposed to a Western diet in Arizona and New Mexico developed unusually high rates of obesity and type 2 diabetes.

Evolutionary arguments are tricky, though, with regard to explaining contemporary differences in obesity among racial groups. Nevertheless, it is important to have some way to talk about preexisting morphological and functional differences, since African Americans and Latinos are often singled out as problem populations in discussions of obesity's causes and consequences. For example, African Americans and, to a lesser extent, Latinos have higher BMIs than whites and Asians, while Americans of East Asian descent tend to have lower BMIs than European Americans but similar percentages of body fat (Power and Schulkin 2009: 308–311). Higher BMIs among African Americans has been attributed to higher bone density and muscle mass, neither of which is generally seen as pathological. The problem is that "social race" and human evolutionary variation are weak substitutes for each other. Social race refers to categories, such as black, Hispanic, or Asian American, that have been produced socially and historically and are meaningful despite the lack of biological bases (Anderson 2001). Note that "Caucasian," "black," "Hispanic," and "Asian" are all problematic aggregations, too, but reflect the level at which most data are collected. (Such aggregations are therefore often the only source of statistics without sampling insufficiencies.) Margery Fee (2006) writes about the inaccuracy of and ultimately the damage caused by using genetics as a "rough proxy" for "social race." She notes, for example, that sickling gene, which is an evolutionary response to malaria, is found in people with origins in north and west Africa and parts of the Mediterranean, geographical patterns that do not map onto "social race." Fee's point is that the importance of genetic disposition pales in comparison to social environmental influence and that efforts to find a genetic basis for particular conditions effectively work to reinscribe the idea that race is biological. As put by Linda Nash in her book *Inescapable Ecologies* (2007), "race is a crude approximation for genetic and lifestyle factors but race is also already entangled in access to medical care, long term and cumulative exposures, and presence in certain environments." "These histories," she goes on to say, "have helped produce race as a meaningful epidemiological category to begin with" (p. 198).

Nash's words illustrate the need to adopt a very different way of thinking about bodily ecologies—and bodily difference—than is typical. Rather than viewing the biological body as either a blank slate for social forces (and calories) to inscribe or a preset genetic inscription, it is critical to think about the body as a site where the biological and the social constantly remake each other (Haraway 1991). This is true even for class, the most indisputably social of all categories of difference. Yet, class most definitely becomes manifest in bodily difference, considering long-term differential exposures to particular labor regimes, toxins, health care, diseases, nutrients, and so forth—exposures that are themselves created by social forces (Harvey and Haraway 1995). This is in addition to what the sociologist Pierre Bourdieu called the habitus, referring to everyday performances of class cultures that materially shape the body in stature, posture, and manner (Bourdieu 1984). Indeed, the increase in size may be the paradigmatic case of this social-biological coconstitution, given the emerging evidence that class-related environmental exposures, stress hormones, and sleep patterns, in addition to food and exercise behaviors, may be creating adiposity. At the same time, some of these exposures have the ability to change genetic inheritance through "epigenetic" effects and, in a world where fat people face deep discrimination, thus to reinforce or worsen class status. One need not rely on evolution, in other words, to discuss bodily difference.

In what immediately follows, I lay out three important anomalies that not only are particularly confounding to existing explanations but also are suggestive of the ways that bodies have already been reshaped as a result of exposures. Thereafter, I present the emergence and state of the science of obesogens that addresses how these anomalies might have manifested.

SOME USEFUL ANOMALIES

One anomaly is the significant increase in very big people since 1980. When BMIs are plotted on a bell curve, not only has the curve shifted to the right but also the skew of the curve is such that the right tail is further above the x axis than the left is (Flegal, Carroll, et al. 2010; Freedman et al. 2002). What this means is that the proportion of big people has increased, and that some people have become very big, while the proportion of very thin people has dwindled. Parallel evidence exists that very big kids are getting bigger while other increases in size among children are flattening (Ogden et al. 2010). At some level, of course, it can only be that way: very thin people have very high rates of mortality; the upper side of the BMI range is less constrained by morphological possibility or mortality. Nevertheless, the higher proportion of the very obese is meaningful in at least two ways. One is that it drives mean BMI up and thus entails a smaller increase in BMI among the many—perhaps, even, an increase that represents less than twenty pounds. Put differently, an increase in the "morbidly obese" category may account for a good proportion of the rapid increase in mean BMI since 1980. A relatively minor increase in size among people categorized as overweight or mildly obese is neither particularly mysterious nor particularly startling. Remember that people in the overweight category have longevity on their side, and it is relatively plausible that caloric excess has contributed to the increased prevalence of "overweight" people. This is not to concede the energy balance model in totality but rather to note that it may have greater explanatory power for this group than for the increased proportion of people weighing more than, say, 400 pounds. The other, then, is that it suggests the possibility of different biological causes for "overweight" versus extreme obesity, with the latter just as likely a consequence of some medical problem than a cause of it. Indeed, evidence exists that high proportions of fat tissue play a direct role in begetting more fat.

A second anomaly, or perhaps lack thereof, is the fairly similar increases in obesity prevalence across racial/ethnic groups (at least those tracked) over the three decades since 1980. For example, in 1971 the prevalence of obesity was 15.4 percent for white women and 29.7 percent for black women; today's rates are about 25 percentage points higher for each (Wang and Beydoun 2007). (Statistically reliable data to make a similar comparison do not exist for Latino Americans before the late 1980s, and few data for Asian Americans exist at all.) What that means is that the differences in today's rates of prevalence are largely a reflection of different baselines and thus already existing bodily difference; the fact that rates of increase are similar across different populations with ostensibly very different cultural practices (but apparently similar caloric intakes) opens the possibility of a similar source of change.

Finally, and most critically, the significant increase in "obese" newborns presents a huge anomaly for existing understandings. Although few studies actually measure newborn infants (0–6 months) as a stand-alone category, a major study of well-baby care visits at a Massachusetts HMO found a 73.5 percent increase in prevalence (from 3.4 percent to 5.9 percent) of overweight infants between 1980 and 2001 (Kim et al. 2006). Although that may not appear substantial, it is highly significant for this particular segment of the population. As put by the pediatric endocrinologist Robert Lustig of the University of California, San Francisco, typical explanations cannot account for "a segment that doesn't go to movies, can't chew, and was never that much into exercise: babies. This epidemic of obese 6-month-olds," as Lustig calls it, "poses a problem for conventional explanations of the fattening of America.... [S]ince they're eating only formula or breast milk, and never exactly got a lot of exercise the obvious explanations for obesity don't work for babies" (Begley 2009). The prenatal and perinatal exposures that must be the sources of these changes may well help explain the rise in childhood obesity, as well. Let us now turn to the source.

MAKING THE CASE FOR OBESOGENS

The first person to make the case for the role of environmental toxins in obesity was Paula Baillie-Hamilton (2002a). In her article, she pointed the finger at the proliferation since 1940 of synthetic organic and inorganic chemicals, in the form of pesticides, dies, perfumes, cosmetics, medicines, food additives, plastics, fire retardants, solvents, surfactants, and so forth, all of which are regularly ingested, inhaled, and absorbed in the practices of life. In making her case, she cited a number of studies that had shown that exposure to the pesticides lindane, dieldrine, and hexachlorabenzene in lab animals had produced significant weight gain, with the last having done so while caloric availability was cut in half. She noted that these results had been ignored, explained away, or even missed by other scientists because weight gain was a nonhypothesized consequence and thus had not been included in scientific abstracts.

Her claims were logical as well as evidence-based. For instance, she discussed not only the abruptness of the BMI change relative to the introduction of these chemicals—a correlation that is specious at face value since so many phenomena have increased in tandem with one another since 1980, from soybean production to home movie viewing. She also mentioned signs that others had set aside, such as the failure of calorie-restrictive diets to promote weight loss or the widely known and often unwanted side effect of many pharmaceuticals, from antidepressants to birth control pills to steroids, that promote weight gain. In fact, the antidiabetic drug, rosiglitazone (brand name Avendia) has subsequently been associated with metabolic syndrome and obesity (Grun and Blumberg 2009). That treatments for diabetes or depression, the latter perhaps triggered by feeling bad about one's weight, are now known to contribute to obesity proves Baillie-Hamilton's point in the most ironic of ways. Still, her point was not only that many people use prescribed drugs that could be causing population-level weight gain. Rather, prescription drugs could be the tip of the iceberg of substances designed for other uses that somehow are contributing to increased adiposity. But the dots weren't being connected.

Apparently, few scientists took her seriously because she lacked scientific credentials, had published this article in a nonmainstream medical journal (the

Journal of Alternative and Complementary Medicine), and had written a popular book promoting a diet to detoxify the body (Begley 2009). Remarkably, in the emerging literature on environmental toxins and obesity, several authors have subsequently conceded that she was on to something. Since she wrote that article, a number of scientific findings have emerged that together point to the strong possibility that environmental toxins (and many other substances and stressors) are directly contributing to obesity. In what follows I review some of the most compelling, starting with an overview of the phenomenon of endocrine disruption.

DISRUPTIONS IN THE ENERGY BALANCE MODEL

Endocrine disruption refers to a range of biochemical processes that alter developmental pathways. The endocrine system, like the nervous and immune systems, signals cells to make particular proteins, and proteins are the building blocks of bodily function. It is "endocrinal" (as opposed to autocrinal) because the signaling organs relay "information" to parts other than the signaling organ (Power and Schulkin 2009). The endocrine system is typically thought to comprise the glands and pathways that emit hormones, for example, the thyroid, pituitary, and hypothalamus glands. *Endocrine disruption* thus entails interference with the action of these hormones. The ones of specific concern are external agents (xenobiotics) that behave like, interact with, or alter the function of hormones produced by the body—mimicking, enhancing, or inhibiting them (Krimsky 2000: 116). These are commonly called endocrine-disrupting chemicals (EDCs).

Critically, postpartum changes in the endocrine system can affect development permanently—as least as much as genetic coding—since hormones can control the expression of inherited genes, by, for example, silencing them (Colborn, Dumanoski, and Myers 1996: 40). In the scientific literature, this effect is referred to as "epigenetic," and it is an important piece of the puzzle.

> Like an organism, a gene is not expressed in isolation but rather in the context of other genes and their products, cells, and tissues in a temporal/spatial dimension. This might be thought of as the ecology of gene expression. It is well known that EDCs, and very likely endogenous hormones, can act on a gene's developmental mechanisms, altering phenotype expression. We are now seeing that the mechanism of these phenotypic changes is probably epigenetic; in other words, they cause mitotically heritable changes in gene function without changing the

> DNA sequence, *i.e.* without mutation. In fact, EDCs do not act on genes alone but on developmental mechanisms that integrate genetic and epigenetic interactions, resulting in the phenotype. (Crews and McLachlan 2006: S4)

Put more plainly, EDCs can interfere with genetic expression in ways that permanently transform bodily form and function, and these changes can be passed on to offspring. Epigenetics could thus account for the genetic contribution to the abrupt increase in obesity.

Sheldon Krimsky's *Hormonal Chaos* (2000) discusses a number of other aspects of endocrine disrupters that matter in terms of what, if any, effects they will have. First, minute changes can have large effects. Therefore, standard toxicological models don't work for testing the effects of EDCs. Toxicology aims to find out tolerable dosages and assumes a linear relationship between dose and toxicity—the more you take or are exposed to, the harder you die. In processes of endocrine disruption, in contrast, a moderate exposure can have the largest effect. What are called dose responses to EDCs are therefore best represented by an inverted bell curve, with minute and very large exposures having nonexistent or even inverse effects. Second, the timing of the exposure matters tremendously in terms of what effect, if any, it will have. It appears that exposure to a disrupter at a critical moment in development can shape bodily function forever or at other moments might not matter at all. Scientists, though, have yet to pinpoint when those critical moments occur. Third, the effects can be additive or complementary and similar substances can induce or suppress a response. Among other things, these qualities make it difficult to isolate the effect of any one substance. Fourth, not all organisms are affected equally, even if exposed at the same time; genetic variability makes some people more susceptible. Fifth, because species already tend to vary for all sorts of vital and beneficial reasons, "disruption" may not produce something bad. Hormones can change developmental trajectories but not necessarily to something worse. This is particularly important insofar as "disruption" is used to explain differences in sex, gender identification, and sexual preference. Insofar as hormone disruptors *can* alter sexual development in ways that *may* affect sex and gender identity, they can alter them in a number of directions. In that vein, it is important to consider that endocrine disrupters affect human variation but do not create human variation (Langston 2010: 144). Among other things, this again argues against pathology as the right metaphor for understanding many aspects of obesity.

Finally, and most critically, there can be a huge, even intergenerational lag time between the exposure and the response. In fact, the accidental discovery of intergenerational effects of diethylstilbestrol (DES) ingestion was one of the primary prompts that led to the discovery of EDCs. During the 1950s, pregnant women were prescribed DES, a synthetic estrogen, to prevent miscarriage and promote lactation. (It was also given to livestock to encourage growth and to menopausal women to deal with "the change.") Mothers who took DES during pregnancy not only had rates of miscarriage at least equal to those who didn't; they also gave birth to children prone to rare forms of reproductive cancers and infertility, harm that was often not discovered until late adolescence or adulthood, making the widespread provision of DES one of the most tragic human biomedical experiments on pregnant women, along with the use of thalidomide.[2] The lag time between dose or exposure and response presents all sorts of scientific problems in terms of detection, invisible damage, and questions of what might have been without such exposure (Colborn, Dumanoski, and Myers 1996: 171). It also provides a huge clue to our puzzle: if people began to be exposed to EDCs in the postwar period and then were barraged with them thereafter—and the effects are intergenerational—it would make sense that more recent generations would express the conditions and traits precipitated by those exposures (Langston 2010).

Besides the theory of endocrine disruption and related discovery of epigenetics, two other important scientific contributions have augmented understanding of possible biological pathways to obesity besides caloric intake and expenditure: the so-called Barker hypothesis and the discovery that adipose tissue is an endocrine organ. The Barker hypothesis (named for the hypothesizer) was premised on well-established observations that small gestational size often results in adult obesity. Upon being fed, formerly small infants will catch up with and even surpass the norm (Barker 1998). The underlying theory is that low birth weight fosters a "thrifty metabolism," which can lead to adult obesity. Bearing out this thesis, studies have shown that very small as well as large birth-weight babies are more likely to have high adult BMIs and may be susceptible to metabolic syndrome (Power and Schulkin 2009: 263). Developmental biologists now believe that anything that hinders fetal growth, including, for example, maternal exposure to secondhand smoke, toxics, or even stress, can manifest in adult obesity (Hatch et al. 2010).

Equally important was the mid-1990s discovery that adipose tissue secretes hormones that are active in regulating appetite and metabolism. What this means is that adipose tissue not only stores fat but actually participates in the body's signaling function (Kershaw and Flier 2004). The probable role of fat in leptin activity, for example, is that high adiposity induces leptin resistance so that leptin cannot suppress appetite as strongly as it otherwise might (Power and Schulkin 2009: 180). (This mechanism should not be confused with the gene mutation that reduces leptin production.) Adiponectin, another hormone secreted in fat cells, plays a protective role against insulin resistance and inflammation; insufficient adiponectin is often associated with obesity (Kershaw and Flier 2004). These discoveries not only acknowledge that signals of appetite and satiety can be distorted and disrupted; they show that fat itself is implicated in such interference.

Nevertheless, the discovery of fat as an endocrine organ does not break far from the energy balance model. That is mainly because it points to already credible ideas about how appetite and metabolism are mediated. Since then, studies have indeed found that EDCs can interfere with more commonly known mechanisms of homeostasis, including insulin response, brain communication, and other conditions that affect metabolism and appetite (Tabb and Blumberg 2006). As it turns out, though, hormonal disturbances can do much more: they can actually stimulate the production and growth of fat cells. This is the aspect of the theory that portends a major paradigm shift.

ENDOCRINE DISRUPTION AND OBESITY
Pathways to Discovery

Until the mid 2000s, most of the research on endocrine disruption focused on the reproductive, immune, and nervous systems, with "little information of the possible direct effect of endocrine-disrupting chemicals on fat cell differentiation or physiology" (Heindel 2003: 248). EDCs had been associated with developmental changes (precocious puberty), reproductive disorders (low sperm count, infertility), behavioral disorders such as attention deficit hyperactivity disorder (ADHD), and various cancers (breast, testicular, vaginal, prostrate) (Krimsky 2000). Since then, evidence has mounted that EDCs are directly implicated in fat tissue development, particularly via estrogen, the main sex hormone in females but also present in males.

In some sense, estrogen was the obvious place to look, because of the DES debacle and because of its known ability to provoke cell growth, particularly in fatty tissue such as animal breasts. This highly relevant discovery of the role of EDCs in cell multiplication came as a surprise, however. In 1987, two researchers at the Tufts School of Medicine (Carlos Sonnenschein and Ana Soto) were attempting to do breast cancer experiments with highly estrogen-sensitive cells. After setting up the experiment and before they introduced the estrogen, they unexpectedly discovered a wild proliferation of cells. After much frustration involved in redoing the set-up of the experiment several times over, they eventually deduced that it was the plastic tubes and dishes used in the laboratory experiments—the presumably biochemically neutral equipment—that contained the chemicals that were causing cell multiplication (Colborn, Dumanoski, and Myers 1996: 122–30). Scientists have subsequently established that estrogen plays a key role in transmitting the effects of chemicals. Receptors present in the body easily bind to many different environmental substances, which then direct cell division (Colborn, Dumanoski, and Myers 1996: 84; Krimsky 2000: 41). Therefore high estrogen circulation is associated with higher incidence of breast cancer, fibroid tumors, and endometriosis.

Still, the role of estrogen in obesity came as a surprise, not a hypothesized finding, according to Retha Newbold, who works at the National Institute for Environmental Health Sciences. I met with Newbold in November 2009 and learned that for thirty years she had conducted research on the role of DES in development. She could tell DES was affecting body size just by looking at the lab animals. Because the DES-exposed animals were unusually large, she had to decrease the number of animals who lived in a cage. She notes that others studying nonestrogenic chemicals didn't have the same problem. Now her research, discussed in the next section, looks directly at the relationship between estrogenic compounds, both natural and synthetic, and obesity.

Another scientist who works on these topics is Bruce Blumberg, a professor of developmental and cell biology at UC Irvine. His research on the chemical tributlyltin (TBT) is the most definitive yet on the specific cell biological pathways leading from EDCs to obesity. His first finding also came as a surprise, although one less serendipitous than the others. As he told me in June 2010, he and his research team were looking at how various external chemical compounds activate various receptors within the cell's nucleus. They found that one such compound, TBT, sex-reversed fish. They decided to expand their experiments to other nuclear receptors and found that TBT also affected those that direct fat cell creation. After that discovery in 2003, he too turned his attention to the roll of EDCs in obesity.

Evidence, Both Animal and Human

Thus far, the direct evidence for the role of environmental estrogens has come from animal experiments. Retha Newbold has conducted probably the most extensive research. She has controlled for diet and exercise in all of her animal studies, with the only variable being the dose of estrogens. The results have been consistent, conclusive, and convincing. One experiment gave both low and high doses of DES to mice during gestation and immediately following birth. Although the estrogen seemed to have no or a negative effect on size at birth and during infancy, in adulthood these mice had significantly higher body weight than control groups and had elevated levels of leptin, insulin, and blood glucose. Demonstrating an epigenetic effect, this study also found that the genes that direct fat distribution had been permanently altered by DES exposure, meaning that the tendency toward high-fat tissue would be passed on to offspring if the mice reproduced (Newbold et al. 2008).

Newbold's research has demonstrated that it is not only synthetic estrogens that are implicated, however. Significantly, she has replicated these results with genistein, a natural estrogen found in soybeans, a source of livestock fodder and a major ingredient of manufactured food. Newbold fed genistein to newborn rats at doses analogous to those in soy formula. Without having eaten more calories, at age three to four months these rats had higher stores of fat and noticeably more weight than the controls (Newbold et al. 2008). In keeping with this, babies fed with soy formula have been found to be bigger than those fed on dairy-based formula or breast milk (Stettler et al. 2005). After conducting the experiment with genistein, Newbold recommended against soy formula for her newborn granddaughter (Begley 2009).

Crucially, Newbold's research has demonstrated age-related effects, in keeping with theories about the timing of EDC exposures. Soy, it should be noted, seems to protect against obesity in adults. Notwithstanding its contribution to adverse health conditions, estrogen replacement therapy can reverse truncal fat accumulation in postmenopausal women, for example (Grun and Blumberg 2009). Newbold's research on "natural" estrogens thus furthers the proposition that, depending on an organism's age at the time of exposure, estrogen may stimulate or suppress fat growth. In addition, and crucially, the presence of estrogen in the body appears to produce sex-specific as well as age-specific effects. In Newbold's experiments, male infant mice exposed to DES or genistein did not become obese and some lost body weight.

Independently, studies that expose pregnant mice to bisphenol A (BPA, a chemical used in many plastics and resins and often used to store beverages and foods) and perfluorooctanoic acid (PFOA, a grease-proofing agent used in microwave popcorn bags, pizza box liners, and other food containers) have produced nearly identical results. Female mice whose mothers were exposed to BPA from early pregnancy through lactation weighed more than controls in adulthood (Rubin and Soto 2009). Mice exposed to PFOA during pregnancy gave birth to smaller offspring that became much bigger as adults, but mice exposed as adults were not affected. PFOA has been detected at up to one hundred times higher concentrations in people living in industrially polluted areas than elsewhere (Hines et al. 2009).

Other animal studies have determined some of the specific biological pathways to obesity. One in vitro (test tube) study of mouse cells showed that the chemical 4-nonylphenol (NP), a by-product of wastewater treatment for plastics, stimulated growth of existing fat cells as well as the development of fat cells from stem cells—those with undefined identity that can develop into any type of adult cell (Masuno et al. 2002). Research on TBT in vivo (live animal experiments) has shown, similarly, that estrogenic chemicals encourage the division of fat cells into more fat cells or stimulate precursor cells to become fat cells. One study included dosing pregnant mice with TBT. These mice gave birth to mice with more fat cells and that became 5–20 percent fatter than controls by adulthood (Grun et al. 2006). It turns out that the antidiabetic drug Avendia causes weight gain along identical biological paths (Kirchner et al. 2010).

As summed up in a 2009 review article on the laboratory research to that date on the role of EDCs in obesity, their probable effects are significant and lasting, and can work independent of caloric intake and expenditure. First, they can directly precipitate cell creation and cell division. Insofar as existing fat cells are not only very hard to get rid of but can produce even more fat cells, nonexceptional exposures to EDCs may produce large increases in adiposity. Second, prenatal and early postnatal exposures may induce changes that may not be visible until adulthood. Third, exposures affect genetic networks epigenetically, meaning that these changes can be passed on to offspring. Finally, and crucially, environmental estrogens involve multiple modes of action, meaning that there's not just one biological pathway through which chemicals are contributing to obesity (Grun and Blumberg 2009). With many possible chemicals and pathways at work, the extent of the problem may be very large indeed.

Given that most of the existing research has been conducted on animals, what does it mean for humans? Although in some cases the pathways are identical, humans still are a different animal. Human experimentation obviously entails enormous ethical issues, however, and even testing for the presence of exogenous chemicals circulating in the body is controversial. Therefore, epidemiological evidence remains the primary way to cross-verify the experimental data. Clearly, epidemiological data are not foolproof or unproblematic. Yet, spotting trends in virulent disease or toxic exposure does seem a more appropriate use of epidemiology than as a medical diagnostic tool or reference for self-management, as discussed in chapters 2 and 3.

The epidemiological data, although thus far limited by the number of studies, do provide important associative evidence (see Hatch et al. 2010 for an overview). For example, scientists in North Carolina found that children exposed to higher levels of polychlorinated biphenyls (PCBs) and DDE before birth were fatter than those exposed to lower levels (Gladen, Bagan, and Rogan 2000). DDE is a by-product of DDT and is still found in soil in the United States, despite DDT's having been banned more than three decades ago. Highly toxic PCBs, despite the fact that they are banned worldwide, routinely show up in human body burden tests everywhere (also in highly fatty animals). Another epidemiological study found a positive association between the level of phthalate metabolites in urine and increased waist circumference and insulin resistance in men. Phthalate plasticizers, widely used to soften plastics and as surfactants and surface repellents, can negatively affect fat tissue homeostasis by mimicking one or more of the hormone receptors involved in this process (Stahlhut et al. 2007). An additional study demonstrated a relationship between insulin resistance and exposure to high levels of persistent organic pollutants (POPs) through diets composed of fatty fish (Ruzzin et al. 2009). It should be noted that such evidence is not easy to come by, given the ubiquity, variety, and persistence of EDCs in the environment. Furthermore, much of the epidemiological evidence came from studies not designed to measure the effects of EDCs on obesity (Hatch et al. 2010).

Finally, although disturbance of thyroid function is a less direct path to obesity than fat cell creation, the release of thyroid hormone is central in regulating metabolism, and hypothyroidism can cause weight gain. A multiyear agricultural health study of more than 16,500 women living in Iowa and North Carolina found that those living on farms who had been exposed to organochlorine insecticides such as aldrine and lindane had a 12.5 percent incidence rate of thyroid diseases, whereas the incidence of thyroid disease in the general population ranges from 1 to 8 percent. Those who were exposed to certain fungicides had a 1.4-fold likelihood of hypothyroidism (Goldner et al. 2010).

WHAT ABOUT THE FOOD SYSTEM?

Many EDCs are found in household items such as furniture, cosmetics, and clothing; many more in air and water. Importantly, though, many of those that have been identified as possible obesogens are prevalent in the food system, including a few I have already mentioned (e.g., pesticides, BPA, PFOA, and soy). It appears that obesogens are present all along food supply chains from farm production to transportation and storage to food processing.

Obesogens are present in meat production as well as crop production. For several decades, DES was given to beef cattle as a growth hormone. Although it has since been banned, several other natural and synthetic sex hormones, including estrogen-based compounds, are routinely used on up to 80 percent of cattle raised in the United States (Raloff 2002). Research on the human health effects of hormones used to plump up livestock is far less developed than it ought to be, in part because it has met with substantial pressure from industry. Nevertheless, what research has been published suggests more of the same. For example, one study found that men born to mothers who consumed substantially more beef than controls during pregnancy had significantly reduced sperm count in their semen (Swan et al. 2007). If estrogen hormones given to cattle affect human development through in utero exposures in this way, it is surely likely they could also affect cell differentiation leading to obesity, just as DES was found to do in mice. Notably, until quite recently the European Union banned US beef because of the use of hormones. Is it possible that the absence of hormones in meat is an alternative explanation of Europe's relative thinness, which is often attributed to "lifestyle"?

A couple of the most established obesogens are used in the transportation and storage of food. Besides BPA, this includes TBT, discussed earlier. TBT is an organotin, a class of POPs that are used across the food system in, for example, plastics, crop pesticides and fungicides, and slimicides in water treatment. TBT in particular is a disinfectant, fungicide, and wood preservative for fishing boats and thus enters the food chain in seafood and drinking water (Grun and Blumberg 2006).

Food ingredients and processing agents may be part of the mix, as well. Soy, now shown to be associated with obesogenesis, is not only a major source of livestock feed but also a microingredient in many processed foods. A computer modeling study used to identify additives that have molecules that bind with estrogen receptors found at least two commonly used additives that have estrogen-mimicking properties: propyl gallate, used to prevent fats and oils from spoiling, and 4-hexyl resorcinol, used to prevent discoloration in shellfish (Amadasi et al. 2008).

In addition to these substances associated with endocrine disruption, other commonly used ingredients of processed foods are implicated in obesity in more commonsense ways, namely, by altering metabolic function. Much attention has been given to high-fructose corn syrup (HFCS), the primary caloric ingredient in sodas, which are coming to rival cigarettes as the bane of public health. HFCS has been subject to much debate regarding whether it metabolizes differently from regular old sucrose, the chemical constituent of beet and cane sugar. There seems to be some agreement that fructose acts differently from glucose (sucrose is made up of both). Fructose consumption does not stimulate either leptin or insulin secretion. Therefore, ingesting a particular caloric dose of fructose will produce a less robust insulin response than the same caloric dose of glucose and will insufficiently signal satiety, presumably to encourage more eating (Power and Schulkin 2009: 118).

Strikingly, a study of overweight or obese adults that compared the effects of beverages sweetened with glucose and sucrose found similar overall weight and fat gain, but the group that had consumed the fructose-sweetened drinks had substantially greater increases in visceral fat than in subcutaneous fat (Stanhope and Havel 2010). Similarly, a study of trans fats, another food ingredient of growing concern, found that monkeys fed trans fats gained more weight and visceral fat than control monkeys given nontrans fats of the same caloric constitution. They also exhibited heightened insulin resistance (Kavanagh et al. 2007). That these studies highlight how substitute food ingredients can affect fat disposition as well as metabolism serves as a reminder that we need to pay much more attention to what exactly is pathological. Concern with just calories, or just BMI, occludes concern with how various food substances affect bodily ecologies in ways that do not necessarily materialize as fat.

As put by Bruce Blumberg, the substances discussed here are just the "tip of the iceberg" of known obesogens, and many of these are found in the food system. Surely, a food system perspective must include a hard look at the chemicals used in food production and distribution, alongside the calories. It must also take into account the chemistry of newer ingredients in food processing, ingredients that have been introduced precisely because they are cheap substitutes for less toxic ingredients. That, though, I save for chapter 6.

PUTTING THE PUZZLE TOGETHER

Putting all of the evidence together creates a strong case that the increase in size is not all about soda, fries, and video games. Rather, much of this upward trajectory in BMI values appears to be a consequence of exposures to a set of barely regulated chemicals and food substances. Many of the problem chemicals were introduced in the 1950s and 1960s, during an era in which the slogan "better living through chemicals" did not provoke incredulity (Langston 2010). They then became "truly ubiquitous" at just about the same time that BMI values began to increase—in the 1980s (Baillie-Hamilton 2002a). Notwithstanding accusations of spuriousness, the relationship seems much more plausible in light of what scientists have found about the timing of exposure, the time lag of manifestation, and the epigenetic effects of EDCs in particular. Other possible obesogens, such as HFCS, which became widely available in the 1980s, can affect people at any time in the life cycle.

In addition to the overall timing, the science of obesogenesis gives plausible answers to some of the anomalies I introduced earlier. For instance, the significant increase in extreme obesity may have to do with the way that obesogens affect fat cell regulation so that fat cells become active in their own replication. The all-important timing of uterine and neonatal exposures to some obesogens helps explain why some people have remained thin despite their ubiquity, notwithstanding that genetic inheritance, maternal nutrition, and, yes, even calories also play roles. The increase of infant obesity certainly suggests gestational exposures or epigenetic effects on mothers. The growth in childhood obesity may also be a consequence of EDC exposures, as well as soy-based formula feeding during infancy in bottles made from BPA.

The findings also help explain some of the gender and racial differences in rates of obesity—or lack thereof. Recall that despite what seems significant differences, black, Latino, and white women have seen obesity prevalence increase at very similar rates since that 1980 baseline, again suggesting similar exposures. Also recall that women show more variance in obesity than men. Because women produce more estrogen and have higher percentages of body fat, they are blessed at birth with the propensity to store fat.

Even geographic and class variation in obesity rates may be partially explained by the science of obesogens. Although some obesogens are indeed ubiquitous, others tend to be more present in certain environments. For example, obesogenic agricultural chemicals are, obviously, used in rural agricultural areas. And rural agricultural areas tend to have higher rates of obesity prevalence than cities do (Jackson et al. 2005), as well as other health problems related to EDCs (Steingraber 2003). Remarkably, studies that look at rural obesity do not consider agricultural chemicals as a possible source. As for class variation, the USDA data I provided earlier on daily caloric intake certainly undercuts the presumption that low-income people eat more calories. It is probably demonstrable, however, that low-income people eat more foods produced with the most obesogen-intensive industrial farming and food-processing methods, because these are cheaper. As I will discuss in chapter 6, the intensification of agricultural production that has allowed cheap food has been made possible by the use of materials and substances now considered obesogenic, with HFCS being the example par excellence. That being the case, the cheap food hypothesis that attempts to account for class differences in obesity prevalence may actually be less about how much food is eaten and more about the conditions under which it was produced. Beyond the food system, other physiological processes that tend to be experienced by those in precarious economic situations, such as sleep deprivation and chronic stress, have all been consistently associated with obesity in epidemiological studies (Hatch et al. 2010). Again, in the case of stress, this appears to be related to the secretion of stress hormones, not simply stress eating (Rosmond 2005).

Finally, the strong case I have presented that environmental toxins play a significant role in the rise of obesity does not concede that fat is necessarily pathological. On the contrary, to the extent that the chemicals are toxic, the increase in adiposity may be an adaptive response. Biological adaptation is twofold: it can regulate physiology around a set point (homeostasis) or change the state of the organism to deal with external conditions (allostasis) (Power and Schulkin 2009: 95). In keeping with calls to pay attention to the tropes we use to describe nature, rather than view increasing BMI as a deviation from homeostasis, we can read it as an allostatic adaptation by which bodies transform to deal with environmental changes. Moreover, this adaptation is arguably protective because it stores lipids away from places where it could be toxic to bodily function—delaying, for example, the onset of metabolic syndrome (Unger and Scherer 2010). In contrast, fat that plays a role in pro-ducing more fat, as appears to be the case in extreme obesity, would appear pathological rather than adaptive. As Grun and Blumberg (2009: 1131) state, "The physiological process of diverting excess calories toward lipid storage may be benign or pathological depending on the mechanism and site." The point is that we need to look carefully at the specificity of fatness, including how and where fat is deposited on the body, rather than simply condemn it wholesale. The fact that some food substances more directly produce abdominal obesity is an example of where more detailed understanding matters. More broadly, we need to abandon models that neglect pathological environmental conditions *and* continue to define the problem as nonnormative bodies and the behavior that presumably begets them.

WHAT'S NOT EATING THE FOODIES

The research I've discussed here is still in its infancy and the connections I have made cannot, of course, solve the puzzle of abrupt and differentiated increases in obesity once and for all. But at the very least they should cast doubt on the energy balance model as the ultimate explanation. As put by two leading scientists on the issue, "The existence of chemical obesogens in and of themselves suggests that the prevailing paradigm, which holds that diet and decreased physical activity alone are the causative triggers for the burgeoning epidemic of obesity, should be reassessed" (Grun and Blumberg 2006: s54). If what is altering bodies is not just food excess and exercise dearth, though, this means that solutions cannot tenably boil down to personal choice and lifestyle. As we have seen, timing is everything with endocrine disruption, and it is time to look elsewhere than eaters' lack of self-control.

Why, though, *does* the energy balance model remain sacrosanct? To be fair, the answer must lie in part with the newness of the science and the relative sparseness of evidence. Much of the research on EDCs has not yet cleared the radar. It is possible that by the time this book reaches the online book sellers' warehouses, many will be talking about environmental obesogens. At the time of this writing, high-level news sources such as the *New York Times*, the *New Yorker* magazine, and *Time* magazine have already published pieces on BPA, for example.

Nor is proving the effects of EDCs easy, especially given the nature of the scientific object in question. Existing models of environmental toxicology don't apply. Unlike arsenic and other poisons, substances for which the first models of environmental toxicology were established, EDCs do not sicken or kill people. EDCs can alter, diminish, or arguably enhance humans without making them sick (Colborn, Dumanoski, and Myers 1996). Furthermore, even though some of the same chemicals that appear to be endocrine disrupting are also carcinogens, their mode of action is different from carcinogenesis, which, as Krimsky (2000: 2) notes, has become the "dominant lens through which the study of toxic chemicals has been viewed." Finally, trying to establish proof means going up against the very powerful chemical industry—an industry that has the resources to commission many studies designed to prove no harm from these chemicals. Establishing the environmental causes of cancer has not exactly been a political cakewalk; establishing the environmental and chemical causes of obesity will be no easier.

There is much prosaic resistance to these ideas, too. Bruce Blumberg encountered such resistance when he began his research on EDCs. Initially, he found it somewhat difficult to get his research published and even more difficult to get it funded. As he told me, one grant proposal referee wrote in his review, "Why would you even imagine such a thing?" Efforts to hold the energy model together—to defend the dominant paradigm—are akin to what Thomas Kuhn, in *The Structure of Scientific Revolutions* (1962) (discussed in Gard and Wright 2005), described as the defense of "normal science" against paradigm shifts, by which the investment in existing models precludes investigation of possibilities outside the model.

Still, I want to suggest that the lack of attention to toxic exposures is not just a sin of omission or a problem of normal science. Rather, the deep investment in the energy balance model also reflects the deep investment in healthism. As I was developing this chapter and discussing it, I was surprised by the level of surprise and then skepticism it has evoked. An op-ed piece I wrote for the *San Francisco Chronicle* drew shocking vitriol and exoneration of the chemical industry in the online comments. One referenced concentration camps as proof of the energy balance model; another reminded me that "everything is chemical; look it up"; another suggested I go on a diet.

Meanwhile, the fact that some of the very things that come from the making (and storing) of the cheap food supply, including pest-control chemicals, livestock growth enhancers, food and water containers, and synthetic food-processing ingredients are implicated in making fatness the new normal is precisely the place one ought to look in adopting a food system perspective. A food system perspective asks us to consider the entirety of social and ecological issues that arise from the production, distribution, and consumption of food. Therefore, many of those (including the foodies) attempting to change the food system should be deeply concerned about the human biological effects of environmental toxins and food additives. Nonetheless, they remain wedded to the energy balance model in the face of this emerging evidence, I argue, in part because it fits better with their prevailing theory of change. As I discuss in chapter 7, food system activists have tended to focus more on consumption than production, and more on markets than policy. Although they have done so for understandable reasons, they ignore industry's role and the government's responsibility for regulating that industry at considerable peril, for they then become complicit in the neoliberal project to make health and well-being a matter of personal responsibility. For, as I show in the next chapter, policy has created some of the most reviled aspects of the existing US food system, including those profoundly implicated in obesity.

CHAPTER 6

Does Farm Policy Make You Fat?

Since the mid-1970s, farm productivity in the United States has grown tremendously (US Department of Agriculture, National Agricultural Statistics Service 2009). Corn and soy, major inputs to food processing, have seen especially dramatic increases in yields per acre. Between 1974 and 2007, corn yields rose from about 73 bushels per acre to 155, while soy yields rose from about 23 to 41.4 bushels per acre (US Department of Agriculture, National Agricultural Statistics Service 2007). The aggregate food supply rose from 3,300 calories per capita per day in 1970 to 3,800 per capita in 1994, although in 1994 about 1,100 of those calories were lost to spoilage, plate waste, cooking, and "other uses" (US Department of Agriculture 2002). In roughly the same period, the percentage of disposable family and individual income spent on food declined from 13.8 percent in 1975 to 9.8 percent in 2007, even with the increase in away-from-home eating (US Department of Agriculture, Economic Research Service 2009).

These sorts of statistics, which roughly correlate with increases in mean BMI, have inspired many scholars, activists, and journalists concerned with sustainable farming, food security, and public health to identify farm policy as a major culprit in the so-called obesity epidemic. The commodity subsidy system that provides price supports to corn and soy has been the most specific target, thanks to Greg Critser's *Fat Land* (2003), Michael Pollan's *Omnivore's Dilemma* (2006), and films such as *King Corn* (2007). As Pollan tells it, corn is omnipresent in a fast-food meal: the high-fructose corn syrup (HFCS) that sweetens the soda; the feed of the steer that goes into the hamburger beef, often the oil that fries the potatoes, one of the many microingredients that stabilize the bun. Corn by-products, it turns out, are used even in the packaging and serving utensils. The problem, he and others (e.g., Drewnowski

and Specter 2004) have argued, is that commodity subsidies make these ingredients artificially cheap, especially in comparison to fresh whole foods. That's
these authors' primary explanation for why Americans are getting fat: food
is so cheap that they eat more of the high-calorie cheap stuff and less of the
lower-calorie and more expensive good stuff. This analysis then leads to a set
of solutions: remove the subsidies and have food prices reflect their "real" cost.
Then maybe people won't eat as much—or an apple will be as appetizing as
a bag of Cheetos.

This long-in-coming attention to farm and food policy, evidenced particularly in a groundswell of activism surrounding the 2008 farm bill, is unques-
tionably salutary. The persistence of costly commodity subsidies that benefit
some of the wealthiest farmers and work against more ecological farming
practices warrants a serious reform effort. Nevertheless, there are many ideas
and assumptions embedded in this analysis that bear more scrutiny. One is
the idea, examined in chapter 5, that people, especially less well-off people,
are fatter because they eat more. If you believe the national health surveys,
that is not necessarily the case. It may be, though, that they eat differently,
or differently enough that other qualities of the food they eat, along with
environmental exposures, are contributing to obesity. Another embedded
assumption is that the commodity programs that subsidize farmers make
this food artificially cheap.

This latter assumption is the focus of this chapter. Although these subsidies
contribute to the overproduction of certain commodities, and overproduction brings prices down for those commodities, in actuality a much broader
set of practices, industrial dynamics, and policies make food in the United
States cheap. Some of these practices and policies are indeed consequential
for obesity, since in the interest of productivity they encourage the use of the
very sorts of "obesogenic" inputs and processing aids discussed in chapter 5.
Thus, what may be making us fat is what has been allowed in the production
of food rather than how much we eat.

The analysis also misses something else—and that is the way these policies have contributed to the need for cheap food. Cheapness, that is, has been
accomplished through uneven access to land, racially segmented labor markets,
and more recently through a concerted effort to lower wages and prices for
those who work directly in food production. Practices that ratchet down wages
and income, many of which originated in the food industry, have been adopted
elsewhere, contributing to the more general decline in real wages among

America's so-called middle class and poor and hence, to growing inequality. To the extent that many people can afford only cheaply produced food, the industrial food system has made a virtue of necessity.

By drawing these connections, my overarching goal is to suggest that the problem of cheap food represents a set of political choices that could possibly be reversed, but only with more focus on the political economy of food instead of what and how much should be eaten. A more dynamic reading of the role of policy, in particular, may lead to a different response than the call to just pay more, including more attention to the environmental health aspects of the food system, no matter how they manifest bodily. First, though, I want to discuss how and why the commodity subsidies exist and to suggest that they are not fundamentally responsible for cheap food, much less obesity.

DO SUBSIDIES MAKE FOOD CHEAP?

Farmers, as many scholars of agrarian political economy have noted, tend to be price takers—meaning they take what they can get. In a climate of routine oversupply, which has characterized much of basic commodity farming, high profits come only when someone else's misfortune reduces such supply through pests, drought, and other "acts of God." The problem of routine oversupply can be attributed largely to two fundamental tendencies of agricultural production, one related to its basis in land and the other related to its end in food (Fine 1994; Kautsky 1988). Regarding land, those who already have access to the most critical means of production (land) are loath to give it up. In wanting to hold on to their land, farmers are notorious for operating not fully in accordance with market signals. Getting some return is sometimes better than none, especially with a crop already planted, so farmers will often harvest and sell their crops no matter what the price consequences. Regarding food, the problem, known as Engel's Law, is that as individual income increases, people do not generally buy or consume more food proportionate to those increases, although they do indeed buy different food as income increases—an observation that has relevance for the shape of food politics today. So unless population grows and markets otherwise expand, demand remains flat.

The problem of oversupply was particularly acute in the late nineteenth and early twentieth centuries due to widespread imperial expansion. In the United States, generous resource policies (at least for whites) were a key strategy of expansion. Throughout much of the nineteenth century, the federal government distributed much of the public domain cheaply or even free, including mining claims, grazing rights, and farmland. Most famously, through the 1865 Homestead Act white farmers obtained access to land at rock-bottom prices, notwithstanding that land speculation was rampant (White 1991). The rationale of such handouts was not only to sow Jeffersonian democracy but also to further continental aspirations of (white) settlement from "sea to shining sea," no matter what or who stood in the way (Limerick 1987). Meanwhile, the British and other European powers continued to pursue colonization to provide industrial inputs and food stuffs to their rapidly industrializing economies. By the latter part of the nineteenth century, an extensive, trade-oriented world food system had developed and many British colonies, in particular, were growing wheat (Friedmann and McMichael 1989).

Since this was also the period of the industrial revolution, much of the agricultural expansion was accompanied by the opening of new urban markets. Inevitably, though, new supply would exceed new demand, and prices would fall. The world grain economy was thus plagued by boom and bust cycles: expansion when prices were good and then collapse when price competition ensued. The first of these collapses in world grain markets took place in the 1870s, followed by another in 1897, the trough of a major depression (Cochrane 1993). In the United States the farm sector recovered nicely after 1897, as the grain glut was absorbed by new immigrants who arrived in the cities to provide a labor force for America's industrial revolution. Farm prices remained high through World War I, when the disruptions of war abroad heightened the demand for exports (Cochrane 1993). The decline in foreign demand after the war led to yet another glut, however. The Capper-Volstead Act of 1922, which exempted farmers from antitrust legislation and allowed them to cooperate in marketing their products, did little to stem the tide of declining farm prices that were the first signal of the great slump of the 1930s (Cochrane 1993). The "dustbowl" in the American Southeast was a symbol of much that was lacking in agricultural policy. Without production controls or orderly marketing, that is, farmers would produce and sell irrespective of market conditions in order to receive some return on their investments. Of course, this exacerbated problems of poor crop prices and, unable to pay off creditors and landowners, resource-poor farmers were forced to leave farming altogether.

Today's disparaged commodity supports owe much to New Deal farm policy, which was originally designed to mitigate these boom-bust cycles and stabilize the agrarian sector by ensuring more orderly marketing. New Deal policies were loosely based on Keynesian economics, which calls for an expansion of government expenditures in times of recession and retraction in times of economic strength. Farm policy was based on a variation on the theme: enhanced government spending to restore farm prices and hence farmers' incomes. Specifically, the Agricultural Adjustment Acts of 1933 and 1938 legislated government loans that would allow farmers to store commodities rather than market them, to avoid glutting the market. The loan program provided a minimum price support because if market prices fell below the set rate, farmers would then put excess grain in storage; if the crops were never sold, the government effectively bought them (Cochrane 1993). This was the origin of government surplus food, which became a mainstay of food aid both domestically and abroad. At first, the adjustment acts applied to "basic commodities" (e.g., wheat, corn, cotton, rice, tobacco, peanuts); eventually price supports were extended to other commodities, including soy, hogs, and dairy products. Production controls were also instituted, often taking the form of incentives to avoid farming on marginal land.

Because most subsidies were tied to "base acreage" on specific pieces of land, it put the owners of that land on a much stronger footing politically. It also, eventually, increased the value of that land. These farmers could stay in business when otherwise competition would have driven them out of business. Their profitability—government-supported—helped support organizations such as the Farm Bureau, which became an effective lobby for large farm interests. The subsidy system thus gave rise to a powerful farm bloc that continued to advocate for more of these types of programs—including guaranteed prices and export supports (McConnell 1953). The specifics of the programs shifted over the years, but the basic mechanism to support prices became production controls, and most production controls took the form of acreage restrictions. It was these sorts of programs that were later characterized as paying farmers not to grow crops.

But, as is the case with many policies, these policies produced unintended consequences. Mainly, acreage restrictions effectively encouraged growers to increase output on the ground they could cultivate. In that way, the subsidy programs most definitely fed into the cycle of overproduction. What is not so clear is that these programs caused the problem and that removing the subsidies would solve it. Farmers who make so little money at the margin would still need to grow as much as possible to get a return on their investments. For that reason, Tom Philpott, a farm commentator in the online magazine *Grist*, argues that commodity subsidies are more of an effect of overproduction than a cause of it (Philpott 2007). For that matter, these days few farmers receive these subsides. Approximately two-thirds of farmers did not receive any direct payments during 2007, while the top 10 percent of payees received 60 percent of the payments (Cook and Campbell 2009).

It is even less clear that these subsidies have expanded the domestic food supply much, especially during the period since 1980. Surpluses became so chronic after the New Deal that policy makers looked for ways to get rid of them by selling surplus foodstuffs abroad. Putting surplus commodities to strategic use abroad proved a way to kill at least two birds with one stone. Most famously, Public Law 480, also known as Food for Peace, enacted in 1954, allowed the US government to dispose of crop surpluses through direct aid, barter (for strategic raw materials), and concessionary sales. As put by President Dwight Eisenhower, the purpose of Public Law 480 was to "lay the basis for a permanent expansion of our exports of agricultural products with lasting benefits to ourselves and peoples of other lands" (US Agency for International Development 2004). Never intended for charity alone but rather to increase the consumption of US agricultural commodities and improve foreign relations, the law proved to be an invaluable weapon for extracting political and military concessions (McMichael 2004).

Alas, though, food "dumping" fed into the boom-bust cycle, most dramatically illustrated by the Soviet grain sales that precipitated the 1980s farm crisis. In the years 1972–73 the United States sold thirty million metric tons of grain to the Soviet Union as part of détente. This represented three-quarters of all commercially traded grain in the world at that time (Friedmann 1993). Almost instantly, US grain supplies shifted from surplus to scarcity, leading to soaring prices for meat and grain alike. US farmers, typically responsive to price signals on the high side and egged on by Secretary of Agriculture Earl Butz, did as they were told and planted "from fencerow to fencerow." In doing so, they brought marginal land back into production—the very land they had been encouraged to set aside through previous policies. To plant and market this grain, they mortgaged themselves to the hilt. When the grain sales to the Soviet Union ended, grains yet again glutted the markets. Predictably, prices plummeted and farmers no longer had the income to pay their mortgages.

After 1980, the United States redoubled its efforts to expand exports, both to manage the chronic surplus and to address the emergent and substantial balance of payment problem. This was in large part a success. In 2008, for example, the United States exported 40 percent of its food grains and 43 percent of its oilseeds (US Department of Agriculture, Economic Research Service 2010). What made these exports competitive on the world market was the commodity program, which relieved farmers of having to recoup all of their production costs. This has hardly gone unnoticed; many of the issues that have bogged down the international trade ministerial meetings (e.g., in Cancun, Doha, and Hong Kong), are related to the recalcitrance (and hypocrisy) of the United States (and European Union) in refusing to terminate these direct subsidies, which are currently out of compliance with international trade agreements. It bears mentioning that one of the most subsidized export crops for which the United States takes flack is cotton, not a food crop. It also bears mentioning that two other normally subsidized crops, corn and sugar, are being used for biofuel production, sold both domestically and abroad. Biofuels, actually, have proven to be a powerful, if temporary, fix for overproduction. High demand and high prices have decreased subsidy payments. Unfortunately, this has led to huge increases in food prices and food shortages around the world, at considerable detriment to food security.

Although the role of subsidies in overproduction is debatable, it is patently false that subsidies make junk food more affordable than fresh fruits and vegetables, a claim that Michael Pollan (2007) has promoted. He based this on a finding by obesity researchers Adam Drewnowski and S. E. Specter (2004) that a dollar could buy 1,200 calories of cookies or potato chips but only 250 calories of carrots. Although the latter may be true, the reason that processed food is cheaper than fresh fruits and vegetables has little to do with subsidies. It is in small part due to market structure; it is in much larger part due to the cost of growing. Simply put, many processing ingredients, such as potatoes, corn, and wheat, are far less costly to produce on a mass scale than fresh fruits and vegetables. Potatoes, corn, and wheat, all primary ingredients in snack food, can be tilled and harvested by machine, whereas fresh peaches, strawberries, and lettuce require a great deal of hand labor in weeding and harvesting. This is not to say that fruit and vegetable production has not been intensified; intensification through breeding, postproduction practices, and sped up crop rotations make crops such as tomatoes and iceberg lettuce, for example, cheaper than they would be, but not nearly as cheap as grains.

These last points serve as an indication that the connection between subsidies, commodity overproduction, low food prices, and domestic obesity are a bit more tenuous than is often proclaimed, especially given the time frame of obesity's increase. Aside from the question of calories, the trip from farm to stomach is quite a lengthy and complex one, especially when it involves commodities such as corn and soy that have been at the center of this critique. An assessment of this claim must therefore be founded on an understanding of the dynamics of farming, how farming has intersected historically with the industrial food production and distribution system, and how government goals and interests have furthered certain tendencies and thwarted others. This will further show that subsidized commodities most definitely play a role in the cheapening of food, but they're not driving it.

POWER BEYOND THE FARM

The primary reason that farmers tend to be price takers is because the buyers of farm products have had the power to set prices. This was a historical development that the Czech-German Marxist Karl Kautsky had already noted when he wrote *The Agrarian Question* in 1898. Seeking to explain the persistence of the peasantry, he posited that capitalism was taking hold around the farm but not on the farm, a proposition that largely remains true today. Much later, the food economist David Goodman and his colleagues (1987) added why it is that capitalism seems to take hold in the businesses that sell inputs to farmers and buy crops *from* them. Farming is an economically risky business, they posited, given its basis in land and the centrality of biological production. Industry would prefer to take on the more certain and profitable aspects of food production such as producing farming inputs and selling them back to farmers—what they called *appropriationism*—and adding value to farm commodities after they leave the farm through processing, distribution, and marketing, and even making synthetic substitutes for agricultural commodities—what they called *substitutionism*. And so it is. Industries that surround the farm, including the seed, farm machinery, and chemical companies that supply farm inputs and the grain buyers, meat packers, and food processors that purchase farm commodities, continue to enjoy a privileged position relative to farmers, and they are the ones driving the heavy economic machinery.

Indeed, it was the granary system of marketing that first made US farmers "price takers" and set in motion the problem of overproduction. Granaries bought crops from farmers and then would sell them en masse to millers, brewers, and other processors for urban users. By 1860, the granaries and food processors controlled much of the marketing, and to meet their needs farming was already highly specialized and regionalized (Cochrane 1993; Danhof 1969). Commodity farmers (i.e., those that grow and sell basic, undifferentiated crops such as grain) were beholden to the quality controls as well as the price setting of the granaries. Commodity farmers could persist only so long as price takers, though. Eventually they would have to pay the mortgage or borrow money to plant next year's crops. Without returns from the previous years, they would go out of business. Therefore, the only way farmers could compete was by producing more, by expanding production (Cronon 1991). The imperative to intensify, to improve output per unit of land, was fully established after the closing of the frontier in 1890, when the federal government declared that it would no longer give away land. The proliferation of labor-saving steam-powered farm machinery in the 1890s, even among family farmers, constituted the first major wave of intensification, giving rise to the bonanza farms that soon led to glut (Friedmann 1978).

Farmers quickly learned that to stay alive they had to improve output, and to do that, they had to adopt the latest in yield-producing as well as labor-saving technologies. Many of these technological developments were subsidized indirectly by the federal government beginning with the Morrill Act in 1862. The Morrill Act granted land to every state to establish agricultural colleges (later called land grant universities). Later legislation established experimental stations and cooperative extension, which would develop and disseminate these technologies. Technical support set in motion the classic treadmill of production, which, among other things, fed into boom-bust cycles (Cochrane 1993). Early innovators would adopt the technologies first and make healthy profits because they were selling more, others would jump in, and thereafter prices would drop further. Investment in machinery to produce enough to pay the land rent was one of the primary causes of the dustbowl disaster in the 1930s that forced many tenant farmers out of business (Worster 1979).

Yield-enhancing technologies played a huge part in the major intensification in agriculture that characterized the post–World War II period. The widespread adoption of hybrid corn in the 1940s (though it had been invented twenty years earlier) provides a critical example of the multiple ramifications of intensification. Hybrid varieties did produce enormous yield increases—166 percent increase in corn yields between 1945 and 1971 (US Department of Agriculture, National Agricultural Statistics Service 2001)—and they were widely adopted. Since hybrid varietals do not "breed true," however, farmers were compelled to return each year to the seed company to buy more seed. Hybridization thus hastened the process of *appropriationism*, which squeezed farmers on the upstream as well as the downstream end. In addition, hybrid seeds were often designed to work with particular chemical inputs; what made the seeds vigorous in yield made them more vulnerable to pests. Farmers had to buy these chemical inputs—another squeeze—and use them (Kloppenburg 2005). Hybridization thus created an entire package of social and ecological consequences, some of which we still don't comprehend.

Many of the technologies that followed hybridization were likewise designed to speed up or enhance biological processes and minimize loss. It is true that plant breeders had long been making plants grow faster or produce more fruit, just as livestock breeders had been making bigger and faster-growing animals. In the postwar era, however, an ever-increasing proportion of the speedups and loss prevention was chemically induced. Beef producers began to use growth hormones to bring animals to size, as well as pharmaceuticals to deal with the inevitable increases in disease. In crop agriculture, farmers began to rely on petrochemical inputs to enhance soil fertility, synthetic pesticides and fungicides to reduce crop loss, and herbicides to save manual labor. Many of the chemicals that allowed farmers to stay in business are now well-known carcinogens, established endocrine disrupters, and likely obesogens.

Import substitution also played a large part in the cheapening of food. Before World War I, the colonized world's major involvement in the world economy was as exporter of key food and fiber materials: rubber, tropical oils, ground nuts, and sugar, along with those not easily substituted desirables that are still widely traded: coffee, tea, bananas, and cocoa. In the face of growing political instability, early twentieth-century US food manufacturers looked for cheaper, more reliable sources of these crops, and the US government encouraged development of internal supplies by providing subsidies (Friedmann 1993). Commodities that could be grown in temperate climates substituted for tropical imports. Beet sugar replaced cane sugar before HFCS derived from corn became the most prevalent sweetener in processed foods. Corn, safflower, and rapeseed (canola) oils substituted for palm and coconut oils and dairy-produced butter. At some point, virtually all of these import substitutes were subsidized as so-called strategic commodities.

In this case, subsidies most definitely contributed to excess, and food processing proved to be one solution to deal with the excess. Many of these became the ingredients for the sort of cheap processed food that defined postwar modernity: cake mixes, margarine, Hamburger Helper, and so forth (Friedmann 1992). Intensified feedlot and factory livestock production proved a much grander solution, however (Friedmann 1993). Grain feeding addressed two problems with land-extensive grazing and foraging: competition from other uses for ranching land and insufficient demand for produced grain. Today, 94 percent of soy meal and 80 percent of corn goes to livestock feed (Environmental Protection Agency 2007; United Soybean Board 2007).

But again, it was industry that gave farmers, ranchers, and fishers little choice but to adopt intensive practices, especially in the emerging political and economic climate that rewarded cutthroat competition. Beginning around 1980, and in part spurred by the weakening of antitrust regulation, intense consolidation took place among those companies that purchase crops and livestock, creating some of the largest corporations in the world: Pioneer Hybrid, Unilever, ConAgra, Cargill, and Tyson (Heffernan 1998). Often being the only game in town enabled these companies to put inordinate pressure on farmers and livestock growers to sell at the lowest possible prices. So, for example, Iowa Beef Packers, now owned by Tyson, set extremely low prices for beef that forced many ranchers into feedlot husbandry, which then compelled them to use intensive regimes of hormones, antibiotics, and other agents to bring animals to their killing weights as quickly as possible. President Hoover's promise of "a chicken in every pot" was far surpassed, and perverted, by a chicken industry that took a no-holds-barred approach to cheapening chicken, beginning in the 1960s. Its success began with a regional shift to the American South to take advantage of rural poverty that would make farmers and laborers willing to accept low prices and wages. There, Tyson, Perdue, and the other big chicken "integrators" began to contract the grow-out phase of chicken production to economically marginal "family farms," making chicken a "good crop on bad land." Working with breeders, they produced broiler chickens that would grow faster and plumper but that were also subject to more disease. Since the ever-shrinking (currently, thirty-eight-day) period from chick to broiler is the most biologically risky for the already overbred chickens, the economically marginal farmers were made to comply with highly specified production standards while taking the most risk, while the integrators took advantage of the chief asset of family farms: cheap, docile, and flexible labor (Boyd and Watts 1997). These are the kind of practices that drove production costs down and made meat dramatically cheaper relative to historical prices.

Players closer to the consumer, such as chain restaurants, food service, and retailers, also have had a large hand in the price squeeze, given their increased economic importance as purchasers of mass-produced agricultural commodities. In 1996, for example, McDonald's purchased 2.5 percent of all beef and 3.2 percent of all potatoes produced in the United States. Pizza Hut used 2.5 percent of all milk produced in that year for its cheese requirements alone (Jekanowski 1999). One of the strategies employed by Wal-Mart and other large retailers to shore up their market share is volume pricing, which, along with store location and in-store geography, entices consumers to buy more than they otherwise would. They are able to offer low prices by dictating terms upstream to suppliers (Burch and Lawrence 2005).

These cost-cutting strategies play out in the international arena, too, again suggesting that commodity subsidies play a lesser role in making food cheap. Shrimp, once a luxury item, has become a regular feature of all-you-can-eat chain restaurants such as Sizzler as well as low-cost "gourmet" markets such as Trader Joe's. Today, shrimp is farmed in tropical mangrove swamps that once supported many fishers. Countries that have become export platforms for shrimp have done so largely to comply with structural adjustment policies that insist on increasing export revenue. Shrimp farming has developed at tremendous ecological and social costs to coastal fishers in those export areas, and the unfolding price competition has ruined the livelihoods of shrimpers who catch shrimp in the wild (Bell 2006). Farm-raised shrimp and salmon live in a soup of chemical pollutants, including PCBs, dioxin, mercury, and TBT, which are passed on to humans who eat the shrimp or salmon, counteracting many of the health benefits that fish are supposed to provide (Mansfield 2011). Some of these pollutants are probable obesogens.

Meanwhile, food manufactures have taken substitutionism to a whole new level that sometimes has little to do with subsidies—or even farmers. Much of this substitutes ingredients made in factories for those produced on farms. Consider, for instance, the shift from fruit juice to fruit drinks. The way substitutionism has worked is not only to substitute HFCS for cane sugar (two different subsidized commodities), but also artificial flavorings for fruit extract (no subsidies involved, just that artificial flavorings are produced in factories and not on trees). Substitutionism, in fact, uses all sorts of microingredients to impart particular food qualities and enhanced shelf life. This is where generic processing additives such as wheat gluten, lecithin, guar gum, "natural" flavors, and so on come in. They cheaply (and hence profitably) add all sorts of qualities, from mouthfeel to sweetness to sometimes bombastic flavor. A bag of Cheetos today has far more microingredients than one did twenty years ago and much more intense flavors, and some of these come from products that are possibly obesogenic through paths other than caloric intake. That said, it is not only the processing aids and soy by-products in that bag of Cheetos that may make people fat. There is little doubt that the recipe for Cheetos is carefully designed to make it very difficult to eat that portion size of, say, twelve chips once the package is open. What we don't really know is whether the calories from a bag eaten in its entirety are in excess of or substituted for a meal with less toxic ingredients.

It is worth considering that substitutionism is the process that allows the development of diet foods. These days, many diet products attempt to thwart the metabolism of food calories into body fats. Splenda (or sucralose), a low-calorie sugar substitute, is ten times less dense but six hundred times sweeter than sugar. Very little of Splenda's sweet component—sucralose—is metabolized. The very few calories it does contain come from dextrose or maltodextrin filler. Olestra, a fat substitute designed to provide mouthfeel without caloric intake, literally passes through the digestive tract without being absorbed. Of course there are limits to products that thwart metabolic function, as the anal leakage and vitamin depletion associated with Olestra so vividly conjures. Surely, if the same policy environment that allows the production of "fattening" food also produces nondigestible or noxious (but cheap) "diet" food, we have to rethink the problem statement.

THE SUBSIDY OF FAILED REGULATION

The use of toxic inputs in farm production and nutritionally questionable ingredients in food production most easily takes hold in a regulatory climate that favors productivity over ecological and public health concerns or, put more favorably, defines the health of the food system in terms of being able to provide (more than) sufficient food for its public. This pretty much characterizes the US approach to food regulation since the inception of agricultural policy, with some occasional blips of activity on the side of health and environmental caution. Since 1980, neoliberal approaches to governance have weakened enforcement and regulation of what little was established during those blips at the same time that nutritional and toxicological science has strengthened the causes for concern. It is therefore a curiosity that food advocates and activists have paid so much attention to the subsidy program and so little to environmental and health regulation. It is easily arguable that lack of regulation itself is a huge subsidy to the food industry.

The US Department of Agriculture (USDA), created in 1862, was the first federal agency that had anything remotely to do with regulating the quality of food. Charged with ensuring a sufficient and reliable food supply, it interpreted this charge as encouraging food production, and thus supporting agriculture. Its role in protecting consumers was always interpreted through the needs of farmers. It was again on the basis of killing two birds with one stone that the USDA first distributed food surplus and eventually took on the role of administering the major food assistance programs. The USDA-run national school meal program, initiated in 1946, was precisely to "safeguard the health and well-being of the Nation's children" and "encourage the domestic consumption of nutritious agricultural commodities and other food" (Gunderson 1971). Accordingly, schools received reimbursements from the federal government for meals provided to income-eligible children, and they were encouraged to prepare these meals with surplus commodities purchased directly by the federal government and donated to schools. Moreover, the USDA mandated proportions of milk and other proteins that were made from overproduced commodities (Poppendieck 2010). It took hard-fought campaigns by antihunger activists, which resulted in the 1960s enactment of two other assistance programs specific to food purchasing, the Food Stamp program and WIC (Women, Infants, and Children Supplemental Nutrition Program), to allow recipients more options in obtaining food rather than have the government dictate that they procure surplus food (Gardner 2002: 229).

And thus the primary way in which the USDA became involved in food quality was in providing dietary advice and guidelines that would support farmers. To some extent, these nutrition guidelines reflected extant scientific and medical thinking regarding the public health ills and risks of the day. For example, in 1900 the leading causes of death were tuberculosis and diphtheria, related to malnutrition among the poor. So for a long time, nutritional advice encouraged people to "eat more" (Nestle 2002). Yet, as Nestle points out, these guidelines were not necessarily aligned with good nutrition. Recommended foods have often reflected the type of crops grown in any given period, rather than the inverse. For example, a 1917 pamphlet of recommendations made sweets and fatty foods distinct food groups as a means to encourage their consumption; by 1958, dietary experts were focusing on what became the "four food groups": dairy, meat, vegetables/fruit, and bread/cereals, and had established a recommended number of servings for each (Nestle 2002). Needless to say, few recommendations encouraged eating whole foods or hormone-free beef or avoiding additives, and those who espoused such goals were deemed quacks (Belasco 1989). To the contrary, the USDA dragged its heels on developing an organic standard and for a long time disallowed labeling of meat as organic, fearing that it would disparage the ways in which livestock is conventionally produced.

Another agency of the federal government, the Food and Drug Administration (FDA), has had a more direct role in regulating food safety and to some extent nutrition, although its use of sticks rather than carrots has been surprisingly minimal. The FDA was established by the 1906 Pure Food Law, a response to widely reported adulteration of packaged food. During the New Deal, the 1938 Food, Drug, and Cosmetic Act broadened the FDA's charge to mandate legally enforceable standards for food ingredients and for labeling nonstandardized ingredients as artificial. Yet, it was not until the Delaney hearings that a series of laws addressing pesticide residues (1954), food additives (1958), and color additives (1960) were passed to give the FDA much tighter control over the growing list of chemicals entering the food supply. Most famously, the 1958 Delaney clause ordered zero tolerance for food substances deemed to be carcinogenic. As it turned out, very few such substances were actually banned from use following that amendment. Saccharin was the most notable exception, banned when it was found to cause cancer in laboratory rats in the early 1970s. Yet, thanks to the "saccharin revolt," it was put back on the market in 1977, with the stipulation that it be marketed with a warning label that it has been known to cause cancer in lab rats. Incidentally, this revolt came from largely white middle class women who feared getting fat without access to artificial sweetener, further calling into question the idea that thinness equates with health (de la Peña 2007). One can only wonder what the public reaction would be if it was found that artificial sweeteners are demonstrably causing obesity (as some evidence already indicates).

Up until 1970, no federal agency was charged with food and agriculture regulation from the perspective of environmental health. The creation of the EPA in 1970, as part of the Environmental Protection Act, owes much to Rachel Carson's *Silent Spring* ([1962] 1987), which first publicized the potentially grave ecological consequences of the use of DDT. For a very long time, the EPA's sole success was the 1972 banning of several chlorinated hydrocarbon pesticides including DDT, while the organophosphates, which were much more toxic but had shorter half-lives, stayed on the market (Shrader-Frechette 2005). Then, the notoriously weak Toxic Substances Control Act of 1976 grandfathered in more than sixty thousand chemicals that were already on the market. In any case, the EPA's effective life was largely cut short in the early 1980s by an abrupt shift in ideas about the proper role of government.

Those on the Left were skeptical of the government's ability to regulate, which was understandable in light of the industry-friendly ideas of nutrition and food safety that had been guiding much food and environmental regulation. Such skepticism had spurred the alternative-food and medicine movements and other practices associated with early healthism (Crawford 2006). Meanwhile, the New Right had developed its own head of steam regarding the government and sought to get rid of regulations seen as bad for business. As Rose (1999) has observed, it was precisely an alliance of the New Left and the New Right, in their shared distaste for the state, that allowed neoliberal notions of governance to take hold. Ironically, this antistatist turn came at a time when stronger health and environmental regulation was finally gaining a tiny bit of traction.

To be clear, health and environmental regulation was already lax in terms of controls on and prohibitions against potentially harmful substances, or else the era of "better living through chemicals" would have been more obviously nonsensical. After 1980, however, very few new regulations came into existence and agencies ceased to enforce those that did exist, owing either to underfunding or to the appointment to agency leadership of people who would not enforce regulations. The regulations that did come into being favored regulatory approaches more in keeping with neoliberal norms of governance, such as cost-benefit analysis (which had already been mandated in the Toxic Substances Control Act) and providing consumer information.

The most substantial change in environmental health protection came through the Food Quality Protection Act (FQPA), passed in 1996. The FQPA overturned the zero-tolerance Delaney clause and reinforced old norms of risk assessment that weighed regulatory costs to business against public benefits. On the one hand, many chemicals previously slated for review and discontinuance were allowed to stay on the market (Wargo 1998). Similarly, the synthetic hormones currently allowed to be used in beef cattle, which are known to leave measurable residues of known carcinogens and are now suspected obesogens, would have been outlawed under the Delaney clause (Langston 2010: 115). On the other hand, the FQPA did mandate review of cumulative and interactive risks and those associated with environmental illnesses other than cancer, a regulatory change that has pleased environmental toxicologists (Krimsky 2000). Under the FQPA, methyl parathion, one of several highly toxic organophosphates, was finally banned in 1999, although many of its cousins remained registered with the EPA as allowable pesticides. Although the FQPA has both strengths and weaknesses, the main problem has been lack of enforcement. The EPA has been so slow and reticent that in 2009 a bill was introduced in Congress to move review of endocrine disrupters to the National Institute of Environmental Health Sciences, a research agency that is part of the National Institutes of Health.

Since most questionable substances affect human health incrementally or long after exposure occurs, it is highly problematic that they are primarily regulated through the requirement of "buyer beware" warnings, to the extent they are regulated at all. That is, without proscriptions on the use of toxic substances, consumer-oriented labels have become the primary mechanism of regulation. Even then, for a health claim (positive or negative) to be allowed on a label, "significant scientific agreement" must exist regarding the relationship between the substance and the disease.

One major piece of legislation since 1980, the 1990 Nutrition Labeling and Education Act, reformulated and standardized the way that food products convey nutritional information. It also essentially curtailed the ability to make evaluative claims on food labels. Potential obesogens that are ingredients in food are unlikely to meet the standards for evaluative claims. The FDA's recent efforts to deal with trans fats are illustrative in this regard. Trans fats, a type of unsaturated fat originally developed to be healthier, cheaper, and more convenient than the saturated fats of butter and lard (hence, substitutionism) have been found to be not so healthy after all. The FDA's stance has been to institute a requirement that use of trans fats be listed on the label, although foods containing less than 0.5 grams per serving are not required to be labeled as containing trans fats. The FDA also rejected requiring an additional footnote that would state that intake of trans fats "should be as low as possible." That leaves it to the buyer to decide how much is enough. Crucially, the FDA has been just as lax with antiobesogens as with obesogens. Even with record-setting complaints about the side effects of Olestra, the FDA's primary intervention was to require that snack food containing Olestra state on the label that "Olestra may cause loose stools and abdominal cramping." After one peer-reviewed study showed few side effects, in 2003 the FDA removed all labeling requirements for Olestra.

Although food regulation has always favored invention over caution, today's laxity is particularly painful since ample science exists to make a case for the precautionary principle in regard to many chemically and biogenetically derived pest-control treatments, growth or yield enhancers, taste and palatability enhancers and preservatives, and diet foods. The failure of existing regulatory bodies to curtail the proliferation of junky food in a meaningful way in part results from regulatory capture. Marion Nestle's *Food Politics* (2002) is an exhaustive account of regulatory capture as it applies to the food industry. Specifically, she shows how both the FDA and the USDA have been highly influenced, if not outright controlled, by the industries they are charged to regulate. This has occurred through, for example, congressional lobbying, political campaign donations, the revolving door between industry and government, and the support of industry front groups such as the Center for Consumer Freedom, which produces provocative advertisements to suggest that food regulation curtails liberty. Such capture has also affected the USDA's post-1980s dietary and nutritional advice, which has largely turned on the content and message of the USDA food pyramid, which now doesn't even name food groups or recommended servings. In an odd way, though, Nestle's own intervention suggests the influence of neoliberal norms of governance that give regulatory responsibility to consumers and their choices. Most of her examples are about government oversight of the delivery of nutritional information, and one gets the impression from reading *Food Politics* that were consumer information based on the best, unencumbered nutritional science, it would be sufficient to regulate food. (Her approach in *Safe Food* [2003], however, is more accusatory about the failure of regulatory oversight and corporate responsibility.)

The focus on labeling as regulation assumes that consumers read the label, care about what it says, will make choices based on labeling information, and, if they can find a more healthful or desirable alternative, will have a chance to buy it. In addition to the fact that many of the materials and processes of concern are not labeled, the label in no way addresses the source of the problem, namely, the extraordinary price pressures that have led to unrelenting intensification and substitutionism. Not only does this regulatory laxity provide an enormous subsidy of sorts to food industries (which do not have to pay either the environmental or the public health costs for their practices), much of this cheapness has come from intentional and mean-spirited efforts to reduce the cost of labor itself. How can consumers buy their way out of the problems presented by cheap food when it is also through the ratcheting down of their own labor costs that food has been made cheap?

CHEAP FOOD AND CHEAPER LABOR

The speedups and substitutions that have made food cheap in America are inseparable from their effect on human incomes and work conditions, and it is this piece of the story that continues to get short shrift—with the important exception of *Fast Food Nation* (Schlosser 2001). Yet it is a crucial piece of the story, because the question is not only what forces have come together to produce cheap food, but also what forces have come together to produce the need for it. By leading the reductions of wages and income in the United States, the cheap-food sector has in many ways created a market for its own goods. I have already touched on the way that those who make their living in the most primary businesses of food production (i.e., farming, ranching, and fishing) have been subject to the dictates of food buyers. The substantive lack of control over the production processes and the inability to be price setters has made many farmers akin to "wage labor on their own land" (Watts 1993). These days most farmers are quite poor, which has pushed many farm families to seek off-farm employment.

But wage labor exists throughout the food system and has since the advent of agrarian capitalism in seventeenth-century England. The glorification of the "family farm" in the United States can be pernicious in hiding the fact that wage labor is prevalent even in "family farming," as I discuss in *Agrarian Dreams* (Guthman 2004). Devaluing rural labor to keep food costs low has been one of capitalism's most abiding tendencies, and marginalizing and even rendering invisible those who do the labor has been one of farming's most abiding strategies. This is because the creation of a rural labor force has almost always come by dispossession. Unlike England, though, where in a dialectical process land enclosures simultaneously created a labor force, the United States did not even have a peasantry whose land could be appropriated. Instead, the United States initially prevented land ownership by many of those who were here before nationhood and statehood or by the many waves of migrants who were brought in to work. All of this depended on racial discourses that helped legitimate in the eyes of lawmakers who was not deserving of land, citizenship, and a wage (Almaguer 1994).

Crucially, then, the land giveaways that defined American expansion were coincident with the appropriation of Native lands, the disenfranchisement of Hispanos and Californios from ranches in the Southwest, the failed reconstruction of the plantation South, which made African Americans tenant farmers at best, and, a little later, the preclusion of Chinese and Japanese from land ownership (Romm 2001). As such, the land giveaways extended and solidified the racialized land-labor relationships that had begun with slavery. Whites would own farmland, and others would provide farm labor, either through direct coercion (slavery or debt bondage) or because of economic desperation (sharecropping or wage labor). Except for the white vagabonds who intermittently worked on the wheat farms in the late nineteenth century, and the dispossessed dustbowl migrants of the Southeast (the Okies and Arkies) who came to pick fruit in California until the war industry began providing new jobs in 1940, agricultural labor has almost always been provided by people of color. In addition, the technical support that was offered to these white farmers was generally not available to others, save for the establishment of a few black agricultural colleges. In general, though, technological development benefited the farmer first and then the buyer, so it often worked against laborers and low-resource farmers. The paradigmatic case in point was the University of California's development of a tomato harvester in the 1960s, which cost thousands of farmworkers' jobs and put many small farmers out of business, too, eventually precipitating a lawsuit against the university.

US agricultural and trade policies, as well as geopolitics more generally, contributed to a steady stream of migrant groups who were recruited as or became agricultural laborers. For example, the worldwide collapse in grain in the 1870s brought some of the first Eastern Europeans, who were different enough from native-born whites to be put to work harvesting sugar beets in the upper Midwest, at much lower wages than Anglos would have countenanced (Mapes 2009). Encouraging the adoption of high-yielding grain varieties in places such as Mexico and the Philippines under the banner of the Green Revolution put many farmers out of business in the mid to late twentieth century, farmers who then came to the United States as labor migrants (Ross 1998). The post-1980s flood of refugees from Central America, precipitated by US economic and military interventions, provided another wave of migrants. Most recently, US-subsidized corn, shipped to Mexico, has put many Mexican corn farmers out of business and has thus contributed to the flow of migrants (Fitting 2006). Farmers have used this chronic "oversupply" of labor as well as pitting new migrants against old ones to keep wages low. Groups that have found some political power and organized have often been replaced by even more vulnerable groups. For example, growers began using labor contractors and employing undocumented workers in the 1970s precisely to break the emerging power of the United Farm Workers (Wells 1996). Although this system began in California, where fruit and vegetable production depended on short-term seasonal labor, California is no longer what McWilliams once called "the great exception" in farm labor. Many agricultural states, including Oregon, Washington, North Carolina, Texas, and Florida, have replicated California's "peculiar institution" of reliance on migrant wage labor. Even the dairies of Wisconsin and Vermont now employ Latino immigrants.

The practice of using racial and political vulnerability has extended sectorally as well as geographically. In parallel with the chicken industry's relocation from the central Atlantic states to the American South and Southeast to take advantage of poor farmers and unemployed laborers, the meat processing industry moved from the highly unionized cities of Chicago and Cincinnati to rural Nebraska and Kansas. Meatpacking industrialists were looking to employ a less militant rural labor force and were at first welcomed by the many rural whites who were attempting to hold on to their farms through part-time employment (Fink 1998; Stull and Broadway 2004). Soon, they too turned to an even more vulnerable labor force, replicating the labor market management of farm labor. Today many of the worst tasks of meatpacking are performed by undocumented Latino and Southeast Asian workers, who have little means to contest the work speedups and poor wages notorious in the abattoirs (Gouveia and Juska 2002).

The more recently emerged food service industry has been particularly inventive in driving labor costs down. Labor-saving technologies and union-bashing politics have made fast food what it is today, and in some sense its labor practices define the industry. In a story chronicled in *Fast Food Nation* (Schlosser 2001), the founder of the McDonald's empire, Ray Krok, was one of a group of businessmen in Orange County, California, who had no fondness for unions—or decent wages. Kroc wanted to make his restaurants inexpensive and efficiently run, and to do so he set about mechanizing much of the food production in his restaurants. Former short-order cooks were let go for unskilled teenagers who could put burgers in a warming oven and press a button to draw a milkshake. Krok strenuously subverted all union activity and even gave his franchise owners paltry incomes and little leeway in how they operate. Then, he took this cost-reduction logic to the meat processing plants that supplied McDonald's. As others adopted his model, eventually the rest of the food service sector saw significant deterioration of the labor conditions and wages won by earlier union activity. The food service giants Sodexho and Aramark, as well as the major big-box retailers, used the climate of economic desperation in the postindustrial era to set wages particularly low (Lane et al. 2004). Wal-Mart employees routinely rely on public assistance such as food stamps and Medicare to make ends meet (Dube and Jacobs 2004).

Even though the number of farmers declined significantly during the twentieth century, the food sector has grown substantially, especially in food processing, service, and trade. In 2001 (the most recent available tally), twenty-four million workers were employed in the food sector (Edmonson 2004). According to the Bureau of Labor Statistics, wages for production workers in food manufacturing (one subset of the food sector) averaged $14.00 an hour, compared with $18.08 per hour for all workers in private industry in 2008. Food manufacturing also has some of the highest incidences of injury and illness.

Policies have allowed the cheapening of food workers, as well: not commodity subsidies but labor policies, and, of course, immigration policies. Farm labor was never afforded the same status as manufacturing labor, even after the successes of the New Deal that brought an industry-labor bargain in the form of the National Labor Relations Act of 1935 (the Wagner Act). Farm labor was exempted from the Wagner Act, and it wasn't until 1975 that the Agricultural Labor Relations Act brought farmwork into the fold of collective bargaining law. Farmworkers were soon made vulnerable again by farm labor contractors and the increased use of undocumented workers. It was precisely their "illegality" that made these economic and political immigrants highly exploitable. Illegality was codified in the national immigration reform of 1986, and later the fortification of the border through Operation Gatekeeper in the 1990s (Nevins 2001). Fear of deportation has not only undercut union and other collective action but also thwarted complaints of occupational health and safety violations and minimum-wage violations. It is therefore likely that border policy, more than anything else, has contributed to cheap food.

WHERE'S THE SUBSIDY?

The notion that the commodity subsidies are responsible for the low-quality, high-calorie food associated with the rise in obesity is suspect in a number of respects. The subsidies existed long before the post-1980 rise of obesity, and since 1980 most of the subsidized commodities have been exported abroad. And even though many of these subsidized commodities are key ingredients in processed foods or livestock feed, it is not these commodities that are making food fattening—calorically or otherwise. Rather, cheap, fattening food has come in part from the tremendous power of processors, retailers, and food service, which have used this power to exert downward pressure on farmers, fishers, and ranchers to provide products at ever-lower prices. In farms and in factories, making food cost less has entailed speedups and ingredient substitutions, and the inclusion of all sorts of materials and processes that may be obesogenic in ways we don't yet understand. This is not to dismiss the role of product formulation and marketing—or calories. Supersizing, addictive-styled flavoring, and packaging probably do make people eat more. The important point is that it is the same political-economic logic that is profoundly changing environmental and human ecology, regardless of the biological mechanisms that cause obesity—or cancer, or allergies, or any number of health problems potentially attributable to the food system. Furthermore, the regulatory environment has done little to curb these logics and, if anything, has prioritized productivity over caution.

Yet, to alter these logics takes political will, not will power. Targeting subsidies as the problem carries with it the additional hazard of playing into free market nonsense. The subsidies came into being precisely because of the failures of the free market. It is no small irony that much-extolled fresh fruits and veggies are in fact subsidized, too—albeit in less visible ways. Many of these are grown in the American West and South, in Texas, Arizona, California, and Florida. In most of these places, farmers have depended on federal government irrigation projects for water. They have used the technologies developed through the land grant universities to manage pests. For the most part, they have depended on punitive immigration laws and a militarized border to get access to cheap labor. At full cost without spillover benefits from government-sponsored research, infrastructure projects, labor regimes, and other government investment, fruits and vegetables would be even more expensive to grow and harvest; to suggest that removal of the corn and soy subsidies would make them relatively cheaper is disingenuous. The fact of the matter is that agriculture and food production are subsidized in far more complex, and often indirect, ways than the commodity program or even the land grant system: water infrastructure, immigration policy, and lax regulatory policy have all made it so the food industry doesn't have to pay the "full cost" of producing food. So why should consumers?

The truth is that, by itself, the market cannot simultaneously keep farmers in business and provide good food for workers; paying food workers and farm-workers living wages would make food prohibitively expensive. Although it is flawed in many respects, agricultural policy evolved precisely to address the competing imperatives of farmers, wage workers, and nonfarm businesses that rely on a well-fed labor force. As the food processing and distribution sectors have grown, and as public concerns about how food is produced have multiplied, the juggling act has become even more complex. The problem, in other words, may not be the *existence* of subsidies, but to whom and for what they are directed.

Yet, the very movement that seeks to challenge the food system, a movement that has been wildly successful in bringing people into its fold—the alternative-food movement—is not directly challenging these policies and practices. Instead it is giving well-to-do people an opt-out through free market logics. As I discuss in the next chapter, the reasons for this strategic direction are complex and often laudable, but without such challenges, it is in effect producing a bifurcated food system with great, healthy, less toxic food for the few and cheap, standardized, and nutritionally vacuous food for the masses.

CHAPTER 7

Will Fresh, Local, Organic Food Make You Thin?

[The lecture and video] made me want to eat all organic fresh fruits and vegetables, no processed foods, no meat (except organic, free range), no sodas, no popcorn, and nothing that has corn syrup and corn derivatives. (f)

Whilst it is true that it is expensive to eat healthy (organic, etc.) just because you cannot afford this, and have to buy unhealthier food, does not mean you have to eat enough or so much to become obese. (f)

The obesity epidemic isn't a social problem, it's an economic problem. The way our food structure is set up around the world is creating shitty, unhealthy foods. People should be able to eat local foods that were produced fairly and hopefully organic. Our fucked up globalization is creating unhealthy people. (m)

This chapter begins with another set of quotations from my students. Although they range in tone and analysis, they share an idea that indicates an important rhetorical move that has taken hold in the obesity conversation—one that first motivated this book. It is the idea that education about and access to fresh, local, and organic—or simply "real"—food offers an antidote to the obesity epidemic. Those who adopt a food system perspective are particularly apt to take this position.

Apparently, the idea is catching on. A report released by the Organic Center in 2009 details six ways that organic food can reverse trends in obesity (McCullum-Gomez, Benbrook, and Theuer 2009). In August 2010, the *New York Times* featured an article about "prescription produce." In an effort to fight obesity in children of low-income families, doctors at three health centers in Massachusetts are writing prescriptions for vegetables to be filled at farmers markets. Hoping to instill longer-term behavioral changes, this pilot program issues coupons amounting to $1 a day for each member of a patient's family "to promote healthy meals" (Singer 2010).

How this particular definition of "real food" has come to occupy a privileged place in obesity discourse is reflected in the tendency among adherents, like those quoted above, to lump together all aspects of the current food system that are bad and assume goodness in the opposition to them. So, for example, if globally traveled, industrially produced, highly processed, and cheap food has contributed to obesity, locally sourced, craft-produced, fresh, seasonal, and, thus, expensive food must contribute to thinness. The coherence of this opposition owes a great deal to the alternative-food movement, which has been highly successful in creating a discursive and practical counterpoint to the conventional food system. Inasmuch as the movement has been bolstered by the practical skills of good cooks and farmers and the rhetorical skills of good food writers, it has even come to offer a new kind of hope for dieters: the possibility of eating food that is healthy, delicious, and whole without getting fat.

Alas, though, alternative food is unlikely to prevent obesity, much less cure it, and much of this chapter will be devoted to explaining why it can't. In a nutshell, this is because the alternative-food movement focuses more on what people eat than how food is produced, works through the market rather than contests the policy environment, and for the most part punts on the question of inequality. Efforts to address inequality, through, for example, "food justice" might make good food more accessible, but it still does not fundamentally challenge the dynamics that cause the vast majority of Americans to eat vacuous food and to be exposed to appreciable amounts of toxins by dint of the way most food is produced. The influence of healthism on the alternative-food movement is palpable.

Furthermore, by exalting a set of food choices, the alternative-food movement tends to gives rise to a missionary impulse, so those who are attracted to this food and movement want to spread the gospel. Seeing their food choices as signs of heightened ethicality, they see social change as making people become like them. This gives far too much power to those who happen to be privileged (and thin) to define the parameters of food system change. In addition, it mixes up the effects of their embodiments with the causes. In other words, those who make these choices tend to be already privileged and thin and forget that they probably didn't become privileged and thin through these choices.

To be clear, my issue isn't with activists' amount of effort or even their accomplishments. Changing the dynamics of the food system is a tall order, and it is unfair to hold this movement alone to such a high standard. Nevertheless, as a *set of strategies*, the alternative-food movement has been far too complicit in the neoliberal agenda, with the effect (not the intention) of producing self-satisfied eaters. To make the case for these admittedly jarring claims requires a definition of alternative food and how it became the antidote to obesity, practically and conceptually. That is where I begin.

ALTERNATIVE FOOD AS THE ANTIDOTE TO OBESITY

The alternative-food movement, as I discuss it here, first evolved to support farms with sustainable farming practices. As such, it created a set of institutions that link producers and consumers in close relationships, such as farmers markets, community-supported agricultural programs (CSAs), and farm-to-restaurant sales. I see these institutions as distinct from those that date back to the late 1960s, when the New Left began to organize various food provisioning activities. Taking cues from earlier socialist and communal experiments, those various "co" institutions were explicitly noncapitalist in their organization and ownership, and sometimes were intended to model social forms of organization (Belasco 1989). They included *commune*s where residents grew their own food; *collective* bakeries, cheese stores, and restaurants where workers owned and managed the store; *cooperative* groceries where members pooled their money for food purchasing; and *community* gardens where neighbors farmed small plots of land together or in allotments. In contrast, the alternative-food movement, as I characterize it here, is less concerned with using food practices in the service of social change than with changing the food itself. The movement is not now nor was it ever radically transformative, although certain segments were most definitely anticorporate, and particular individuals in the movement may have such inclinations or may have participated in earlier more radical permutations (cf. Alkon 2009).

Alternative-food institutions are explicitly designed to support producers with good prices and steady markets and to allow consumers access to wholesome, healthy, and sometimes exceptionally tasty food (Allen et al. 2003). Although the movement is hardly unified—it encompasses, for example, radical antistatists and policy reformers, antihunger activists and high-end chefs, urban coastals and rural agrarians—as a whole it has come to put enormous emphasis on providing markets for small-scale, sustainably producing farmers by changing what people eat. Now it's increasingly about simply changing what people eat, often under the banner of food justice.

Many good things have emerged from these efforts, which have produced both better farming and better food. Dedicated farmers and consultants have spent years learning and disseminating farming methods that are far kinder to soils and that depend on fewer and less toxic inputs than are used in what we call conventional agriculture. Thanks to inventive and dedicated food producers, the sustainable agriculture/organic farming movement has broadened its ambit beyond its earlier emphasis on fruit and vegetable crops to pasture-raised meats, eggs, and dairy products. The sustainable farming movement has successfully challenged the idea that "to feed the world" intensive, industrial agriculture is necessary.

Meanwhile, those on the cutting edge of food culture—chefs, food writers, and so on—now champion the fresh whole foods that were once the territory of "health food nuts" and quacks. Through cooking expertise and artistic sensibilities, they have made local, organic, seasonal food into something people *desire* for its taste and good looks. The revolution in taste owes much to the forty-year effort of the chef Alice Waters (of Berkeley's Chez Panisse), who pioneered the inclusion of organic, seasonal ingredients procured from nearby farms in her restaurant cooking to make Chez Panisse synonymous with sustainable food. She then developed a sizable cadre of suppliers and a progeny of trained chefs who carried her torch and went on to experiment with their own ventures in sustainable cuisine. The renaissance of artisan-produced cheeses, breads, and condiments has also contributed to this reenvisioning of food.

As an activist movement, the alternative-food movement is one of the most successful of our day if you consider the numbers of people who identify with it by shopping at alternative-food institutions, attending events, contributing money, and providing countless hours to gardening projects, farm-to-school programs, and "hanging out" with food. Of course, the alternative-food movement has a huge tactical advantage over other social movements in galvanizing support because it champions the pleasure of eating—and, for some, cooking and gardening. Many dollars have been raised of late from fundraisers in high-quality restaurants.

The idea that alternative food is a solution to obesity rests not merely on the conceptual opposition between the bad and the good. Alternative food has also become an antidote to obesity as a practical matter, specifically another tactic to secure new markets for farmers—and grants from funders. As I mentioned in the introduction, my research on the farm-to-school movement first brought obesity discourse to my attention. Seeking to understand how and why farm-to-school programs were becoming so popular, my colleague and I were surprised by how frequently promoters invoked childhood obesity (along with enhanced scholastic performance) as a rationale for these programs. Advocates who came from the alternative-agriculture movement were painting farm-to-school as a "win-win" that would both support farmers and galvanize the support of nutrition professionals and funders who were concerned with the obesity epidemic (Allen and Guthman 2006).

Apparently, the explosion of cooking, gardening, food provisioning, and environmental programs since we conducted that research has developed on similar premises. My students routinely return from their field studies with such organizations with stories of how leaders rerationalized program goals around combating obesity to attract fundraising dollars. For example, the annual fundraiser for one food justice organization featured testimonials from women who had taken its nutritional cooking class, taught by someone who condemned fat for being "just unhealthy." Graduates of the program took the stage to talk about how they had learned to buy and prepare appealing and healthy food, and many commented that they had lost weight by doing so, one exclaiming that she had dropped two whole dress sizes (Tattenham 2006: 25–26). Even when alternative-food advocates do not explicitly promote thinness or dutiful adherence to what Campos (2004) has called "chronically restrained eating," in problematizing fat bodies in their rhetoric they are complicit in enforcing bodily norms.

Outside of movement politics, there is another, more publicly salient reason that alternative food has caught on as an antidote to obesity: the growing acknowledgment that diets don't work in part because they are punitive and abstemious. The sensual pleasures of fresh, local food seems to promise a different route to bodily salvation than calorie counting and Olestra.

A KINDER AND GENTLER DIET?

If people were better educated in nutrition, "diets" would no longer have to be an unhealthy suppressant of what you cannot have, but simply the usual nutritionally fulfilling food one has been educated to eat.

—Student comment

As exemplified in the epigraph to this section, some people no longer believe that an optimally healthy diet must be composed of diet food, latter-day health food, or even the "brown food" associated with what the food historian Warren Belasco (1989) once called "countercultural cuisine." They reject nutritionism, with its reductionist approach to food intake that emphasizes particular components of food (Scrinis 2008). Whole food, referring to food that has been minimally processed, has (once again) taken its place. With minimal processing, all of the interactive goodness of a food's constituent parts can presumably be retained and the nasty processing aids and chemicals designed to impart taste, durability, and mouthfeel, but which might compromise the food's health-giving properties, can be avoided. Supporting this move, many nutritionists today, at least the ones not bought off by the food industry, say that virtually all of the nutrients "you need" can be found in a diet that has a variety of whole grains, legumes, meats, fruits, and veggies. And so they recommend a balanced approach to eating with the simple message of "eat less" (Nestle 2006).

Along with those in the nutrition profession who have heeded shifts in nutritional science and have recognized that cajoling is ineffective, the alternative-food movement can take credit for this shift. Through better farming and better cooking, the movement has in an important sense redefined good food from "healthy" to "real." These ideas have been promulgated by food writers, of course. The tagline of Pollan's *In Defense of Food* (2008b) reads: "Eat food. Not too much. Mostly plants." In the book, he contrasts "food" (that is, "real" food) with "edible foodlike substances."

The alternative-food movement has attempted to influence the way we eat in addition to what we eat. Rejecting the idea of food as simply functional, to be ingested solely to fuel the bodily machine (the approach many diets take), much of alternative-food discourse emphasizes conviviality and the social context of the meal. Food should be eaten at the table, not gobbled down in the car or at a desk, with plenty of time given over to civil discussion (Pollan 2008b). The importance of conviviality is a theme clearly borrowed from the Slow Food movement. European in origin, one of its rallying cries is to bring together pleasure and social responsibility in eating. The Slow Food movement clearly rejects the abstemious approaches to eating championed by latter-day health foodists, some of whom, at their worst, recommended thorough mastication! It also rejects dieting, instead embracing meals made from plenty of fat and salt (after all, the movement emerged in Italy, and traditional approaches to cheese making and pork curing figure prominently in it).

And yet, with all this emphasis on the pleasure of eating, subtle references to and preferences for thinness, akin to healthism, appear in the alternative-food movement. Whereas more mainstream healthism promotes counting calories and standing on the scale, alternative food merely hints at this kinder, gentler way to manage weight. Michael Pollan has been explicit in positioning alternative food against the food qualities and practices that make you fat. In a widely circulated *New York Times* piece about the movie *Julie and Julia*, he correlated the rise of obesity and the decline of home cooking (another potentially spurious correlation) and concluded that you can eat anything you want as long as you cook it from scratch (Pollan 2009c). Some sections of *In Defense of Food* read like a masculine version of *Why French Women Don't Get Fat*. (Apparently, it is because they eat those yummy croissants and duck confit very delicately and slowly and never finish, and then they walk long blocks with baguettes under their arms without taking one bite on the way home.) At times *In Defense of Food* even reads like a diet book, when, for example, Pollan suggests using smaller plates to trick yourself into eating less, or when he says that "another important benefit of paying more for better-quality food is that you're apt to eat less of it" (2008b: 184). As he says, *Not Too Much*. To be sure, *The Omnivore's Dilemma* and *In Defense of Food*, along with Pollan's newest *Food Rules*, developed by eliciting rules from readers in the *New York Times*, all seem to suggest that if you act like him, by spending more money and time procuring, preparing, and eating food, you'll be thin (Pollan 2006, 2008b, 2009b).

It is easy to take issue with Pollan on these points, especially since he appeals to a European aesthetic that is unlikely to resonate with the lower- to middle-income rural and suburban white Europhobes who are some of the prime targets of current-day nutritional advice. Nor, for that matter, do these Europhilic foodways actually represent how most Europeans eat (DuPuis 2010). Nevertheless, the implicit promise of alternative food is that if you have a more natural, sensuous relationship with your food, you will also have one with your body—which will somehow manifest in being not too fat. Is this "natural" relationship easy to find? In her important book *Unbearable Weight*, the feminist theorist Susan Bordo (1993) discusses how, in the face of a tyranny of slenderness that makes the vast majority of women extraordinarily weight conscious, the goal of having a more natural relationship with food can be doubly oppressive for women. Not only must they watch their weight, they must also watch themselves to make sure they appear to eat what and all they want. I've noticed that in the many alternative-food events (conferences, fundraising dinners, on-farm dinners) I've attended over the past several years (for research, of course!), attendees are generally thin and take great care to enjoy and comment on the visual, olfactory, and taste sensations of the food but not eat too much.

To the extent that eating alternative food is discussed, if not explicitly promoted, as a weight-loss strategy, it is reminiscent of what Skrabenek (1994) called lifestylism, in which disease prevention morphs into moral prescriptions as to how one should live, an issue to which I will return. In any case, there are many other ways that alternative food is a weak antidote to obesity. These lie with change strategies that do not address the political-economic foundations of the larger food system.

CAN WE CHANGE THE WORLD ONE MEAL AT A TIME?

It sounds like a grass-roots rebellion—literally—and that's pretty much what he [Pollan] has in mind. But to his critics on the left, the very notion of starting a food revolution by changing what you personally eat is wrong-headed, and Pollan is Exhibit A.

—Laura Shapiro

The Omnivore's Dilemma concludes with a description of a meal that Pollan helped to forage and hunt—and cooked all by himself, which, as he puts it, "gave me the opportunity, so rare in modern life, to eat in full consciousness of everything involved in feeding myself: for once, I was able to pay the full karmic price of a meal" (Pollan 2006: 9). Besides overlooking the role of laborers in the food system in contemplating the full karmic price, Pollan seems to suggest that if we eat as he does, we can fix the food system. At the end of *Fast Food Nation*—in my view the very best of the food exposés, true to the muckraking style of Upton Sinclair—Schlosser (2001) tells us to "have it your way," suggesting that we can choose not to eat at McDonald's. Even the 2009 documentary *Food Inc.*, which presents a scathing critique of the livestock industry, concludes with the message to vote with your dollars three times per day. It's understandable that the producers of these media want to end on an upbeat note that gives people a sense of what they can do or, better yet, what they can eat. But I want to argue that, indeed, "the very notion of starting a food revolution by changing what you personally eat is wrong-headed."

Changing what you eat may provide new and different pleasures—and I have little to quibble with in that claim. But what to eat is the wrong question to ask in order to transform the food system into one that is more just and less toxic.

It rests on the theory of change. The theory of change begins with the proposition that those who can afford it and are more conscientious should pay for high-quality food. This proposition grows out of the analysis discussed in chapter 6: that food in the United States is artificially cheap due to commodity subsidies especially but also other forces of agricultural intensification. It would seem to follow that food produced in more ecologically sustainable and socially just ways would necessarily cost more. Many advocates of alternative food—and here I am referring to food writers, chefs, nongovernmental organizations, and those in the alternative-food business—seem to agree that educating consumers to the provenance and qualities of the food, along with some good muckraking about the conventional food supply, will turn people into believers, willing to pay more for their food. And then, so the logic goes, the market will respond to consumer demand and the food system will eventually transform to one that is ecologically sustainable and socially just. Consumer choice is thus seen as the primary vehicle for transformation. The notions of "voting with your dollars" and "changing the world one meal at a time" are popularizations of these ideas.

First, I want to point out that the idea that the food system can be transformed by selling and buying good food (through informed choice) is a huge concession to the neoliberal idolatry of the market. As I detail in *Agrarian Dreams* (Guthman 2004), the organic farming movement was a progenitor of the market-based approach to food system transformation, having developed in opposition to the state and particularly the USDA. In the minds of many, the USDA had utterly failed to regulate agriculture in a way that would conserve soil and reduce the use of toxic materials. Having given up—or never having believed that chemicals could be sufficiently regulated through government action—the original organic farmers, both large and small, developed a set of techniques to grow crops without synthetic inputs. As the organic moniker began to have cachet, they needed to secure markets with a guarantee to consumers that what the latter bought was indeed organically grown. The necessity to differentiate their products eventually led to the complex system of rules, material verification, and certification that allows farmers (and now food processors) to be rewarded with a price premium for their efforts. "Organically grown" was thus the "mother of all eco-labels." Today the organic standard is sanctioned through the USDA's National Organic Program, but enforced largely through nonstate institutions.

The organic program thus works in distinction from other strategies that might reduce toxins in food production, including gradualist approaches to pest management such as integrated pest management or materials restrictions that would force producers to adopt less toxic ways of producing food. Rather than putting a lid on production practices deemed dangerous or unjust, incentive-based regulation such as the organic standard is based on the principle that people who want, say, pesticide-free food should pay for it. Regulation through market choice rather than command and control is a decidedly neoliberal approach to regulation.

Organically produced food was thus designed to cost more, to incentivize organic production. One unforeseen consequence of this approach to regulation is that it allowed significant appropriation and cooptation. As the organic sector grew, some farmers began to lose out on the price premiums associated with organics due to intense price competition. Farmers in the Northeast, for example, were particularly miffed that organic produce from California was coming their way and hurting their markets. Moreover, as with all farm production, buyers of agricultural products gained market power relative to growers in the organic sector. Corporate involvement in shipping, processing, and retailing, including by giants like Wal-Mart, led to further price erosion. Meanwhile, some producers and consumers grew frustrated that the organic standard never really encompassed concerns such as the treatment of workers, the scale of operations, or the wholeness of foods. In general, the organic production system seemed less different from the conventional food system than some had hoped. The limited ability of the organic label to address many of the issues associated with the industrial food system led to many different efforts to go "beyond organic," some of which manifested in other labels with more stringent or targeted standards (e.g., salmon safe, fair trade) and some of which manifested in discursive shifts, such as "buy local." But in almost all cases, the impulse was to support prices for particular farmers (and later ranchers).

Of the various postorganic manifestations of alternative food, by far the most popular is "local food." Although a variety of claims are made about local food, it primarily gained traction through promulgation of the food miles concept, which draws attention to how far food travels from farm to plate (Kloppenberg, Henrickson, and Stevenson 1996). One strategy was to develop another label, for example, to codify the local into a specific distance:

say, within a hundred-mile radius of a given center or farmers market. Most agree that is a fairly silly endeavor. (Radius of what center? What about topography?) Instead, local has come to be promoted in more generic ways, for instance, in "buy fresh, buy local" campaigns that direct consumer purchasing toward businesses in close proximity (Allen and Hinrichs 2008).

For curious reasons, local food has come to stand in for the social justice issues absent in organics, as if being in close proximity to one another makes people care more (Barnett et al. 2005; DuPuis and Goodman 2005).[1] This association conflates geographic scale and justice, however (Born and Purcell 2006). Suffice it to say that there is nothing inherent about proximity that makes farmers pay their workers more, makes food affordable, makes profits stay in the region, or allows citizens to participate meaningfully in decision making about food (cf. Hassanein 2003; Kloppenberg, Henrickson, and Stevenson 1996; Lyson 2004). Indeed, the fact that upscale and hipster restaurant chefs helped popularize the idea that local is better means that local, too, has become a way to valorize food, not make it more affordable. Nor is there anything inherent about the local that makes it the place of resistance to the global (DuPuis and Goodman 2005).

Nor is "local" immune from appropriation. Whole Foods and other natural food supermarkets, and even Wal-Mart, now sell "local" food, and the vibrancy of "local food systems" has become a quality used to market particular places, especially at a time when competing for capital and tax dollars defines regional development possibilities (Brenner and Theodore 2002). Since not all locales are created equal in terms of climate and soil, or even community interest, "local" food systems, like leptogenic environments, potentially bring wealth to certain places at the expense of others.

Remarkably, the community food security (CFS) movement, which emerged explicitly to address the affordability issue of alternative food, has hedged with its dual support of farmers. Domestically, the CFS concept came into being in response to the normalization of emergency food institutions such as food banks and soup kitchens that persisted well past the emergency of the early 1980s recession that repopulated them (Poppendieck 1998). Early CFS activists wanted to combat the causes of hunger rather than just its symptoms. They took this to mean limiting dependence on outside, charitable sources of food (Fisher and Gottlieb 1995). Demonstrating the influence of localism and their own involvement with the sustainable agriculture movement, many CFS activists focused on programs that would link up consumers and producers, through community-based institutions such as urban gardens, farmers markets, community-supported farms, and other food delivery services. These were premised on the idea that bringing consumers and producers together (and cutting out middlemen) would benefit both producers and low-income consumers. This entrepreneurial approach, as Patricia Allen (1999) dubbed it, put CFS at odds with more "traditional" antihunger approaches that continued to emphasize the protection and expansion of food assistance such as food stamps and WIC. Moreover, it put food security on a par with farmers' incomes, with the result that most of these market-based institutions have come to serve farmers much more than low-income consumers unless their internal mandates are otherwise. Those that do serve low-income people tend to rely on subsidies from the nonprofit sector or government grants to do so—or expect that low-income consumers will use traditional food assistance programs (Guthman, Morris, and Allen 2006).

In other words, through its abiding support of producers who employ more sustainable methods, the alternative-food movement creates a problem of affordability—by design. Among food writers there is some shame about this. Pollan writes in *In Defense of Food*, "Not everyone can afford to eat high-quality food in America, and this is shameful; however, those of us who can, should" (Pollan 2008b: 184). James McWilliams, the author of *Just Food* (2009), makes a similar appeal to the choices of conscientious eaters in his assessment of which claims of alternative agriculture should be heeded (coming remarkably close to a defense of industrial agriculture at times). But if the Malthusian specter about which he writes—the specter of not enough food, depleted soil, and poisoned air and water—looms so near, it's unclear that the problem can be rectified by the action of conscientious consumers. Are their actions supposed to make up for all of the actions of nonconscientious consumers? Analogously, if only those who can afford to buy high-quality food—an increasingly small group, given the dynamics of neoliberal capitalism (see chapter 8)—do so, what will it add up to? On its own terms, that is, the theory of change cannot amount to a huge shift in market demand. It is doubly problematic that the theory of food system change neglects the millions of low-wage earners who work in the food system. Asking people to pay more for food gets it really wrong when it asks people who have paid with their lives, land, and labor to pay even more. Farmers and agricultural and food workers have to eat too, and yet, the incomes they receive are barely adequate to pay for cheap food, much less the more extolled variety.

At its core, then, the existence of alternative food allows relatively well-off consumers to "opt out" of conventionally grown food because of whatever bad characteristics they attribute to it. Along the way, they may procure and eat some very tasty food (especially in some regions of the country). Some refer to this sort of consumption politics as a "buycott," where you reward the good players, as opposed to a boycott, where you punish the bad ones (Allen and Hinrichs 2008); others, less generously, refer to this as "not in my body" politics (DuPuis 2000), or "inverted quarantine" (Szasz 2007). For, to the extent you can buy your way out, you are trying to purchase relative safety that others can't afford. As Andy Szasz argues in *Shopping Our Way to Safety* (2007), commodified alternatives to regulatory failure tend to accentuate class inequality rather than ameliorate it.

As it happens, purchasing safety is rarely effective in issues of toxic air and water pollution, exposures that are so ubiquitous that they cannot be avoided by purchasing, say, an organic apple (Szasz 2007). (Paula Baillie-Hamilton, the woman who first made the claims about environmental toxins and obesity, encapsulates that contradiction in her book [2002b] on how to avoid toxic exposure through diet.) It is surely striking that the organic farming movement has failed to curb the use of agricultural chemicals in any significant way. Although it may be true that organic agriculture continues to grow, so does the use of toxic chemicals, and those who work or live in or near fields experience the worst exposures (Kegley, Orme, and Neumeister 2000). The problem of pesticide drift has therefore led to activism that is much more confrontational than organic farming is (Harrison 2008a).

Thus, the most profound problem with the alternative-food movement as an activist endeavor is that building the alternatives does not regulate bad practices but, instead, allows them to coexist with good ones (Harrison 2008b). Moreover, not regulating bad practices puts the cost burden on good practices, so that either less economically powerful producers or better-off consumers pay for them. Leaving bad practices unconscionably underregulated means that some will produce food that necessarily will be cheaper than it would be if such practices were prohibited. The food so produced will also be as nutritionally debilitated, toxic, or "fattening" as agribusiness can get away with. Some of these qualities are prevented by occasional rounds of acute illness (for example, *E. coli*) that are traceable to particular meals and thus embarrassing for their purveyors. Fears of future embarrassment may encourage them to clean up some of their act. Yet, where does that leave chemically produced cancers or endocrinal problems that show up years later?

In crucial ways, then, making an *alternative* actively contributes to the bifurcation of the food system (Allen et al. 2003). Put another way, too many carrots (incentives) and not enough sticks (regulations) has meant that some people have come to eat fresh, organic, local carrots while others eat cheap, dangerous, and fattening sticks (Harrison 2008b). Of course there is crossover: Trader Joe's and Wal-Mart sell organic food; Whole Foods sells "healthy" snack food. Nevertheless, the "true" alternatives of local, seasonal, and farm-direct foods are, by definition, not mainstream—and not cheap.[2] How, then, do those who are trying to address the affordability of and access to real food alter the conversation?

WHAT ABOUT FOOD JUSTICE?

The problem that alternative food is often economically inaccessible has not gone unnoticed, and some in the alternative-food movement shun the organic label for that reason. There is also broad recognition that nutritious food defined in less rarefied terms than local or organic is lacking in many urban environments, creating a problem of geographic as well as economic access. The obesogenic environment thesis discussed in chapter 4 thus shares an analysis with the food access critique that the CFS movement has generated. In addition, there is an emerging critique that alternative food is culturally elite. Many alternative institutions are coded as "white" spaces that do not seem to resonate in communities of color or working-class neighborhoods (Guthman 2008a). And again, the emphasis on slow food, with its shades of Europhilia, may not appeal to working-class sensibilities (Gaytan 2004).

All of this has given rise to a "food justice" movement that endeavors to change the practices and idioms associated with alternative food to make good food more culturally and economically accessible. The food justice movement explicitly adopts concepts from both the environmental justice movement and the local food movement (Alkon and Agyeman 2011). Like the environmental justice movement, the food justice movement has arisen in response to a more mainstream movement dominated by privileged whites. Food justice activists have attempted to make alternative food more accessible and attractive to people of color (less so to working-class whites) through setting up shop in their neighborhoods and employing "culturally appropriate" symbolism. For example, they might publicize the plight of African American farmers or promote foods and recipes associated with black cuisine, such as collard greens and beans (Alkon 2008). Like the local food movement, though, the primary endeavor is to shorten the distance and strengthen the connection between food producers and food buyers as a way to support small-scale, relatively resource-poor producers and provide healthier food to consumers. So even though this food justice movement is far more race- and class-conscious than the mainstream alternative-food movement, much of its on-the-ground work is more or less the same: educating people to the provenance of food, having them taste food cooked by trained (albeit hipper) chefs, and making it available in low-income neighborhoods and communities of color, on the assumption that if you build it, they will come (Short, Guthman, and Raskin 2007).

Interestingly, the issue of obesity is in some respects more prominent in the food justice movement than in the alternative-food movement more generally. This is because another key idea that food justice draws from the environmental justice movement is the association between place-based toxic exposures and poor health among low-income people and people of color (Bullard 1997; Sze 2007). The food justice movement aims to bring analogous focus to food-related environmental conditions (e.g., food deserts) and income insufficiencies that lead to ill health. Obese bodies are seen as evidence of injustice, with lack of access to good food assumed to be the cause. Therein lies the problem.

Constructing obesity as a health disparity growing out of food injustice stems from the methodological biases of environmental health scholarship. Having emerged from efforts to prove the existence of environmental racism (Bullard 1990), much of environmental health justice scholarship seeks to establish a positive association of an *illness* with a *race* (or other group) (Brown 2007). Finding positive associations between populations and illnesses is assumed to be morally positive since it demonstrates distributive outcomes that can be acted on in courts or legislation. Yet, such treatments can also help stabilize categories of race and, thus, the association between pathology and certain groups of people (Moore, Pandian, and Kosek 2003: 16). They also elide "the ways in which biological disease processes associated with environmental change intersect with culturally mediated interpretations of health and disease" (Harper 2004: 298). Who gets to define lack of real food as a health disparity or bigness as a disease?

So, even through the problem of differential access to "good" food is a felt problem in certain communities, efforts to redefine it through a particular lens have consequences. It is worth noting that the problem construction assumes the energy balance model and the pathology of nonnormative bodies. What about the injustices that arise from renewed stigma of fat bodies? Since obesity can be a cause of lower socioeconomic status as much as an effect of it, calling out fat bodies under the aegis of "food justice" can also work at cross-purposes to justice. At the very least, it occludes the injustices that ensue when some bodies and self-practices are exalted and others disparaged, injustices such as employment and health care discrimination against fat people (Julier 2008; Kirkland 2010). Although food activists may see inequitable access to good food, as it putatively manifests in the body, as a form of oppression, others (including fat activists, disability rights activists, some queer activists, and some feminists) see the problematization of nonnormative bodies as a form of oppression.

Furthermore, the existing food justice perspective, which emphasizes the absence of fresh fruits and vegetables in neighborhood venues, can obscure the sources of injustice in the food system. Not only does the food justice movement define high-quality food much as the alternative-food movement does (fresh, local, and seasonal, albeit with less emphasis on organic per se), it also gives scant attention to other injustices in the food system, particularly those arising in food production: exposure to toxic chemicals, poor working conditions as they apply to health and safety, and disparities in wages and employment. All of these affect people's capacity to live as they want and some can actually be the cause of these consumption-based disparities. For that matter, defining food justice as an issue of unequal distribution seems to thwart a more process-oriented approach, in which those who are most affected by injustice substantively participate in deciding how injustice shall be defined and redressed (Shrader-Frechette 2005). Arguably, for example, undocumented migrants who work in the food system might prioritize being able to cross the border without fear of death above having a community garden in their neighborhood. (I write this having observed many such projects created in Latino migrant communities—some to teach farmworkers' children how to grow food!)

In other words, the food justice critique, although an important antidote to the class and racial indifference of the mainstream alternative-food movement, is nonetheless politically ambiguous. This becomes especially clear when we see the sort of interventions it inspires. That is, defining the problem of injustice as being about food tends to make the solution "bringing good food to others" or "teaching people how to eat." Thus, bringing or growing food in areas with limited access to good food has become a major strategy of the alternative-food movement. Although there is enjoyment to be shared in home-grown tomatoes, pasture-raised eggs, and food made from scratch, teaching people what and how to eat does appear to have many of the trappings of a civilizing mission, including the sense that the missionaries know what's right. That is where it recalls the worst aspects of healthism.

FOODIES ON A MISSION

Exposure is the only form of aid to these people. (m)

As I have mentioned, many of my students are very excited about the idea of food justice, and every year an increasing number secure field study placements with organizations that claim to promote food justice. As suggested, most of this involves bringing fresh fruits and vegetables and other healthy food into communities of color, sometimes explicitly in the hope of combating obesity. Many of these students return from field study to tell stories about how little the food or the mode of food delivery resonated with the target populations. In one memorable thesis, my student reported a conversation with her African American neighbor. My student had mentioned that she worked for the organization that brought a truck of organic fruits and vegetables to her neighborhood. Her neighbor's response to why she did not shop from the truck (which was convenient and sold at below-market prices) was, "Because they don't sell no food! All they got is birdseed." She went on to exclaim, "Who are they to tell me how to eat? I don't want that stuff. It's not food. I need to be able to feed my family." When my student asked her what she would like the truck to offer, the neighbor said, "You know, what normal grocery stores have" (Tattenham 2006).

When I've shared this story with people involved in the food justice movement, they generally nod their heads and agree that the food promoted should be more "culturally appropriate." That would be a good thing, but what I am *not* trying to do with this story is suggest how such projects could be more effective in reaching their target constituency. Instead, I want to highlight that woman's astute observation about being told what to eat as a way to bring into focus the civilizing mission that inheres in the alternative-food movement. By *civilizing mission*, I mean to connote the early colonial encounters between Europe and others. When confronted with others' ways of life, Europe saw lack and tried to convert these others to the ways of Europeans, most obviously in the realm of religion but also in government, art, and everyday manners. Today, missionary work still involves civilizing, improving, and even providing charity to the "downtrodden," but rarely addressing the source of inequality. Missionary work, thus, often entails *bringing* individual improvement rather than *allowing for* (or supporting) collective action. And, of course, the missionary's life is the one that neophytes are expected to emulate.

Countless historical examples exist of the tendency to teach people about food in relation to other social ends. For instance, in the Progressive Era, white middle-class reformers, primarily women, sought to acculturate newly arrived European immigrants to the diets (in all of their blandness), dress, drinking habits, and manners of Anglo Protestant Americans in the name of Americanization (Levenstein 1988). Today's concern with health and responsibility has provided fertile ground for many programs and projects designed to encourage weight loss and to produce more empowered and self-actualized citizens. We see that on *The Biggest Loser*, where fat people compete to lose the most weight and where the emphasis on losing weight is continually coupled with putting one's life in order or aspiring to a new one. It is worth noting that the contestants are treated paternalistically by the hard-body trainers, whose higher status accrues by dint of their bodies. With bodies as credentials, the trainers readily and regularly bestow life wisdom on their charges. We see something similar in many of the food and gardening programs for both children and at-risk adults that have sprung up around the country. Organizers see their role as changing peoples' relationships to nature, food, and their bodies by encouraging self-efficacy, often under the rubric of empowerment. Much of what goes on in school food programs is training students in norms of civil eating, complete with scripted questions to initiate polite conversation (Hayes-Conroy 2009; Pudup 2008). Even programs designed just to distribute good food have an educational quality to them and occasionally use slogans of empowerment.

What is particularly striking in terms of contemporary food-oriented efforts is the sense that exposure to real tastes *will* unearth the desire for whole, real food and create the more natural relationship between food and the body I alluded to earlier (Hayes-Conroy 2009). Many in the foodie world have heard, loud and clear, of the inequities in access to high-quality food. Their reaction, however, has been to educate in matters of taste. This is the impulse that led Alice Waters to pioneer the Edible Schoolyard and other efforts to rethink school lunch, efforts that were heavily endowed by the Chez Panisse Foundation and have been replicated elsewhere through the largesse of others. School food and gardening programs are part of what Waters now calls "a delicious revolution." The premise of Waters's delicious revolution is to get kids to experience the taste of high-quality food, so they will then "make the right choices." Crucially, Waters treats the particular tastes she espouses as universals—and preaches that if children are properly taught they will, well, taste the light. As noted by Jessica Hayes-Conroy (2009), whose research involved long-term observation of two different school gardening and cooking programs, the very idea of taste education contradicts that premise. If taste must be taught, it is not something naturally given. It is striking that many critics of the existing food system (e.g., Brownell and Horgen 2004) imply an opposite point: that the problem with Cheetos and other junk food is that they are taste-engineered to make them irresistible (once you eat just one). So which is it? Which kind of food *really* tastes good?

Nevertheless, I contend that one of the reasons these conversion projects have the character they do is because they reflect the desires and aesthetics of those who lead them. Project leaders assume that food associated with the local, the organic, and the slow is universally good, desirable to all, neglecting that such food draws on rather rarefied food cultures. Thus, these projects reveal a problem associated with "whiteness": that ideals, aesthetics, and experiences held primarily by whites are assumed to be normal and widely shared (Kobayashi and Peake 2000: 394). Importantly, the assumption of universality allows the problem to be defined as one of access and affordability: if only people had access, they would buy and eat this food, so the logic goes. And, when seemingly universal ideals do not take hold, it is assumed that those for whom they do not resonate need to be educated to these ideals. "If people only knew where their food comes from," as my students often say, or, more tellingly, "exposure is the only form of aid to these people."

Yet, like most missionary work, the message speaks mainly to the almost or already converted. Just as the audience for the obesity statistics is those who are most invested in upholding bodily norms (the already thin or just slightly "overweight"), the audience for organic local food is those who already have a stake in good eating and status. Although I have no ultimate proof of Michael

Pollan's audience, I have come across many of his fans in classrooms, speaking engagements, and public forums. Without an obvious exception, I've noticed that they are white, educated, urbane, and thin—and already quite convinced of alternative food's goodness. It may be that Pollan's iconic power has less to do with changing minds than with animating something latent. In a funny way, even Michael Pollan knows this. *In Defense of Food* is full of appeals to "us." In other words, it's not so much that the discourse of good food convinces its subjects; rather, the discourse chooses subjects who are ready to believe it (Robbins 2007). Think about it: If you eat the Pollan diet, will it make you thin? (It hasn't worked for me.) Or is it that because you are thin, you are more likely to read about and eat the Pollan diet?

HAVING YOUR CAKE AND EATING IT TOO

Aside from missionary zeal, much of what is limiting about the contemporary food movement turns on its emphasis on alternatives. To be clear, when organic agriculture first developed as a kinder and gentler way to manage crops, it made sense to develop an alternative to conventional agriculture. Not only were government agencies completely unsupportive of the movement's critiques, but also those in the movement felt it was important to develop positive models while they contested negative ones. The development of alternative institutions was thus imagined to take place alongside more confrontational strategies against states and corporations. Even today, there continues to be a place for both those who confront and those who develop models. But what I've seen of late is that the alternatives have sucked the air out of the oppositional room. The types of field studies available to my students stand as a mountain of evidence of where social movement activity lies. Those who want to confront immigration policy, trade policy, agricultural biotechnology, industrial meat processing, or pesticides find that organizations that do this sort of work are few and far between, and those that exist are woefully underfunded. Meanwhile, the myriad organizations that are creating alternative-food institutions—whether CSAs, urban farms, farmers markets, community gardens, food delivery services, or farm and garden education programs—are spreading like, well, pollen.

In many respects, the character of these projects simply reflects a politics of the possible, specifically as it applies to nonprofit work. Clearly, food positive activity is now part of the national zeitgeist. Furthermore, in a funding climate for so-called social change that insists on deliverables, with ideas often generated by the funders themselves, projects that focus on self-help, practical skills, and providing specific goods are easier to get funded (Guthman 2008b). They are also easier to mobilize around. Volunteers and interns are much easier to come by when the work involves gardening, cooking, or food distribution rather than the long-term, arduous, and often frustrating work of effecting policy change (Poppendieck 1998). I can attest that many of my students want to work with cooking or gardening—"to get their hands dirty"—rather than sit behind a computer. Of course, the crucially important but also politically challenging work of making demands on the state or changing corporate practices yields few immediate tangible rewards, and, in threatening the powers that be, it is not often fundable (Arnove 1980; INCITE! Women of Color Against Violence 2006). In other words, there are some real structural reasons that the focus of action in food politics, in particular, has become better growing and eating, rather than, say, organizing collective action to ban a certain food ingredient with known adverse health effects. Nevertheless, especially as food system change may relate to obesity, it is surely ironic that the very issue that once animated the organic food movement—the use of synthetic chemicals in the production of food, stemming from the industrialization of agriculture—seems culpable in the very problem that the movement now claims to solve through better diets.

In closing this chapter, I want to follow on the words of the author and literary critic Toni Morrison (1992: 90), who once wrote that her project was to "avert the critical gaze from the racial object to the racial subject; from the described and imagined to the describers and imaginers."[3] Analogously, I want to shed light on the promoters of good food rather than the targets of that promotion. I do this with the concern that a very vocal subset of the thin and privileged are shaping the strategies and practices of the food justice movement and the alternative-food movement more broadly, based on their own desires and aesthetics, and perhaps their own fears, and in ways that don't challenge their own privilege in wallet and body. As I have tried to suggest, framing the problem as one of inaccessibility to local, organic, seasonal food seems to reflect the desires of foodies more than those of people subject to injustice.

Then the question pointedly becomes what they get out of it. One thing they get out of it is affirmation that their investments in their own embodiments and self-practices—in healthism—are indicative of goodness. Issues of status, real food, good bodies, and ethics are so entwined these days that it is easy to wonder how much of the interest in alternative food is related to the personal fear of getting fat, which gets cover in concern about environmental sustainability, public health, and even justice. In that vein, it has been argued that eliminating particular foods from the diet under the aegis of health or animal rights or ethics (through, for example, vegetarianism, veganism, or raw foodism) can become an excuse for being extraordinarily weight conscious (Maurer 1999). Regardless of whether eating alternative food is explicitly embraced as a weight-loss strategy, the inflection of healthism into projects that are otherwise intended to effect social change allows the conflation of eating well (and having a thin body) with doing good.

The option to purchase alternative food affords relatively privileged people the opportunity to feel that they're doing even more, to have their own consumption habits confused with philanthropy, even though, in practice, pleasurable and ethical shopping can be contradictory (Johnston 2008). Insofar as eaters of alternative food are largely those who have been fortunate in the economy and with their bodies, they may even have a personal stake in upholding market alternatives rather than addressing structural inequality, which might lead to their losing wealth or income. In contrast to, say, paying higher taxes so that others may eat well through food assistance programs, participating in the pleasures of alternative food requires little sacrifice at all. Basically, it allows foodies to have their food and eat it too. Those of us who are lucky enough to live in centers of local, seasonal food have much bounty—and those of us who *want to* and can *afford* to eat at the restaurants that use this bounty may indeed live charmed lives. But good eating cannot be conflated with ethical eating and effecting social justice; to suggest otherwise contributes to a sense of deserving that isn't quite deserved.

It seems to me that when food itself becomes the locus of social change, it tends to erase from consideration the countless ways in which the food system has gone awry socially and environmentally, especially for those who labor in the food industry. Supported by healthism, that is, the alternative-food movement helps convince people that the injustice is unequal access to high-quality food rather than, say, disparities in wages, employment, or working conditions as they apply to health and safety—or exposures to toxic chemicals. Bringing good food to others isn't changing the conditions of exploitation and oppression or addressing the privilege that also results from pervasive inequality. And in saying what is good for others, preaching good food crowds out the ability for others to define their own political projects. The alternative-food movement is the problem, I am arguing, not only in its inability to seriously challenge the cheap-food system, but also in its production of self-satisfied customers who believe that buying, eating, and promoting good food is enough. It is not. So, regardless of whether alternative food really is better tasting and good for you and maybe even will help you lose weight, it is this sort of indifference to class, race, and, frankly, the dynamics of capitalism that ultimately limits what a food movement can do. To capitalism I now turn.

CHAPTER 8

What's Capitalism Got to Do with It?

On October 14, 2009, the *Colbert Report* (a faux news/comedy television show) featured Amy Farrell, a contributor to the newly released *Fat Studies Reader*. Before introducing his guest, Steven Colbert warmed up with a monologue that, among other things, poked fun at Senator John Ensign for his proposed amendment to what was then the still-being-formed health care bill that would have mandated lower premiums for those who lost weight. To that Colbert said, "The government is really sending mixed messages here. First, they subsidize corn, making it so cheap we can gorge on subsidized corn syrup, and then they charge us more for health insurance just because our organs have caramelized. . . . Well, I'm sorry," he quipped, "but our bodies are the only growth industry America has left."

With one quick barb, Colbert captured my most central argument: in the interest of economic growth, contemporary US capitalism has helped to create obesity as a material phenomenon and then made it a moral problem that must be resolved in a way that is equally kind to capitalism. This political economy of bulimia, as it were, is indicated by the mixed messages Colbert highlights. The fact that obesity (as well as responses to it) is utterly wrapped up in the fate of America's place in the global political economy presents quite a challenge for the alternative-food movement, which has largely steered clear of policy approaches that address capitalism's excesses.

The purpose of this chapter is to expand on Colbert's argument, to demonstrate how bodies have emerged as a growth industry in the context of contemporary capitalism. Here I want to work more thoroughly with neoliberalism as an explanatory concept. Of course, not all current policy and norms that affect our bodies can be tied to neoliberalism, especially since many agricultural policies remain protectionist (rather than free trade–oriented).

Yet, insofar as neoliberal economic policies have unleashed a no-holds-barred approach to capital accumulation, worsened inequalities, and generated ideas of self-governance that encourage both excessive consumption and not having it show, much can be tied to it. Neoliberal policies have helped produce many of the food qualities, built environments, and chemical exposures associated with obesogenesis. At the same time, these policies have made available for investment and marketing many (but by no means all possible) solutions to problems they have generated. Thus, the body has become a site for a spatial fix for capitalism's inherent growth problems—for capitalism's limits, such that the political-economic contradictions of the neoliberal era are literally embodied in ways that run up against the limits of the body.

It is the inequalities that neoliberalism has exacerbated that reveal the limits of the alternative-food movement, however. Recall that the theory of change for the alternative-food movement asks that people pay more for better food. It is certainly puzzling that this market-driven approach to food system change entirely concedes neoliberalism's parameters. It is maddening, though, that this theory of change feeds into neoliberalism's culture, which has allowed those who have fared the best to trump the moralities of those who have fared the worst with discourses of healthy bodies and foods. In this chapter I want to show that the intense moral outrage with fatness gets it wrong. I want to begin, though, by explaining the limits of capitalism—and, specifically, how the twentieth-century crises of capitalism led to neoliberalism.

LIMITS TO CAPITALISM

What some have called the most important book in academic geography, *Limits to Capital*, written by David Harvey and first published in 1982, is the starting point for this chapter. When Harvey invoked the limits to capital, his meaning was double-edged. Writing this book as an exegesis of Marx's *Das Kapital* (or *Capital*), on the one hand he was qualifying the book he otherwise much admired. The primary limitation was that Marx failed to consider fully how geographic space figures in capitalism's persistent tendencies toward crisis. On the other hand, he was speaking to the limits to capitalism itself, given its self-destructive tendencies. Capitalism, that is, experiences periodic crises because it must always find new sources of accumulation or profit. Without new profit opportunities, those with capital lose value. Most of capitalism's crises, then, are crises of "overaccumulation." When there is too much capital in circulation and not enough profitable investment opportunities, capitalism stagnates, sometimes profoundly. And, indeed, at the time that *Limits* was penned, around 1980, prospects looked bleak, as many of the available fixes had already been played out.

As spelled out by Harvey in *The Condition of Postmodernity* (1989), there are several ways to fix a crisis of capitalism, some more painful than others. Historically, the easiest fix to crises of overaccumulation was geographic expansion—or what Harvey famously called the spatial fix. By this, he meant the displacement of the problem of overaccumulation elsewhere in space. Pretty much all rounds of global capitalist expansion, whether classic colonialism, "development," or "globalization," are versions of the spatial fix, which creates the conditions for capitalism to develop in areas of the globe that are not yet fully subsumed by it. The colonial project that dominated the later part of the nineteenth century was thus precisely about solving the problem of overaccumulation precipitated by the industrial revolution. Likewise, the Great Depression was precipitated when the world's industrial capacity and raw material production outdistanced effective demand from both industrialists and individual households alike. Simply put, all that had been produced could not be profitably sold, especially given the skewed income distribution that characterized the late 1920s.

To understand why capitalism is prone to these periodic crises, it is critical to grasp that the primary source of capitalism's contradictions is the wage. In capitalist economies, most people work for wages; in turn, they buy the goods that capitalism produces. Even though profits are made in production, it is an economic system that still depends on consumption. (It is also important to keep in mind that capital is also a consumer of goods—machinery, tools, software, etc.—to make salable goods.) So, to generate demand for the goods produced, capitalists need to pay out wages. That was the heart of the Fordist social contract that first emerged in the second decade of the twentieth century (but truly solidified after World War II), named after the Ford Motor Company, which was the first among American corporations to pay a good family wage. Henry Ford realized that to sell his cars he needed to guarantee a decent income for his workers. But wages also cut into profitability, so capitalists have a contradictory imperative to keep wages low enough to shore up profits but not so low as to quash demand for consumer goods.

To characterize the antidote to economic collapses as "fixes" may falsely suggest that such fixes are deliberate and explicit. This is not necessarily the case. Rather, Harvey's notion of the fix turns on the absorption of excess capital so that investment becomes profitable again. Indeed, the cruelest fix is to allow assets to devalue. Devaluation is inevitable when no policy exists to moderate the booms and busts. In boom times, that is, when many people are earning money, assets—be they factories, homes, inventories, financial investments, or pension funds—gain value both because they are in demand (i.e., people will buy them) and because people speculate that such values will continue to rise. However, when buying power dries up, through, for example, layoffs, wage reductions, or poor sales of commodities produced, those assets lose value. Those who own the assets lose a great deal of wealth, as do those who lose their jobs, who must live on whatever savings and pensions, if any, they have accumulated. Devaluation is only a "fix" inasmuch as some usable assets and inventories eventually become so cheap that people will buy them up and put them back to work. Such massive devaluation was one of the "fixes" for the Great Depression of the 1930s.

Indeed, the severity of the devaluations of the Great Depression is in part what allowed the ideas of the economist John Maynard Keynes to become influential, ideas that neoliberal economists have reacted against. Keynes observed that capitalist economies systematically fail to generate stable growth or fully utilize human and physical resources, leading to systematic inefficiency and unemployment. Crucially, he also argued that the market operating by itself *cannot* eliminate economic crises and unemployment. Instead, he argued, the state has a large role to play in moderating business cycles. It can use deficit spending (debt) to create labor-intensive jobs or use direct payments to individuals to stimulate economic growth when times are tough. When times are good, direct payments automatically slow down as people find lucrative employment. This is the time to tax income and save those surpluses for the next rainy day. Many of the entitlement programs established during the New Deal or shortly thereafter, including unemployment insurance, Social Security, and welfare, were based on the ideas of Keynes. Remember that the agricultural subsidy program was also developed under the New Deal and, along with cooperative marketing agreements, was at least originally intended to ensure fair prices for farmers (see chapter 6).

Whether through infrastructural development or redistributive economic policy, much, though not all, of American economic policy from the New Deal to about 1980 was roughly Keynesian. This was especially so in the late 1960s, when state expenditures on welfare, health care, education, and housing grew considerably, thanks to Lyndon Johnson's Great Society programs. The development of a set of institutions governing wage determination and collective bargaining, such as the National Labor Relations Board, also helped stabilize the economy. Well-paid workers disrupted less and some of the bargain enjoined them from disruption (so-called corporatism). The public safety net of entitlement programs, together with the unprecedented social compromise between owners and workers, made for improved income security and much less inequality. Putting money in lots of people's pockets spurred demand for consumer goods, and consumer purchasing also helped boost the economy (Cohen 2003). Accordingly, the postwar period was characterized by considerable economic growth, much of it spurred by pent-up demand after the war and Fordism's decent family wage. This golden age of capitalism wasn't perfect—indeed, white male workers fared much better than everyone else—but it was a huge improvement over the economic hardship that preceded and followed it.

Although the combination of Fordism and Keynesianism was the most activist and widely beneficial of fixes for the economic crisis of the Great Depression, it turned out that it wasn't stable for the long haul. It reached its limits—and the chickens came home to roost during the 1970s. The expansive state, together with the cost of the war in Vietnam, produced a huge federal debt. The oil crises, as well as high wages and demands on the state, led to rampant inflation. Inflation was particularly harmful to people dependent on fixed incomes, such as retirees who were beginning to draw on Social Security. In addition, the United States had amassed an unprecedented trade deficit because Americans had begun the habit of buying cheaper goods from abroad, cheaper in part because they were made in places with lower wages. US profit rates were falling, causing considerable frustration to investors, which led many major companies to shut down old, unprofitable plants and set up shop abroad—an example of the spatial fix (Harvey 2005). And, frankly, many (white) taxpayers, who were happy that an expansive state during the New Deal had brought them Social Security and unemployment insurance, were far less pleased when welfare expenditures began to target urban African Americans in Johnson's Great Society programs (Quadagno 1996). So racism played a big part in the emerging tax revolt. All of this paved the way for a new configuration of state and society, a putative fix for the manifold crises of capitalism that manifested in the 1970s. This fix has since come to be called neoliberalism in academic circles, although it was called "trickle-down economics" at the time.

CONSUMING NEOLIBERALISM

Although much neoliberal thought has come to be taken for granted, it wasn't always that way. Harvey (2005) explains that neoliberalism originated with a group of thinkers who were considered extreme in their views. Like the Far Right of today, Friedrich von Hayek and Milton Friedman saw socialism everywhere they looked, including in "embedded liberalism" (the economic system described in the previous section), and thought that anything that interfered with the market was an attack on freedom (thus the term *neoliberal*, which was applied to this school of thought by others). They didn't obtain prime time for their policies, however, until the elections of Margaret Thatcher in the United Kingdom in 1979 and of Ronald Reagan in the United States in 1980. Reagan's election, as well as the broader agenda to reduce wages and social programs, was in large part built on demographic and racial resentments. The white working class resented job loss and black welfare, and retirees resented paying taxes for, among other things, public education. More generalized fears of foreign economic competition played a big role, too.

In practice, the effect of neoliberalism on policy has been quite mixed, especially if you consider the huge public expenditures in prosecuting wars and imprisoning people (Peck and Tickell 2002). The protectionist agricultural policies discussed in chapter 6 are hardly in keeping with neoliberal principles either. Still, using the pretense that the market was the optimal allocator of goods and services—and, thus, government was the problem—the Right steered the agenda to a set of policies that would erode the tax base by reducing the tax burden for corporations and wealthy individuals, lower wages, keep entitlement programs at bay (preventing some from expanding, capping others, and cutting still others), and decline to enforce many health, safety, and environmental regulations (sadly, just as the effects of the postwar chemical revolution were becoming more broadly understood). From the vantage point of 2011, as I write this, it is clear that these policies also failed to create employment-generating economic growth (much less stability). Thus, the neoliberal agenda has been an utter disaster: economically, socially, and ecologically.

After Ronald Reagan was elected president in 1980, one of his first agenda items was to break the power of organized labor. Flaunting the optimism enshrined in his "morning in America" speech, he saw strategic potential in using the strike of the well-paid air traffic controllers' union, PATCO, to gain support for his agenda. He knew that PATCO workers would gain little sympathy from those who were losing their jobs from plant closures or whose retirement income had lost buying power in a period of rampant inflation. The broken PATCO strike marks a watershed in US labor history, and union membership declined steadily in the years that followed, until very recently. So did wages—and they are not recovering. According to statistics gathered by Working Life (n.d.) (formerly the Labor Research Association) from the Bureau of Labor Statistics, inflation-adjusted weekly earnings of privately employed nonfarm workers declined from $302.52 in 1964 to 277.57 in 2004—and that statistic does not even address increasing disparities between different segments of the labor force. The long-term decline in wages, as well as the much greater number of people who are only partially, insecurely, or not employed, has in many ways contributed to the contemporary economic crisis, reducing, as it has, what economists call "effective demand."

For a while, the economy muddled along through the massive entry of women into the workforce, prompted at least as much by necessity as by feminist proclivities. Two-wage-earner households kept the economy afloat, and, in turn, "the market" met their needs and provided more goods and services outside of the household (takeout and ready-made meals being chief among them). With growing costs for services such as education and health care, and steadily declining wages, economic growth faltered again, substantially, in the early 1990s. This time it was saved by a huge expansion of consumer debt in the form of car loans, mortgages, and credit cards, to the extent that consumer debt as a percentage of disposable income doubled between 1975 and 2005 to a record 127 percent (Foster and Magdoff 2009: 29).

Nevertheless, what consumers bought with their credit cards was generally not domestically produced goods. One important exception to this trend was the tract houses purchased with subprime mortgages, although many of the materials with which they were built were imported. So, what also has kept the US economy nominally afloat is what can be called globally disarticulated production-consumption relationships (deJanvry 1981). Production takes place in sweatshop economies where workers' wages are so low and their free time so limited that they are unlikely to buy much of the goods they actually produce (notwithstanding new consumption centers in Singapore, Bangalore, and Shanghai). Instead, much of what is produced in Bangladesh, Vietnam, and Honduras, for example, is exported and sold to American consumers who would not be able to afford the goods if they were made with domestic union labor. Making those jeans and other goods available for sale through retail is one of the few sectors, besides food, that provides nonprofessional jobs in America.

In other words, Wal-Mart capitalism (low-cost retail that rests on exploited labor abroad) is one of the few means that have allowed the United States to retain a toehold in the global economy. Let me be clear. Consumption was also a mainstay of the golden age of capitalism and greatly contributed to postwar growth (Cohen 2003). Yet, in that earlier period, American growth was based on production as well as consumption; in this more recent period of offshoring production, only the consumption side contributes much to the economy. Inasmuch as middle-class consumers actively participate in this economy by purchasing goods from abroad, they have effectively accepted the bargain of having access to cheap goods rather than high wages (Miller and Rose 1997). For the (low-paid) US middle class, that is, Wal-Mart producer-consumer relationships have become one of the few ways to maintain middle-class status.

Although cheap goods made by cheaper labor (involving the super-exploitation of labor in the global South) have propped up the low-cost retail sectors of the US economy, they have also contributed to unprecedented trade deficits, deficits funded primarily by government debt. As such, they concatenate with the deeper problem of financialization, which threatens to undermine the entire global economy. For, on the other side of consumer debt have been investors willing to extend credit because that was the only game in town, owing to the lack of potentially profitable investments in the production of goods and services. More generally, financial instruments themselves have proliferated as sites of investment, indicating a crisis of accumulation of the highest magnitude. Without good investment opportunities, that is, those with money to invest either will put it in places that protect what they have (e.g., savings accounts that pay interest) or will use it to speculate in financial markets (stock and bond markets, government borrowing, and foreign exchange) to see their money grow. Yet, with little capacity for the economy to make good on these financial instruments, the markets for them crash. And that is precisely what happened in the 2000s. Especially following a slump in the early 1990s, a huge proportion of economic activity was not even nominally linked to productive investment. Rather, capital was being put into various combinations of safe havens (e.g., offshore banks), government debt instruments, and more speculative financial instruments, such as mortgage-backed securities. The problem, as the 2008–9 banking crisis made clear, is that more credit was extended than there was income generated to pay off the debt.

When all is said and done, neoliberal policies have actually done very little to restore profitability or otherwise stimulate the economy since 1980. Sure, there was growth in what some call the "real economy," particularly in information, communication, and media technologies, with huge fortunes made by tycoons like Bill Gates. By the *real economy*, I am referring to industries that actually employ people, including services. Yet, statistics of GDP per capita, nonfinancial-sector profit rates, and unemployment suggest that the 1990s and into the 2000s were not a high-growth period at all (Brenner 2002).[1] To the extent that labor productivity slightly improved, this resulted from all sorts of cost-cutting measures that either deny jobs or make them nearly unbearable, as the speedups in meat processing attest. And in some industries, such as the airline industry, price competition has led to such deep cost cutting as to compromise the very services that the industry offers. (In this light, the focus on the obese as a problem for the airlines seems particularly perverse.) Speculation, rather than "real" economic growth, has ruled the day, as the bursting of the high-tech, dot-com, and housing bubbles of the 1980s, 1990s, and 2000s, respectively, surely indicate.

Tragically, the main achievement of neoliberalization, besides controlling inflation, has been to redistribute rather than generate wealth and income (Harvey 2005). Bush's tax reductions didn't spur investment, nor did the Federal Reserve's low interest rates. Nor did deregulation and the proliferation of new sorts of financial instruments unleash market forces to develop new enterprises. What they did instead (as Harvey so pointedly wrote) was to restore class power. Tax breaks made rich people richer, offshore banking provided rich investors with safe havens from taxation and scrutiny, and a lack of oversight allowed the sort of outright fraud of which Bernard Madoff's Ponzi scheme may be the tip of iceberg.

In short, neoliberalism has put the US economy in a bad way, and the fixes available aren't pretty. The gentlest way to fix the economy would be to tax and spend. This was the heart of Keynesianism, but it was expensive and was bad for US international competitiveness, and its proponents lost their political will in the face of the New Right's attack on welfare. Obama's tepid attempt at stimulus has been dismal in part because of previously accumulated debt, the US economy having had the Keynesian cake of high government expenditures and eaten it too with reduced taxes. The bailout following the 2008 banking crisis was a poor substitute for putting people to work through direct government investment (as in New Deal work programs); that such a direction seemed pie in the sky (to continue with the just desserts theme) speaks to the continued rhetorical power of the Right, which as of this writing is now blaming America's financial problems on public-sector workers.

A lot more possibility exists for a spatial fix, if you consider that at least one-third of the world's population is utterly impoverished and, if paid wages, would create markets for goods. But there are political costs to such expansion, quite obviously, and it's unclear that American capitalism and American militarism are on the same page (Harvey 2003). Still, if you think about the 2008 Olympic Games in Beijing, during which companies like Coca-Cola, GE, McDonald's, and Johnson & Johnson had access to the largest barely tapped market in the world, you can see that the strategy has hardly been abandoned. Neoliberals know that the spatial fix is a path out of the economic slump. That's why they call for free trade. But they really have no way to clear the path politically—nor should they, morally speaking.

The only fix to this sort of crisis is a massive devaluation of existing assets (be they factories, homes, currencies, securities, or commodities) that had gained value in the good times through speculation—a purge, that is, after the binge. And that is what has been happening. While all lose, the middle class has lost a huge percent of its wealth to home foreclosures, bank failures, and devalued pension funds, and the poor had no safety net to begin with. So only those with remaining assets stand to recover. Yet even if such massive devaluation may in time provide a new fix, since it will release a set of assets at fire-sale prices that can be put to profitable use, who will be able to purchase these assets? And who will buy the goods that are produced with them? The contradictions are far from resolved. Capitalism appears to be up against its limits.

So, you may ask, what does all of this have to do with obesity? Much, I am going to argue. For along with making the economy thoroughly dependent on (low-cost) consumption and exacerbating inequalities in wealth, neoliberal logics have helped produce many of the food qualities and environmental features associated with obesogenesis. In keeping with a political economy of bulimia, they have also produced opportunities to profit from having created obesity as a problem.

THE POLITICAL ECONOMY OF BULIMIA: MAKING A VIRTUE OF NECESSITY?

As I discussed in chapter 6, the US agriculture economy is entrenched in long-term dynamics that tend toward overproduction, a tendency that has been exacerbated by existing food and agriculture policies. The US food sector, in other words, has its own problem with excess. In *The Omnivore's Dilemma*, Michael Pollan (2006) argues that those crop surpluses end up in our bodies; subsidized crops like corn and soy are most likely to go into the processed foods that have become a mainstay of American diets. In turn, these processed foods may contribute to fatness (although not necessarily in the ways he discusses). But he pretty much leaves it there. My argument is much more expansive. I argue that a much broader set of food and agricultural policies are implicated in fatness—but also thinness, and a host of other health conditions that may not manifest in either direction. The food economy, that is, mirrors the larger economy: it is full of contradictions, some of which are literally embodied. But I take it even a step further, to consider policies not even directly related to food and agriculture, such as taxation, financial regulation, and economic development policies that have created huge disparities between rich and poor. To the extent that socioeconomic status and body size are associated, these policies must somehow be implicated in fatness and thinness. Part of this inverse association between size and class status appears to rest on cheap food and the need that neoliberal policy has created for it.

To begin with the food sector, it is critical to remember that Wal-Mart producer-consumer relationships have their counterparts in food consumption, particularly in the fast-food industry. Mass-produced food was part of the political bargain of the US Fordist period (DuPuis 2001). Yet it was made affordable not only by government agricultural subsidies, but also by the scale economies of industrialized agricultural production and by union wages in nonagricultural production. As discussed earlier, the fast-food industry was at the forefront of attacking wages and thus helped usher in a sharply different social contract from that of Fordism. Unlike Fordism, that is, the fast-food industry has assiduously worked to ratchet down the income and wages of those who work in or for the industry. The industry has been at least as successful as the auto industry, however, in creating a market for its goods. For in a low-wage, low-income economy, people come to depend on cheap goods to make ends meet.

In this light, supersizing, a practice much vilified by food writers, begins to take on a different moral valence. With supersizing, customers are charged a marginal amount extra for receiving several ounces more of, say, a beverage that costs only pennies to produce and pour. The same is true of large portions, the mainstay of the national chain restaurants: the cost of the incremental amount of food served is minor compared to the cost of setting and serving a meal. From the purveyor's perspective, the rationale of supersizing and value meals is that you increase profits by serving more, since the food is cheap and the labor (relatively) expensive. But there is also an inversely related consumer rationale, which is that when real wages are low, in part owing to the practices of the food industry, you need to fill up with the dollars you spend. Is it all that surprising that those with marginal incomes seek out foods that give you more calories for the buck (aside from the pleasure of eating what you want)?

Similar things can be said about ready-to-eat meals and the vilification of convenience. The decline in family wages more broadly has pushed many women into the workforce, and many household providers hold multiple jobs to make ends meet. Having to work several jobs has surely increased the need for fast and convenient food and contributed to the decline of the much-lauded (and perhaps overly romanticized) family meal. Snack foods, heat 'n serve meals, supermarket takeout, and eating on the run are not just "lifestyle choices" or, for that matter, signs of the failure of women to fulfill their familial duty. For many, managing jobs, children, and elderly parents and taking time for the most minimal self-care are real challenges that no amount of cajoling about how we should cook our own meals is likely to solve.

The point, though, is not only to defend those who cannot follow the food gurus. It is to note that these ways of eating are central to the current economy. If anything, fast and convenient food has been a triply good fix for American capitalism. It entails the super-exploitation of the labor force in its production, it provides cheap food to support the low wages of the food and other industries by feeding their low-wage workers, and it absorbs the surpluses of the agricultural economy, soaking up, as it were, the excesses of overproduction to keep the farm sector marginally viable. For that matter, it has also substituted for an adequate social safety net.

Thanks to neoliberal welfare policy, that is, cheap food has also become almost a necessity for those who are food insecure, in contrast to what came before in the form of Keynesianism or embedded liberalism. Keynesian fiscal policy introduced the use of food assistance and other publicly funded safety nets for those with inadequate income to buy what they need. (And remember, food insecurity in the United States results from insufficient income, not insufficient food production.) Beginning in the 1930s, the federal government negotiated the opposing imperatives of keeping farmers in business and feeding the hungry by either directly purchasing food and redistributing it or providing direct payments for those who fell beneath a certain income level (i.e., entitlements). Notwithstanding the dubious nutritional quality of the food that was donated or authorized (in the case of the school meal program) by today's standards, such redistributions did reflect the state's role in mediating incomes for both farmers and the poor (Poppendieck 2010).

Yet at the same time that the fast-food industry was facilitating the spread of the low-wage economy, state-guaranteed entitlement programs were beginning to be dismantled. Having invoked a fictional black welfare queen in his campaign speeches, President Reagan took on the food stamp program almost immediately following his election. He restricted eligibility guidelines and then went after other sorts of direct aid programs. The attack on entitlements continued under President Clinton in his own welfare reform (although championed more visibly by House Speaker Newt Gingrich). Among other things, the Personal Responsibility and Work Opportunity Reconciliation Act of 1996 made both food stamps and WIC subject to even more stringent eligibility guidelines and placed a limit on the amount of time able-bodied adults could receive them. As a result, the number of households receiving government food program assistance decreased at the same time that poverty rates were beginning to rise again (Fitchen 1997). During the same period, the use of the emergency food system (e.g., soup kitchens, food banks, food pantries)—developed primarily through charitable contributions—swelled tremendously, to the extent that many households started to depend on them as a regular source of food (Fitchen 1997; Poppendieck 1998). Completely voluntaristic emergency food assistance was in keeping with calls by both Reagan and the elder Bush to devolve social services to the voluntary sector, the "thousand points of light."

Today, use of the Supplemental Nutritional Assistance Program (SNAP), which replaced food stamps, is on the increase because so many people meet the already raised bar to qualify as in need. Now such assistance is under attack by some nutritionists and foodies because it allows people to buy sodas and junk food. Yet the alternative safety net, food charity, has proven to be a source of low-quality (basically, unwanted) food, too. Consider the handwritten sign I once spotted at the checkout counter of my local Whole Foods supermarket. The sign requested that customers bring in cans of conventional food, for which they would receive the equivalent in 365, the market's private "quality" label. The donated cans would be taken to the county food bank. That sign captured perfectly the limits of food charity as a way to address the problem of food insecurity in America: poor people get the dregs. To be sure, much of the enormous network of food banks, food pantries, and soup kitchens that collect and distribute donated food to those in need relies on the damaged goods of low-cost retailers and the surplus of the government's commodity support programs (Poppendieck 1998). And when people need it most, these programs are least able to deliver, because many who would otherwise donate cannot during hard economic times. For these problems and more, scholars of hunger like Jan Poppendieck have long championed government food assistance, such as the food stamp program, as the most efficient, dignifying, and effective way to provide reasonably nutritious food to people with insufficient income to buy it. Even then, current SNAP benefits are far below what would be necessary to buy fresh meats and fruits and vegetables and whole-grain breads from a high-quality grocery store, much less the farmers market (in 2009, $135 per week for a family of four).

Interestingly, the national school meals program has been one of the few welfare programs to survive the cutbacks of the neoliberal period, in no small part because of the market it provides for the farm sector. Yet, more generalized cutbacks in public education, a consequence of an eroding tax base, have affected this guarantee, as well. Many school districts, no longer able to raise adequate revenue from taxes, turned to fast-food franchises and pouring contracts with soft-drink manufacturers to generate revenue. Many more offered a la carte items alongside school meals to make ends meet. According to the 2000 California High School Fast Food Survey, 95 percent of California school districts were offering a la carte menus from fast-food chains, often in lieu of meals supported by the school meal program. The introduction of fast food went hand in hand with cuts in school service staff, effectively disabling the possibility of serving foods prepared in-house (Poppendieck 2010). Contemporary farm-to-school programs are attempts to redress the nutritional effects of these debilitated school lunches; at the same time, they themselves are uneven, driven by private money and initiative, and have thus far been implemented in few school districts that serve low-income children. For example, one of the first farm-to-school programs was initiated in Santa Monica, with the support of the pop-jazz artist Kenny G, who offered his personal chef for the program's use. The Berkeley program has been mainly supported by the largesse of the Chez Panisse Foundation. These programs also tend to employ volunteers and NGO staff rather than traditional school service workers (Allen and Guthman 2006). In that way they are ironically contributing to the underemployment problem that is the basis of food insecurity. Mostly, though, school districts that have implemented farm-to-school programs using federal meals program money find that the program is inadequate to purchase high-quality ingredients, much less have them tastily prepared.

In other words, it is not only that the junk food that putatively causes obesity is subsidized and cheap; it is also that existing entitlement programs and wages are inadequate to ensure the affordability of the healthy food that is so lauded. As an important aside, it is worth noting that many people involved in the alternative-food movement are quite skeptical of food assistance, favoring instead more entrepreneurial means to deal with hunger (Allen 1999). In 2004–5, my colleagues and I conducted a study to understand to what extent alternative-food institutions, such as farmers markets and CSAs, were trying to address issues of food security (Guthman, Morris, and Allen 2006). Although managers of these institutions generally supported the idea of improving the affordability of the food they provide, most felt that these institutions existed to support farmers first, so prices should be set accordingly. Some were quite antagonistic to customers who used food assistance. I remain haunted by a CSA manager, not atypical, who said, "I'm not sure that I agree that subsidy is the best route. In my experience, the subsidy customers are the least committed/reliable."

Many of the features associated with the obesogenic built environment can be traced back to neoliberal economic policy, as well. Tax rollbacks certainly helped build much of what is associated with the foodscapes of national fast-food chain strip malls, big-box store malls, and even food deserts. Specifically, localities starved for tax revenue encouraged such retail development to generate sales tax revenue, with the effects of California's Proposition 13 providing the example par excellence (Schrag 1998). The rollback of both commercial and residential property taxes to 1976 assessments (with 2 percent per year limitations on increases unless property changes hands) spurred many cities to welcome strip malls and discount centers. Although much residential property has subsequently been turned over and reassessed (with one unintended consequence being that neighbors can have vastly unequal tax assessments), commercial property, including former farmland, has hardly changed hands at all. In addition, many of these strips were built on the outskirts of town where land was cheap, making it necessary to use automobiles to reach them and more generally contributing to urban sprawl (Schlosser 2001). Building these suburbs on cheap former farmland is in some sense a substitute for the affordable housing that might have stayed in urban areas with capital for renovation, the continuance of the Department of Housing and Urban Development, and some curbs on gentrification. The flip side of this kind of retail-oriented economic development was the severe disinvestment that created food deserts, which are largely attributable to the weak buying power of poor urban residents, especially as job training, welfare, and other entitlement programs have been cut in the neoliberal era (Massey and Denton 1998). Notwithstanding the complex ways that class matters in negotiating daily food practices, these "obesogenic environments," in other words, are themselves a result of neoliberal policy.

Yet, it is the failure of environmental and food health and safety regulation that is most directly traceable back to neoliberal policy and forward to obesity. A key objective of neoliberalization was to remove or disable regulations seen as unfriendly to business. Accordingly, regulation of agricultural chemicals especially was put on hold, just a decade after the EPA had been established. It wasn't that the Environmental Protection Act was repealed. Rather, the EPA slowed down and in some cases stopped review of potentially toxic chemicals (not to mention endocrine disrupters), and agency mandates turned to nonenforcement of existing prohibitions. And the FDA became an utter patsy in preventing food substances of questionable safety and necessity from being put on the market.

In short, neoliberal policies may not have solved the problem of profitability for the economy as a whole, but in that endeavor they seem to have greatly contributed to aspects of the built environment and the quality of food that many believe contribute to obesity. By the same token, let us not forget that the obesity epidemic, and its tendency to dignify obsessions that equate thinness and beauty, *is* hugely profitable. It has proved a boon to a $100 billion per year weight-loss industry (by some estimates) that distributes specialized products and services, alongside the money made on bariatric and cosmetic surgery. Television shows like *The Biggest Loser*, sponsored by purveyors of diet foods, fitness centers, and pharmaceuticals, contribute to the false idea that diets work in the long term, and thereby increase the market for such goods and services. Jenny Craig and Weight Watchers frozen dinners, the thousands of diet books, and pay-as-you-go group weight-loss therapy all demonstrate that diets can be sold and bought, and that weight loss itself is a commodity (Austin 1999; Fine 1998; Fraser 1998).

For that matter, the pharmaceutical industry has much to gain by hyping an obesity epidemic, and, in fact, the research-oriented International Obesity Task Force receives much of its funding from the pharmaceutical industry (Campos et al. 2006; Oliver 2006; Saguy and Riley 2005). It appears that the industry is banking on the hope that people will learn, once again, that diets don't work and "lifestyle changes" aren't easy to make, and when one of these companies finally comes up with the magic bullet, profits will be good, at least for a while. In the meantime, industry involvement in setting and lowering thresholds of "at-risk" levels for glucose, cholesterol, and other obesity-associated biomarkers also sells drugs (Angell 2005). Functional and other "health" foods must thus be seen through this lens, too. Functional foods isolate and include specific nutrients and substances believed to promote health, whether vitamin C, antioxidants, or probiotics, even if marketed as alternatives (Scrinis 2008). Whole Foods, a major purveyor of more natural-sounding functional foods, has much to gain as an antidote to cheap food. Again, organics and even "local" food are commodified remedies to obesity, albeit indirectly so.

That producing and selling junk food gives rise to all sorts of investment potential for those seeking to produce and sell solutions to its effects instantiates a political economy of bulimia, as it were. It also puts a dent in the rhetoric of obesity alarmists and public health professionals who urge us to simply follow the money to determine where blame must lie. It is true that the big players in the food industry—from Tyson to Coca-Cola to Jack in the Box—have profited tremendously from selling poor-quality food, but they are not the only ones. If you're really going to follow the money, you might find yourself taking a long, circuitous journey through the entire economy. And you might also discover how central bodies have become to making and resolving capitalism's crises.

BINGING AND PURGING: THE BODY AS SPATIAL FIX

Over the course of capitalism's history, spatial fixes have been politically costly. They have given rise to deserved resistance, to which many of the wars of the last two hundred years can be attributed. They are rife with environmental destruction, as well, whether the killing of the buffalo to make way for the railroad in North America, or burning of the rainforest to make pasture in the Amazon. Although environmental destruction can and does lead to political resistance, it can and does also provide opportunities for capitalism, whether by selling solar panels, recycled paper, or carbon offsets. Still, the tendency for capitalism to destroy its own conditions for reproduction is a second limit to capitalism, one theorized by another noted Marxian scholar, James O'Connor (1989). O'Connor agreed with Harvey that perpetual crises of overaccumulation constitute the first contradiction of capitalism. Unlike Harvey, though, he shared with environmentalists the notion of ecological limits to growth, limits that may manifest as environmental degradation or resource depletion. Therefore, what he called the second contradiction results directly from endless efforts to resolve the first. The specter of continued global climate change may be the most extraordinary example of his second contradiction, a consequence of a spatial fix writ large that seriously compromises the possibilities for capitalist expansion, with its fundamental dependencies on fossil fuels and fresh water (and yet, like obesity, can't be thoroughly understood without a set of measurements and models that have shaped how we know the problem).

These grand (and depressing) contradictions most define the world we live in, and food and body issues seem to exist on another scale of analysis and seem comparatively humble as social problems. I think, though, they are all of a piece. That is because, along with the soils, seas, and air, bodies (both human and animal) are absorbing much of capitalism's excesses. That the fixes are more intensive than expansive and more "in here" than "out there" is perhaps what allows them to be treated as personal concerns rather than political ones. Still, environmental-human interactions are most certainly altering body ecologies, possibly in ways that undermine future profit opportunities.

To the extent that people eat more than they did in previous generations, that is one of the more prosaic ways in which the body is providing a spatial fix. (Again, there is no doubt that people are bigger than they used to be, although whether and how that comes from eating more is somewhat debatable.) Still, markets for food cannot be infinitely expansive because there are limits to how much food any one person can eat, certainly at a sitting and possibly over time. We don't know precisely what those limits are, but we know they exist. This is what economists refer to as the problem of inelastic demand (or Engel's Law), which I touched on earlier.

Remarkably, some of capitalism's efforts to create purchasable solutions to the problems it generates (both materially and discursively) work against those limits. In the case of obesity, this would include the design of food products that do not act like food. Products such as Simplesse, the substance used as fat in low-fat ice cream, or Splenda, the low-calorie sugar substitute, break right through the problem of inelastic demand. The commodity simply passes through—enabling the product to be consumed with no weight-gaining effect. For that matter, some of the new pharmaceuticals (e.g., Xenical) and nutritional supplements designed to reduce the body's absorption of fat (along with essential vitamins and minerals) fulfill a similar function. By thwarting the body's metabolizing functions, these products allow markets, but not necessarily waistlines, to expand, albeit with less than salubrious side effects.

The degree to which people eat more foods of questionably quality provides another fix. Ingesting nutritionally vacuous—or deleterious foods—that exist to solve problems of profitability for the food industry puts the ecological burden on the body, as does inhaling fouled air or drinking fouled water. In effect, individual bodies are absorbing the so-called *externalities* of production processes, so the food companies most definitely do not have to pay the full cost of doing business. And then bodies became a site for commodifiable cures to the conditions and illnesses created through these foods and exposures. Despite the rhetoric about the burden of health care costs, let us not forget that in a for-profit health care system, illness also creates profit-making opportunities, with pharmaceuticals at the leading edge of raising health care costs (Angell 2005). This is something the 2010 health care legislation has not fundamentally altered.

Aside from assisting in the political economy of bulimia, what does this suggest about the role of the human body in capitalism today? In 1995, the science historian Donna Haraway declared that the body has become an accumulation strategy in the deepest sense (Harvey and Haraway 1995: 511). By this she meant much more than the shallow observation that an increasing number of commodities are produced and sold to enhance bodies. She even meant more than the Marxian sense that "bodies" are central to capitalism in their role as both laborers and purchasers of goods and services (Harvey 1998). Rather, she was saying that bodies are now endemic to capital flows in ways beyond their role as human subjects who work and shop. To be sure, as bodies are increasingly used for drug transportation, mined for organs, sperms, eggs, and genetic material, rented out for human reproduction and other biomedical uses, and bought and sold in various trades, it is clear that bodies are involved in capitalism in ways that go significantly beyond the processes of producing and consuming commodities in market exchange.

So, in arguing that the body is part of the spatial fix, I am suggesting something along the same lines: that the body is wrapped up in the material processes of capitalism quite apart from the "decisions" that human subjects make around production and reproduction. Rather, bodies as material entities are literally absorbing the conditions and externalities of production and consumption. Of course in some respects there's nothing new here. Bodies have always been affected by both their working conditions and their consumption practices, which can manifest as strengthening, wasting, hunching, fattening, and so forth. What is new, then, is the convergence of a barely regulated economy that celebrates profit over all other notions of the public good with seemingly endless technological and biomedical possibilities for fixes. Bodies become part of what makes new rounds of accumulation possible. At some point, though, bodies can't absorb any more of capitalism's problems than can geographic expansion. The illnesses and conditions that arise, in their capacity as fixes for capitalism, suggest an internal limit to capitalism—in a way that seriously challenges ideas that these illness are the result of personal lifestyle choices.

This raises the question of where those limits lie. Following O'Connor, I argue that in a theoretical sense the limits are reached when capitalism begins to destroy its own conditions for production. How can this be ascertained with conditions, like obesity, that are contested as illnesses? Limits cannot be defined by what pleases the eye—flab or no flab—and part of what I have sought to show is that thin bodies also absorb these externalities of production. Nevertheless, when bodies start producing their own fat cells irrespective of what is eaten, or are no longer able to metabolize sugars into energy, then that's a limit. When bodies do not produce their own reproductive organs, then that's most definitely a limit. It is also a limit when, under the pressure of the "obesity epidemic," people routinely use laxatives or induce vomiting, thereby upsetting the body's acid-base balance and damaging tissue (Rome and Ammerman 2003)—or, most obviously, when they starve themselves to death. It must also be a limit when the substances and procedures designed to "fix" obesity create digestive disorders, anal leakage, and inability to absorb crucial vitamins and minerals. If all of these latter problems occur because of fear of obesity, then the problem is being conceptualized in the wrong way. There really are limits to what responsible individuals can do faced with a polity that allows food produced with toxic materials or nutritionally vacuous ingredients to be sold in the interest of economic growth and then blames people for eating it or, in the case of endocrine-disrupting chemicals, even breathing them.

CLASS AND THE CULTURAL ECONOMY OF BULIMIA

And yet, that is precisely what we are being asked to do, to resolve an impossible contradiction. For the political economy of bulimia I have just described is supported by a culture of bulimia. On the one hand, we're supposed to keep the economy afloat by consuming and not interfering with the business of business. To be sure, with so much of today's economy based on retail, we have also been led to believe that shopping is good for the nation, to help prop up a fragile capitalism. Let's not forget what Bush stated on the eve of going to war in Iraq: Keep shopping. To argue from the obverse, can there be any doubt that neoliberalism was also a response to the "consume less" ideas that circulated in the 1970s crisis period? "Buy less" is a huge threat to capitalist growth, which is why contemporary capitalism crucially depends on a culture and ideology of consumerism (Sklair 1995: 23). On the other hand, we're supposed to exercise self-control and restraint and not tax our health care system through diet-related illnesses, notwithstanding that our health care system also employs people and contributes to the economy.

Given the accentuation of class disparities much in sync with body size disparities, you would think that everyone might be on at least equivalent moral footing in working out this contradiction. As it happens, though, poor and barely middle-class people have not only been made poorer but also morally punished for their tendency to "overconsume"—and overextend their credit. They are the ones who, in wallet and body, are accused of not being able to control their impulses and failing to make good decisions, although those who are not fat are punished far less. Should fat people be the subject of such moral outrage in the wake of this thirty-year experiment in feeding the rich?

Meanwhile, relatively privileged people have been credited with exalted consumption choices that putatively lead to thinness and, for those attracted to alternative food, environmental sustainability. And those who have fared best in the neoliberal economy—those who are the main beneficiaries of neoliberal capitalism that others' borrowing and consumption habits have kept afloat—have a broad range of ways to resolve the contradiction of spending more and showing less. They can buy houses with nearby walking trails, hire personal trainers, spend hours exercising (especially if they are stay-at-home spouses), and eat at upscale restaurants where the presentation and taste of the food is more important than satiety. They may also be able to afford plastic surgery and other shortcuts to achieving thinness. It is also possible that their chemical body burdens (in regard to potential endocrinal effects) are also lower, given where they live and what food they buy. In fact, their options for resolving the political economy of bulimia may be much less deleterious to health than the options available to those who are stuck with both cheap "fattening" food and cheap "diet" food, and thus are most likely exposed to far more obesogenic substances. The degree of internalization of the spatial fix is therefore another way that class disparities become manifest.

The unkindest cut, then, is that because thinness has been so associated with self-efficacy and control and even achievement, essentially those who are thin and rich are doubly rewarded, not only for having made off with much of the wealth but also for having appeared to earn it by displaying it bodily. This sheds a whole new light on the old quip that you can't be too rich or too thin.

CHAPTER 9

Conclusion

What's on the Menu?

THE OBAMAS' GARDEN

Upon assuming the role of First Lady in 2009, one of the first things Michelle Obama did was to plant an organic garden on the White House lawn. This was not too long after Michael Pollan (2008a) had written his open letter to the president-elect, whom he dubbed farmer-in-chief. The letter provided a long list of recommendations for food and farming policy reform to reduce the use of fossil fuels and wean the US food system off the logic of cheapness.[1] For this, Pollan was himself informally crowned farmer-in-chief, and a huge swell of grassroots support arose to name him secretary of (food and) agriculture. The White House must have been listening. After all, it was one of Pollan's recommendations to "tear out five prime south-facing acres of the White House lawn and plant in their place an organic fruit and vegetable garden."

The garden wasn't without its critics. The Mid America CropLife Association, which represents chemical-agribusiness interests, sent an angry letter to the White House claiming that only conventional agriculture can feed the world. For the most part, though, the garden encountered little resistance and was widely heralded, especially by the alternative-food movement. If nothing else, this demonstrates the huge success of the organic farming and gardening movement in communicating its *ideas*, which used to sit on the countercultural margins, to a much wider audience. To wit, as Pollan also pointed out in the same letter, there is room for food and farming across the political spectrum. "Reforming the food system is not inherently a right-or-left issue: for every Whole Foods shopper with roots in the counterculture you can find a family of evangelicals intent on taking control of its family dinner and diet back from the fast-food industry—the culinary equivalent of home schooling. . . . There is also a strong libertarian component to the sun-food agenda, which seeks to free small producers from the burden of government regulation in order to stoke rural innovation. And what is a higher 'family value,' after all, than making time to sit down every night to a shared meal?" Therein lies the problem: an approach that appeals to all parts of the political spectrum cannot challenge the political-economic forces that are producing cheap, toxic, and junky food—and making some people dependent on it.

Since the Obamas planted their organic garden, the rest of the food and agriculture agenda has remained the same, more or less. For example, the Obama administration, under the guidance of the EPA and the USDA, has been pushing the use of coal waste containing gypsum (a form of calcium) on fields, despite its containing traces of lead, mercury, and arsenic; Obama has been championing immigration reform, which includes paths to citizenship but also tighter border controls, which will continue making the undocumented workers who slip through easily exploitable (see chapter 6); and he has already signed into law a reduction in food assistance to go into effect in 2014. In December 2010, he signed a bill extending the Bush tax cuts, exacerbating the nation's increasing economic inequality. This is not an argument with gradualism—it is painfully evident that the Obama administration has had to seriously tamp down expectations in view of an intransigent and increasingly virulent Right. And it's not even necessarily about scale, that this small garden is a drop in the bucket amid the vast farms and factories that produce cheap food. There is definitely something to be said for creating a highly visible model. My concern, rather, is the absence in the policy agenda of any move that would begin to undermine a food (and industrial) system that simultaneously brings hunger, danger, and unremittingly undercompensated toil; it's the absence from public discussions of acknowledgment that our food system is part of a political economy that systematically produces inequality; and it's the reluctance of much of the alternative-food movement to take on the big fights, instead promulgating the notion that education will change how people eat—and thus transform the food system. Obama's garden, in other words, throws into sharp relief the limitations of alternative food as a change strategy.

Yet, it is the appeals to obesity to which I draw your attention. Naturally, in his open letter Pollan also discussed the health costs and dangers of type 2 diabetes and obesity, which he said could be avoided with changes in diet and lifestyle. In promoting the garden, Mrs. Obama was quick to point out that it would not just "provide food for the first family's meals and formal dinners; its most important role will be to educate children about healthful, locally grown fruit and vegetables at a time when obesity and diabetes have become a national concern" (Burros 2009). How is local, organic, and seasonal garden-grown food a tenable solution to obesity?

In the face of insurmountable evidence that traditional dieting rarely achieves lasting results, exposing people to attractive fresh food, like the kind found at farmers markets and in gardens, does seem a kinder, gentler approach. Even *The Biggest Loser*, a medium for advertising all manner of commodified diet food, has not edited out one of the trainers' recommendations to eat more *organic* vegetables. At one level, it's hard to take issue with this recommendation. After all, who could be against fresh, visually appealing vegetables? And such an approach certainly couldn't hurt, so it seems.

Nevertheless, in urging people to make better "choices," those who advocate for fresh, organic, and local produce as a means of weight loss are not wholly unlike those who want to combat global warming by getting consumers to swap their incandescent light bulbs for fluorescent ones. (Incidentally, buying fresh, local, organic foods at farmers markets roughly covers five different suggestions listed in the top fifty things you can do to stop global warming as listed at http://globalwarming-facts.info/50-tips.html.) These suggestions are based on a singular hegemonic understanding of the cause of the problem: calories and carbon dioxide emissions, which to some degree forecloses efforts to search for other causes (and, remarkably, the proposed solutions to both obesity and global warming have to do with energy). They educe individual, consumerist solutions based on those singular causes, which tends to neglect the sources of the problem in production and lets off the hook those most responsible for the problem (corporate bad actors and policy makers). And they don't consider the consequences of defining problems and solutions in ways that may be damaging to those most vulnerable to the problem (whether resource-poor subsistence producers or very fat people).

In these ways, the current conversation about obesity and good food shares many characteristics of environmental orthodoxies (such as global warming), in which taken-for-granted assumptions are built into explanations and solutions, and urgency to do *something* trumps careful scientific examination (Forsyth 2003: 37–38). Forsyth emphatically does not deny that environmental problems such as global warming exist. Rather, he argues that conventional ways of understanding such problems can be "intellectually constraining in that they delimit the universe of further scientific inquiry, political discourse, and possibly policy options" (originally in Jasanoff and Wynne 1998: 5). As antidote, he proposes what he calls a critical political ecology approach that pays attention to (a) how existing framings shape scientific understandings of the problem; (b) how those framings foreclose or leave out other explanations; and (c) the social consequences of the framings. Looking beyond the standard explanations does not necessarily reveal other certain explanations or falsify myths, he argues, but it can illuminate problems in new and meaningful ways.

BACK TO THE PROBLEM

This critical political ecology approach is what I have tried to take in this book. The orthodoxies I have examined are about obesity and alternative food separately and as they articulate in efforts to address obesity as a health problem. My goal has not been to deny the increase in obesity prevalence, the idea that obesity *can* cause illness, that certain environments lack access to the good life, or that the existing food system produces nutritionally suspect food (quite the reverse). Instead, it has been to challenge the assumptions along various links of the explanatory chain—and particularly at the point at which these two discourses intersect. I have done this in the interest of *opening up the conversation* to other ideas, contending not only that current rhetorical and practical efforts may be ineffective but also that they may do harm in the name of "doing good." With that in mind, let me now review and cross-fertilize the key concerns I have raised, which, following Forsyth, I roughly categorize as representational, causal, and consequential.

There is little question that the significant increase in size between 1980 and the early 2000s is worthy of explanation, keeping in mind that fatness itself is not new. Yet, the ways in which this phenomenon has been measured and represented can obscure as much as they tell. First, as an indicator of obesity, high BMI is crude and doesn't adequately represent aspects of adiposity that may be more or less detrimental to health—for example, differences between subcutaneous and visceral adiposity. Second, the particular ways of categorizing BMI values into definitive ranges of normal, overweight, and obese inflects some of these changes with more drama than they perhaps warrant. Third, because they rely on conventions of averaging to define normal phenotype, they tend to confuse the normal with the normative, "what is" with "what ought to be." The reliance on averages is particularly odd, given that BMIs in the "overweight" range are actually the new normal.

Nor do these BMI ranges match up neatly to health outcomes. Not only is a much broader range of BMI values than those in the "normal" range associated with relatively low risk for mortality; the use of probabilistic risk factors is also a crude and often confusing way to understand and represent how particular body morphologies (i.e., shapes) may lead to disease. One reason is that any given disease or risk factor is associated with a multiplicity of others, and the direction of causality is often indeterminable. Obesity and type 2 diabetes, for example, are risk factors for each other, poverty is a risk factor for both, and obesity is also a risk factor for poverty. It is certainly reasonable to think that . poverty leads people to eat too much low-quality food, and that causes obesity, which then causes diabetes-related death. But it is also plausible that poverty presents an obstacle in seeking preventative health care—or, more likely, is nested in a host of complicating factors that affect health outcomes. It is also possible that toxic exposures are causing both obesity and type 2 diabetes, with each a symptom of the other. The point is that the relevant psychological, economic, social, cultural, biological, and ecological factors are inextricably coconstitutive, and risk factors appear a highly reductive way to represent a problem that is very difficult to sort out. Insofar as the medical costs of treating obesity also incorporate such risk factors in the calculations (as attributable fractions), the idea that obesity is a cost to the nation is sketchy. Rarely do we hear that poverty is a huge cost to the nation. And, of course, rarely do we hear about the calculations of health care costs related to efforts to be thin.

The heart of the representational problem, then, is reliance on epidemiology as a basis of health knowledge and diagnosis. As "surveillance medicine," detached from actual bodies, epidemiology cannot take the place of clinical medicine and laboratory science in determining and treating what exactly is pathological, for which obesity may be a very weak proxy. Although it may be true that the tools of epidemiology are the best available for noting trends in population-level public health, they should nonetheless be understood for what they are and what they can and cannot do.

Moving into the questions about obesity's causes, the period of growth in BMI has seen enormous nutritional changes. To the degree that rising BMIs reflect nutritional changes, at least some of these are for the better. Although many Americans are food insecure, these days few truly go hungry. Many good foods have been made more available, such as fresh fruits and vegetables, and foods that have made people taller, such as milk, seem to generate far less concern than those that have putatively made us fatter, notwithstanding the increasing prevalence of lactose intolerance. Nevertheless, we shouldn't assume that differences in nutritional intake solely explain body size difference along class, race, and gender lines. The assumption that obesity inheres to people with low socioeconomic status because they lack income to buy healthy food, live in food-insecure environments, or are beset with stress-eating and self-medication is belied by data that show little difference in caloric intake among different income groups. In general, steadfast loyalty to a nutritional explanation, via the energy balance model, neglects other possible explanations that may lie in the enormous environmental changes that occurred just in advance of the period when mean BMI began to creep upward. Furthermore, aspects of the increase in size such as the increase in extreme obesity are not well explained by the energy balance model. The increase in infant obesity is most definitely not. Some of these shifts in body size could well have resulted from exposures to endocrine-disrupting chemicals and food ingredients (both related to class but not through the vehicle of "consumer choice") that affect body size in ways other than through caloric intake and expenditure. Conversely, the emphasis on obesity tends to occlude the many diseases and conditions associated with poor nutrition and toxic exposures that don't happen to manifest in fatness.

The discourse of obesity has articulated with efforts to redirect blame for poor health toward certain built environments instead of those who live in them. Pointing out the inequities in access to nutritious food and pleasant outdoor environments is laudable. Nevertheless, since the food side of the obesogenic environment thesis, with its emphasis on the ubiquity of cheap, fattening food, appears to apply to just about all food environments in the United States, it paradoxically provides support to those who say that obesity results from personal choices. For, if some people remain thin amidst the plenty, they presumably are more effective in mediating these environments. More fundamentally, the thesis assumes the energy balance model of obesity causation. Again, to the extent that obesity prevalence does cluster geographically, it could also be a consequence of place-specific toxic exposures or simply that people of the same race and class also tend to cluster geographically.

Even accepting the energy balance model, the obesogenic environment thesis tends to ignore how inequalities in income, employment, and wealth, as well as regressive tax policy (such as reliance on sales tax, which causes the poor to bear a relatively larger portion of the tax burden than a progressive income tax does), give rise to the character of these environments. To be sure, in addition to the many uncertainties and absences in these discourses, the current conversation about obesity and food is remarkably indifferent to the dynamics of capitalism and the long-term production of inequality—and how urban environments reflect the buying and investment power of people who inhabit them. In that way, the current conversation is very much in the vein of what Robbins calls "apolitical ecologies," in which explanations of ecological problems (and obesity *is* that) focus far too much on individual behavior and choices and far too little on the broader political and economic context in which choices are made. This is particularly clear in the discussions of the food system.

To the extent that food system activists focus on policy, they attribute far too much to the role of commodity subsidies and too little to the broader geopolitical concerns and political-economic conditions that have encouraged overproduction of commodities and compelled food processors and manufacturers to cut costs to compete. Additionally, in their desire to support small, agrarian producers, they have almost entirely neglected that the rest of the food system has been a source of tremendous inequality. American agriculture was built on racialized land and labor relationships—many whites received land nearly free, while others were prohibited, discouraged, or disenfranchised from owning land, and worked as slaves, sharecroppers, indentured servants, or undocumented workers, depending on migration histories and the particular racial character in which they were slotted. Since the legacies of unequal access to land and high-paying jobs are far from erased, neglecting the issue of income—and thus whether different groups even have a choice to buy the kind of food they want—is shameful. Eschewing the use of regulatory "sticks" in ways that might curtail the use of some of the worst materials and practices in agriculture and other industrial production is shameful, too.

Altogether, much of the current conversation about obesity and good food is an expression of the ideology of healthism. Healthism makes personal health attainment the highest goal, sees poor health outcomes as a result of behaviors, and conflates personal practices of self-care with empowerment and good citizenship. Recall that healthism is itself a reflection of neoliberal norms of governance, since it concedes the rollback of public-sector responsibility for supporting and protecting the health of all and instead places responsibility on individuals for their own health outcomes. In doing so, healthism tends to neglect—or write off—those without the means or the desire to share in these norms. The way healthism filters both understanding of obesity and conceptualizing of food system transformation has consequences—consequences that can work against social justice and well-being.

First, no matter how worthy the intentions behind it, obesity talk makes fat people a problem and renews the stigma of a population that has had to endure much of it. Healthism gives additional cover for expressing distaste for fat bodies. Swipes at obesity, especially coming from those who have never been subject to such scrutiny or objectification, or the pain and frustration of weight loss, are insensitive at best and seriously damaging at worse. The intense social scolding of fat people (or people who believe themselves too fat) can be costly, too, and can work at cross-purposes to health and well-being. Besides the fact that many fat people are reticent to seek care for fear of embarrassment, scolding, or self-doubt, blaming fat people for health care costs is leading to the denial of health care in the name of health. To the extent that healthism reinforces fat discrimination in jobs, education, and access to health care, it can worsen inequality, adding to ways in which socioeconomic status can be an outcome of size as well as a cause of it.

Second, many of the approaches to redressing obesity and improving the food system exacerbate racial and class inequalities, regardless of body size. This is most obvious with the obesogenic environment thesis, which takes healthism's notion of the good life and projects particular ideals and aesthetics onto the built environment. Such accounts do not address the political-economic circumstances that make some places desirable and allow disinvestment in others. Not only are the ideal, leptogenic environments financially unattainable to most; disparaging certain types of neighborhoods as "obesogenic" does little for those who live in them, including many working-class whites, since such disparagement could contribute to more devaluation. Conversely, trying to solve the problem by making obesogenic places more like wealthy, leptogenic places can push poor people out through gentrification.

Third, the unrelenting emphasis on the putatively tight relationship between calories and adiposity misses serious dangers in food, including those that don't manifest as fatness. The inattention thus far to environmental obesogens is the most telling of all. While there is much discussion about the injustice in access to fresh fruits and vegetables, food movements continue to pay relatively little attention to the daily dousing of pesticides in fields and agricultural communities, which lead to cancer and birth defects, and now, it appears, to fatness (Harrison 2008b). While there is much talk about supersizing and other ways food marketers get people to eat more, there is much less discussion of the ways that cheap food, including many diet foods, alter physiological processes in other potentially debilitating ways. That foods which are nutrient-depleting, cancer-causing, or just hard on the body are promoted for weight loss suggests once more that aesthetic displeasure with fat is driving much of the conversation and even affecting political priorities. I don't say this lightly. Studies have shown that people would rather have heart disease, be legally blind, or have a leg amputated than be fat (Puhl and Brownell 2001). We know that people smoke cancer-causing cigarettes to avoid getting fat.

Finally, the implicit linking of good food, good bodies, and political activism allows those who are already privileged to achieve even higher status by virtue of their bodies and food-purchasing habits. Fat stigmatization neces-sarily accords higher status to those who are not fat (Julier 2008). Bolstered by the ideology of healthism, which suggests a lack of personal responsibility and knowledge among the fat, those who are not fat are positioned as more responsible and knowing, regardless of what, if anything, they do to be thin (LeBesco 2004). Owing to its abiding association with upscale eating, organic, local food also accords higher status to those who buy and eat it (Guthman 2003). With the appearance of alternative-food participation as the paradig-matic way to transform the food system, and food transformation as the social movement issue of the day, eating well (and having a thin body) begins to be equated with creating positive social change. In effect, the alternative-food movement attaches political citizenship and ethics to personal investments in body and health. Those who have already done well in wallet and body get to feel as though they've done even more. It is this most self-congratulatory aspect of the alternative-food movement that is perhaps most consequential for social justice, since it limits what is put on the table politically.

WHAT TO PUT ON THE TABLE

Precisely in this vein, I ask you, the reader, to reconsider where the problem lies. We have a political economy that produces and makes available cheap food and goods, underpays people, and urges them to buy this food and these goods to keep the economy afloat—and then a culture that blames them for consum-ing this food and these goods after all. A large part of this political economy involves barely regulated food, chemical, and pharmaceutical industries that produce materials not all of which are willingly ingested, inhaled, or absorbed but which modify our bodies in ways we barely understand.

And the broadest social force against these, the alternative-food movement, has focused on providing good food and has nearly abandoned changing the regulatory environment to reduce toxic exposures. Nor has it ever really engaged with issues of wages and entitlements so that all people can afford to eat well. To the contrary, the influence of healthism has helped justify individualistic approaches to food system change, and even allowed food injustice to be defined merely as unequal access to high-quality food rather than also including unequal incomes in food work and unequal exposure to pesticides.

That the more radical food justice movement (at least in rhetoric) addresses the access problem but for the most part steers clear of labor and to some extent income issues speaks to a self-perpetuating narrowing of political possibility. Precisely because social movement possibilities are so constrained by neoliberal logics of the market, many dedicated activists barely see other ways forward besides educating people to the qualities of food and bringing good food to low-income people in acts of charity or through nonprofit subsidies and in the name of health and empowerment. The charitable act of bringing good food to others is in no way comparable to transforming the increased class disparities that neoliberal capitalism has produced. To be sure, having come into being in a neoliberal context, the current trend in food activism writ large tends to reflect and uphold neoliberal forms of governance, despite the fact that the particular confluence of problems, in many (but not all) ways, stems from neoliberal economic policy. Accordingly, the alternative-food movement puts a great deal of emphasis on the market rather than the state, on consumption rather than production, and on individual health rather than social justice. And yet, *the current policy environment is a result of political choices, not consumption choices. Therefore, to make different political choices requires much more attention to the broader injustices that the cheap food dilemma rests on and perhaps less attention to what's on the menu.* We cannot change the world one meal at a time.

As for the problem of obesity, it needs rethinking both medically and discursively, especially given the effect of a barely regulated food system on the body. We should give a rest to the idea that "something must be done" to reverse trends in obesity per se. At the very least, we need to consider a broader range of body sizes as nonpathological and to distinguish what's pathological from what's simply not normal (as in average). More to the point, we need to recognize that, even when obesity is pathological, efforts to fix it at the individual level may do more harm to health and well-being than letting it be. A harm-reduction perspective may be in order, which would entail refraining from disciplining people whose health outcomes are not easily determinable by their size and exercising more compassion for those whose condition cannot be cured. More fundamentally, then, we need to understand that, like the ecologies affected by global warming, bodily ecologies are indeed being remade as a result of unregulated capitalism in ways that we don't entirely know or understand. But, also like global warming, the issue is not the fact that we are getting bigger—things change—but what it means for those most likely to be adversely affected by it.

Given the profits that have been made on the binge and purge economy and the inattention to regulating body-changing pollution, it is clear that we must turn away from the current obsession with individual consumption habits and body sizes and engage more deeply with policy. Rather than complicity in market logics, we need to harness this exploding interest in food and use the power of public politics to change food systems. Given the competing imperatives of food production—to support producers and to feed consumers—we need to admit to the need for subsidies, but subsidies of a different kind: subsidies that allow farmers to grow in the most ecologically and socially responsible ways without having to overtax the environment; subsidies that allow all eaters to buy what they want and need. And we need to remove the subsidies of a free regulatory ride. The "free market" will not do.

To their credit, some organizations in food movements have already begun this shift. The discussions that led up to the 2008 farm bill saw unprecedented participation from this movement, which both critiqued the commodity subsidy programs and demanded more programs that encourage fresh fruit and vegetable production, soil conservation practices, and support for low-resource farmers. Community food security activists have redoubled their efforts to expand entitlement support. And those in the nutrition and public health communities have had a modicum of success in banning sodas from public schools and discouraging the use of trans fats through either local ordinances or more generalized shaming. These are all places to start, although policies must be carefully crafted to change the practices of the producers rather than tax and scold people who can least afford it.

Still, in my view, policy must go to an even deeper place. I have tried to show that the availability of cheap food is a deeply structural problem having to do with the logics of capitalism that the neoliberal "fix" has worsened and made our bodies be the site for that fix. The systematic production of inequality has taken place not only through farm and food policy but also through trade, labor, immigration, health care, economic development, taxation, and financial policy—in other words, just about all policies that have kept American capitalism (barely) afloat. While some in the alternative-food movement have been content to use capitalism to change food, others are returning to the idea of using food, the most essential of human needs, to change capitalism. They are rejecting the limited tools of the market and thinking about other ways in which food issues can galvanize social movements for global justice—because, ultimately, what needs to be put on the table is not only fresh fruits and vegetables (and, really, whatever you want to eat), but capitalism.

NOTES

2. HOW DO WE KNOW OBESITY IS A PROBLEM?

1. Even then, the strength of association alone is not a good test. Many spurious correlations are based on "strength." In *Method in Social Science*, Sayer (1992) illustrates the fallacy of regularity with an old joke. A guy goes to the bar on several different nights and orders several shots of a different grain alcohol mixed with soda each time. Aching with hangover each morning, he concludes that his hangovers must come from the soda. As Sayer explains, not knowing the real causal agent (the alcohol) is the problem here, and associations do not always demonstrate the real causal agent.

3. WHOSE PROBLEM IS OBESITY?

1. UCSC's Institutional Review Board for research on human subjects approved the use of student journals on condition that no one in the class but the author him- or herself could identify the author of any given quotation, a condition with which I wholeheartedly agreed. In keeping with this condition, I opted not to track any identifying information except for gender (which I identify here as *f* or *m*).

2. By *enrolled in*, I am referring to the concept of interpellation articulated by the Marxian philosopher Louis Althusser (1971) who theorized how some people come to be associated with a set of ideas and identities and call them their own. Althusser's now-classic illustration of the process of interpellation is the moment of a policeman calling "hey you" to someone. Anyone who pays attention to the policeman is in effect ceding that he or she is being hailed, whereas those who ignore the policeman at that moment are not implicated in the policeman's call. Althusser's point is that subjects are in some sense recruited into particular ideological constructs, and when they turn to them they are giving recognition that they belong. As such, these constructs are

not universal, and those outside of particular race/class/gender formations may not find them legible at all. It's more like: if the shoe fits, wear it.

3. In this way, responses to the course were a good illustration of Michel Foucault's (1985) productive hypothesis, a retort to Freud's repressive hypothesis. Foucault argued that the naming, describing, and dissection of a condition or characteristic does not control or repress the condition, as Freud had theorized, but actually gives rise to its expression (Stoler 1995). For Foucault, it was bourgeois discourses on sexuality that animated and even intensified desires. And so it was with the Politics of Obesity course. Rather than disarming healthism, the course was "productive" of healthism.

4. DOES YOUR NEIGHBORHOOD MAKE YOU FAT?

1. In truth, the *Men's Fitness* methodology is hopelessly flawed. Not only does it mix indicators of health conditions with city characteristics and policy initiatives, it weighs these indicators in nontransparent ways. If you dig around a little, it becomes apparent that the editors choose in advance what cities they want to promote—or disparage—and then find measures to make their case. In a funny way, it is a textbook example of coproduction.

2. Although I prioritized this group, the study ended up including one Latina and one woman of mixed race (Asian/white) because I did not want to be exclusive in a snowball sample.

5. DOES EATING (TOO MUCH) MAKE YOU FAT?

1. The threshold to overweight for children is, by definition, the ninety-fifth percentile of weight. Since percentiles are supposed to capture the distribution of existing values, it seems nonsensical to discuss an increase in prevalence by a percentile. This speaks to arguments made in chapter 2.

2. Thalidomide was widely prescribed to pregnant women in the 1960s as a sedative and resulted in thousands of babies born without limbs. It was never approved for sale in the United States, although American women participated in clinical trials.

7. WILL FRESH, LOCAL, ORGANIC FOOD MAKE YOU THIN?

1. Consider the inverse of that in regards to social justice. Precious little attention is given to what would happen if US consumers all went local. Many third-world farmers, thoroughly dependent on export markets for their livelihoods by dint of colonial legacies, would certainly be relegated to immediate and extreme poverty. As Allen et al. (2003) put it, localism bounds the world to be cared for.

2. This is a crucial insight of the Roots of Change project, a foundation-driven initiative that is seeking to jump-start the transition to a more sustainable food system in California. The project's first report discussed "a new mainstream," although its

key strategies were thoroughly in keeping with the market-happy approach of the alternative-food movement (Guthman 2008b).

3. Morrison wrote this in agreement with scholars of whiteness who have sought to decenter white as "normal," unmarked, and therefore universal, as a way to make whites accountable for their effects on others (Frankenberg 1993; Sullivan 2006). Drawing on the earlier work of W. E. B. DuBois, scholars of whiteness argued that racism itself produced whiteness as the category that needs no explanation, with the effect that many whites deny privilege because they see themselves as without race. These scholars sought to draw attention to what whites said and did, specifically what they projected onto others, as a way to show the stake that whites had in the race of race and thus the persistence of racism. More recently, scholars, including McKinney (2005) and Sullivan (2006), have observed that the prominence given to whiteness scholarship has effectively recentered whiteness. Still, the move was terribly important. Thinness here is not only directly analogous but also intersectional. That is, discussions of fat people are often simultaneously discussions of racialized and classed "others."

8. WHAT'S CAPITALISM GOT TO DO WITH IT?

1. This has become a matter of considerable debate among political economists, with some (e.g., David McNalley [2011]) arguing that these policies generated substantial growth and profits, although not in ways that have had broad benefits. He, among others, attributes this growth precisely to reductions in wages and employment that have given rise to several "jobless recoveries" in which financial markets have boomed.

9. CONCLUSION: WHAT'S ON THE MENU?

1. For the record, I agreed with most of the recommendations and even take some credit for them. This is because I, along with some of my colleagues, participated in a special issue of the journal *Gastronomica* on the politics of food in which we took Pollan to task for his disengagement from policy work. It was after that was published and circulated that Pollan began fervently discussing the farm bill.

REFERENCES

Alkon, A. 2008. Paradise or pavement: The social construction of the environment in two urban farmers markets and their implications for environmental justice and sustainability. *Local Environment: The International Journal of Justice and Sustainability* 13:271–89.

———. 2009. The taste of place: Food politics in the East San Francisco Bay Area. Paper presented at the "Tasting Histories" conference, UC Davis, CA, February.

Alkon, A., and J. Agyeman. 2011. The food movement as polyculture. In *Cultivating food justice: Race, class and sustainability*, ed. A. Alkon and J. Agyeman, 1–20. Cambridge, MA: MIT Press.

Allen, P. 1999. Reweaving the food security safety net: Mediating entitlement and entrepreneurship. *Agriculture and Human Values* 16:117–29.

Allen, P., M. FitzSimmons, M. Goodman, and K. Warner. 2003. Shifting plates in the agrifood landscape: The tectonics of alternative agrifood initiatives in California. *Journal of Rural Studies* 19:61–75.

Allen, P., and J. Guthman. 2006. From "old school" to "farm-to-school": Neoliberalization from the ground up. *Agriculture and Human Values* 23:401–15.

Allen, P., and C. Hinrichs. 2008. Selective patronage and social justice: Local food consumer campaigns in historical context. *Journal of Agricultural and Environmental Ethics* 21:329–52.

Allison, D. B., K. R. Fontaine, J. E. Manson, J. Stevens, and T. B. VanItallie. 1999. Annual deaths attributable to obesity in the United States. *JAMA* 282:1530–38.

Almaguer, T. 1994. *Racial fault lines: The historical origins of white supremacy in California*. Berkeley: University of California Press.

Althusser, L. 1971. *Lenin and philosophy and other essays*. New York: Monthly Review Press.

Alwitt, L., and T. Donley. 1997. Retail stores in poor urban neighborhoods. *Journal of Consumer Affairs* 31:139–64.

Amadasi, A., A. Mozzarelli, C. Meda, A. Maggi, and P. Cozzini. 2008. Identification of xenoestrogens in food additives by an integrated in silico and in vitro approach. *Chemical Research in Toxicology* 22:52–63.

Anderson, K. 2001. The nature of "race." In *Social nature: Theory, practice, and politics*, ed. N. Castree and B. Braun, 64–83. London: Wiley-Blackwell.

Anderson, M. L., and D. A. Matsa. 2009. Are restaurants really supersizing America? Social Science Research Network. http://ssrn.com/abstract=1079584.

Angell, M. 2005. *The truth about the drug companies*. New York: Random House.

Armstrong, D. 1996. The rise of surveillance medicine. *Sociology of Health and Illness* 17:393–404.

Arnove, R., ed. 1980. *Philanthropy and cultural imperialism: The foundations at home and abroad*. Boston: G. K. Hall.

Austin, S. B. 1999. Commodity knowledge in consumer culture: The role of nutritional health promotion in the making of the diet industry. In *Weighty issues: Fatness and thinness as social problems*, ed. J. Sobal and D. Maurer, 159–81. New York: Aldine De Gruyer.

Baillie-Hamilton, P. 2002a. Chemical toxins: A hypothesis to explain the global obesity epidemic. *Journal of Alternative and Complementary Medicine* 8:185–92.

———. 2002b. *The detox diet: Eliminate chemical calories and restore your body's natural slimming system*. London: Michael Joseph.

Barker, D. J. P. 1998. *Mothers, babies, and health in later life*. Edinburgh: Churchill Livingstone.

Barker, K. 2005. *The fibromyalgia story: Medical authority and women's worlds of pain*. Philadelphia: Temple University.

Barnett, C., P. Cloke, N. Clarke, and A. Malpass. 2005. Consuming ethics: Articulating the subjects and spaces of ethical consumption. *Antipode* 37:23–45.

Begley, S. 2009. Born to be big. *Newsweek*, September 21.

Belasco, W. J. 1989. *Appetite for change*. New York: Pantheon.

Bell, T. 2006. Shrimpers tackle a wild market: Supply appears bountiful, but farm competition is one reason Maine fishermen are nervous. *Portland Press Herald*, December 3.

Berlant, L. 2007. Slow death (sovereignty, obesity, lateral agency). *Critical Inquiry* 33:754–80.

Bhattacharya, J., and N. Sood. n.d. Health insurance, obesity, and its economic costs. US Department of Agriculture, Economic Research Service. Retrieved from www .ers.usda.gov/publications/efan04004/efan04004g.pdf on October 8, 2010.

Björntorp, P. 2001. Do stress reactions cause abdominal obesity and comorbidities? *Obesity Reviews* 2:73–86.

Blaikie, P. 1985. *The political economy of soil erosion in developing countries*. London: Longman Development Studies.

Blaikie, P., and H. Brookfield. 1987. *Land degradation and society*. London: Methuen.

Blair, D., and J. Sobal. 2006. Luxus consumption: Wasting food resources through overeating. *Agriculture and Human Values* 23:63–74.

Block, J. P., R. A. Scribner, and K. B. DeSalvo. 2004. Fast food, race/ethnicity, and income: A geographic analysis. *American Journal of Preventive Medicine* 27:211–17.

Boardman, J. D., J. M. Saint Onge, R. G. Rogers, and J. T. Denney. 2005. Race differentials in obesity: The impact of place. *Journal of Health and Social Behavior* 46:229–43.

Bordo, S. 1993. *Unbearable weight: Feminism, Western culture, and the body*. Berkeley: University of California Press.

Born, B., and M. Purcell. 2006. Avoiding the local trap: Scale and food systems in planning research. *Journal of Planning Education and Research* 26:195–207.

Bourdieu, P. 1984. *Distinction: A social critique of the judgment of taste*. Cambridge, MA: Harvard University Press.

Boyd, W., and M. J. Watts. 1997. Agro-industrial just-in-time: The chicken industry and postwar American capitalism. In *Globalising food: Agrarian questions and global restructuring*, ed. D. Goodman and M. J. Watts, 192–225. London: Routledge.

Braun, B. 2007. Biopolitics and the molecularization of life. *Cultural Geographies* 14:6–28.

Breitbach, C. 2007. The geographies of a more just food system: Building landscapes for social reproduction. *Landscape Research* 32:533—57.

Brenner, N., and N. Theodore. 2002. Cities and geographies of "actually existing neoliberalism." *Antipode* 34:348–79.

Brenner, R. 2002. *The boom and the bubble: The US in the world economy*. New York: Verso.

Brotman, D. J., E. Walker, M. S. Lauer, and R. G. O'Brien. 2005. In search of fewer independent risk factors. *Archives of Internal Medicine* 165:138–45.

Brown, P. 2007. *Toxic exposures: Contested illnesses and the environmental health movement*. New York: Columbia University Press.

Brown, T., and C. Duncan. 2002. Placing geographies of public health. *Area* 34:361–69.

Brownell, K. D., and K. Horgen. 2004. *Food fight: The inside story of the food industry, America's obesity crisis, and what we can do about it*. New York: McGraw-Hill.

Buchwald, H., Y. Avidor, E. Braunwald, M. D. Jensen, W. Pories, K. Fahrbach, and K. Schoelles. 2004. Bariatric surgery: A systematic review and meta-analysis. *JAMA* 292:1724–37.

Bullard, R. 1997. *Unequal protection: Environmental justice and communities of color*. San Francisco: Sierra Club Books.

Bullard, R. D. 1990. *Dumping in Dixie*. Boulder: Westview Press.

Burch, D., and G. Lawrence. 2005. Supermarket own brands, supply chains and the transformation of the agri-food system. *International Journal of Sociology of Agriculture and Food* 13:1–28.

Burchell, G. 1996. Liberal government and techniques of the self. In *Foucault and political reason: Liberalism, neo-liberalism and rationalities of government*, ed. A. Barry, T. Osborne, and N. Rose, 19–36. Chicago: University of Chicago Press.

Burros, M. 2009. Obamas to plant vegetable garden at White House. *New York Times*, March 19.

Cafaro, P., R. Primack, and R. Zimdahl. 2006. The fat of the land: Linking American food overconsumption, obesity, and biodiversity loss. *Journal of Agricultural and Environmental Ethics* 19:541–61.

Campos, P. 2004. *The obesity myth: Why America's obsession with weight is hazardous to your health.* New York: Gotham Press.

Campos, P., A. Saguy, P. Ernsberger, E. Oliver, and G. Gaesser. 2006. The epidemiology of overweight and obesity: Public health crisis or moral panic? *International Journal of Epidemiology* 35:55–60.

Carson, R. [1962] 1987. *Silent spring.* 25th anniversary edition. Boston: Houghton Mifflin.

Chan, S. 2009. Data show Manhattan is svelte and Bronx is chubby, chubby. *New York Times,* July 21.

Chang, V. W., and N. A. Christakis. 2005. Income inequality and weight status in US metropolitan areas. *Social Science and Medicine* 61:83–96.

Clement, K., and D. Langin. 2007. Regulation of inflammation-related genes in human adipose tissue. *Journal of Internal Medicine* 262:422–30.

Cochrane, W. W. 1993. *The development of American agriculture.* Minneapolis: University of Minnesota Press.

Cohen, L. 2003. *A consumers' republic: The politics of mass consumption in postwar America.* New York: Random House.

Colborn, T., D. Dumanoski, and J. P. Myers. 1996. Our stolen future: Are we threatening our fertility, intelligence, and survival? A scientific detective story. New York: Dutton.

Cook, K., and C. Campbell. 2009. Amidst record 2007 crop prices and farm income Washington delivers $5 billion in subsidies. Environmental Working Group. Retrieved from http://farm.ewg.org/farm/dp_text.php on January 23, 2009.

Cooper, M. 2008. *Life as surplus: Biotechnology and capitalism in the neoliberal era.* Seattle: University of Washington Press.

Cotterill, R. W., and A. W. Franklin. 1995. *The urban grocery store gap.* Storrs: Food Marketing Policy Center, University of Connecticut.

Courtemanche, C., and A. Carden. 2010. Supersizing supercenters? The impact of Wal-Mart supercenters on body mass index and obesity. Social Science Research Network. http://ssrn.com/abstract=1263316.

Craddock, S. 2000a. *City of plagues: Disease, poverty and deviance in San Francisco.* Minneapolis: University of Minnesota.

———. 2000b. Disease, social identity, and risk: Rethinking the geography of AIDS. *Transactions of the Institute of British Geographers* NS 25:153–68.

Crawford, R. 2006. Health as a meaningful social practice. *Health* 10:401–20.

Crews, D., and J. A. McLachlan. 2006. Epigenetics, evolution, endocrine disruption, health, and disease. *Endocrinology* 147:s4–10.

Critser, G. 2003. *Fat land: How Americans became the fattest people in the world.* Boston: Houghton Mifflin.

Cronon, W. 1991. *Nature's metropolis.* New York: W. W. Norton.

Crossley, N. 2004. Fat is a sociological issue: Obesity rates in late modern, "body-conscious" societies. *Social Theory and Health* 2:222–53.

Cummins, S., and S. Macintyre. 2002. "Food deserts"—Evidence and assumption in health policy making. *British Medical Journal* 325:436–38.

Cuomo, C. 1998. *Feminism and ecological communities: An ethic of flourishing.* London: Routledge.

Danhof, C. 1969. *Changes in agriculture: The northern United States, 1820–1870.* Cambridge, MA: Harvard University Press.

David, R.-J., and K. Rehman. 2007. Insulin-associated weight gain in diabetes—causes, effects and coping strategies. *Diabetes, Obesity and Metabolism* 9:799–812.

Dean, M. 1999. *Governmentality: Power and rule in modern society.* Thousand Oaks, CA: Sage.

deJanvry, A. 1981. *The agrarian question and reformism in Latin America.* Baltimore: Johns Hopkins University Press.

de la Peña, C. 2007. Risky food, risky lives: The 1977 saccharin rebellion. *Gastronomica* 7:100–105.

Demeritt, D. 1998. Science, social constructivism, and nature. In *Remaking reality: Nature at the millennium,* ed. B. Braun and N. Castree, 173–93. London: Routledge.

——. 2001. The construction of global warming and the politics of science. *Annals of the Association of American Geographers* 91:301–37.

Drewnowski, A., and S. Specter. 2004. Poverty and obesity: The role of energy density and energy costs. *American Journal of Clinical Nutrition* 79:6–16.

Dunn, R. A. 2008. Obesity and the availability of fast-food: An instrumental variables approach. Paper presented at iHEA 2007 6th World Congress: Explorations in Health Economics. Social Science Research Network. http://ssrn.com/abstract=989363.

DuPuis, E. M. 2000. Not in my body: rBGH and the rise of organic milk. *Agriculture and Human Values* 17:285–95.

——. 2001. *Nature's perfect food.* New York: New York University Press.

——. 2010. American obesity: S.A.D. or saved by the Mediterranean diet? Paper presented at the "Food: History and Culture in the West" conference, University of California, Berkeley, April.

DuPuis, E. M., and D. Goodman. 2005. Should we go "home" to eat? Towards a reflexive politics of localism. *Journal of Rural Studies* 21:359–71.

Eisenhauer, E. 2001. In poor health: Supermarket redlining and urban nutrition. *Geo-Journal* 53:125–33.

Environmental Protection Agency. 2007. Ag 101: Major crops grown in the United States. Retrieved from www.epa.gov/agriculture/ag101/cropmajor.html on November 2, 2007.

Epstein, S. 1998. *Impure science: AIDS, activism, and the politics of knowledge.* Berkeley: University of California.

Ettinger, B., S. Sidney, S. R. Cummings, C. Libanati, D. D. Bikle, I. S. Tekawa, K. Tolan, and P. Steiger. 1997. Racial differences in bone density between young adult black and white subjects persist after adjustment for anthropometric, lifestyle, and bio-chemical differences. *Journal of Clinical Endocrinology and Metabolism* 82:429–34.

Fadiman, A. 1998. *The spirit catches you and you fall down.* New York: Farrar, Straus and Giroux.

Fairhead, J., and M. Leach. 1995. False forest history, complicit social analysis: Rethinking some West African environmental narratives. *World Development* 23:1023–35.

Fee, M. 2006. Racializing narratives: Obesity, diabetes and the "Aboriginal" thrifty genotype. *Social Science and Medicine* 62:2988–97.

Fendler, L., and I. Muzaffar. 2008. The history of the bell curve: Sorting and the idea of normal. *Educational Theory* 58:63–82.

Fine, B. 1994. Towards a political economy of food. *Review of International Political Economy* 1:519–45.

———. 1998. *The political economy of diet, health and food policy.* London: Routledge.

Fink, D. 1998. *Cutting into the meatpacking line: Workers and change in the rural Midwest.* Chapel Hill: University of North Carolina Press.

Finkelstein, E. A., J. G. Trogdon, J. W. Cohen, and W. Dietz. 2009. Annual medical spending attributable to obesity: Payer- and service-specific estimates. *Health Affairs* 28:w822–31.

Fisher, A., and R. Gottlieb. 1995. Community food security: Policies for a more sustainable food system in the context of the 1995 Farm Bill and beyond. Ralph and Goldy Lewis Center for Regional Policy Studies, School of Public Policy and Social Research, University of California, Los Angeles.

Fitchen, J. M. 1997. Hunger, malnutrition, and poverty in the contemporary United States. In *Food and culture*, ed. C. Counihan and P. Van Esterik, 384–401. New York: Routledge.

Fitting, E. 2006. Importing corn, exporting labor: The neoliberal corn regime, GMOs, and the erosion of Mexican biodiversity. *Agriculture and Human Values* 23:15–26.

Flegal, K. M. 2006. Commentary: The epidemic of obesity—What's in a name? *International Journal of Epidemiology* 35:72–74.

Flegal, K. M., M. D. Carroll, C. L. Ogden, and L. R. Curtin. 2010. Prevalence and trends in obesity among US adults, 1999–2008. *JAMA* 303:235–41.

Flegal, K. M., M. D. Carroll, C. L. Ogden, and C. L. Johnson. 2002. Prevalence and trends in obesity among US adults, 1999–2000. *JAMA* 288:1723–27.

Flegal, K. M., B. I. Graubard, D. F. Williamson, and M. H. Gail. 2005. Excess deaths associated with underweight, overweight, and obesity. *JAMA* 293:1861–67.

———. 2007a. Cause-specific excess deaths associated with underweight, overweight, and obesity. *JAMA* 298:2028–37.

———. 2007b. Supplement: Response to "Can fat be fit?" *Scientific American*, December 16.

Flegal, K. M., C. L. Ogden, J. A. Yanovski, D. S. Freedman, J. A. Shepherd, B. I. Graubard, and L. G. Borrud. 2010. High adiposity and high body mass index-for-age in US children and adolescents overall and by race-ethnic group. *American Journal of Clinical Nutrition* 91:1020–26.

Flegal, K. M., D. F. Williamson, E. R. Pamuk, and H. M. Rosenberg. 2004. Estimating deaths attributable to obesity in the United States. *American Journal of Public Health* 94:1486–89.

Forsyth, T. 2003. *Critical political ecology: The politics of environmental science.* London: Routledge.

Foster, J. B., and F. Magdoff. 2009. *The great financial crisis.* New York: Monthly Review Press.

Foucault, M. 1985. *History of sexuality,* vol. 1: *An introduction.* New York: Vintage.

Frankenberg, R. 1993. *White women, race matters: The social construction of whiteness.* Minneapolis: University of Minnesota.

Fraser, L. 1998. *Losing it: False hopes and fat profits in the diet industry.* New York: Penguin.

Freedman, D. S., L. K. Khan, M. K. Serdula, D. A. Galuska, and W. H Dietz. 2002. Trends and correlates of class 3 obesity in the United States from 1990 through 2000. *JAMA* 288:1758–61.

Friedmann, H. 1978. World market, state, and family farm: Social bases of household production in the era of wage labor. *Comparative Studies in Society and History* 20:545–86.

———. 1992. Changes in the international division of labor: Agri-food complexes and export agriculture. In *Toward a new political economy of agriculture,* ed. W. H. Friedland, L. Busch, F. H. Buttel, and A. P. Rudy, 65–93. Boulder: Westview Press.

———. 1993. The political economy of food. *New Left Review* 197:29–57.

Friedmann, H., and P. McMichael. 1989. Agriculture and the state system: The rise and decline of national agricultures, 1870 to the present. *Sociologia Ruralis* 29:93–117.

Fumento, M. 1997. *The fat of the land: Our health crisis and how overweight Americans can help themselves.* New York: Houghton Mifflin.

Gaesser, G. 2002. *Big fat lies: The truth about your weight and your health.* New York: Burze Books.

Gard, M., and J. Wright. 2005. *The obesity epidemic: Science, morality, and ideology.* London: Routledge.

Gardner, B. 2002. *American agriculture in the twentieth century: How it flourished and what it cost.* Cambridge, MA: Harvard University Press.

Gaytan, M. S. 2004. Slow food and new local imaginaries. *Food, Culture and Society: An International Journal of Multidisciplinary Research* 7:97–116.

Germov, J., and L. Williams. 1999. Dieting women: Self-surveillance and the body panopticon. In *Weighty issues: Fatness and thinness as social problems,* ed. J. Sobal and D. Maurer, 117–32. New York: Aldine De Gruyer.

Gilmore, R. W. 2002. Fatal couplings of power and difference: Notes on racism and geography. *Professional Geographer* 54:15–24.

Gladen, B.C., N. B. Ragan, and W. J. Rogan. 2000. Pubertal growth and development and prenatal and lactational exposure to polychlorinated biphenyls and dichlorodiphenyl dichloroethene. *Journal of Pediatrics* 136:490–96.

Goldner, W. S., D. P. Sandler, F. Yu, J. A. Hoppin, F. Kamel, and T. D. LeVan. 2010. Pesticide use and thyroid disease among women in the Agricultural Health Study. *American Journal of Epidemiology* 171:455–64.

Goldstein, K. 2009. Michael Pollan takes a stand on Whole Foods boycott. *Huffington Post*, August 30. Retrieved from www.huffingtonpost.com/2009/08/30/michael-pollan-denounces-_n_272176.html.

Goodall, J., G. McAvoy, and G. Hudson. 1995. *Harvest for hope: A guide to mindful eating.* New York: Warner Books.

Goodman, D., B. Sorj, and J. Wilkinson. 1987. *From farming to biotechnology.* Oxford: Basil Blackwell.

Gottleib, R. 1993. *Forcing the spring: The transformation of the environmental movement.* Washington, DC: Island Press.

Gouveia, L., and A. Juska. 2002. Taming nature, taming workers: Constructing the separation between meat consumption and meat production in the US. *Sociologia Ruralis* 42:370–90.

Grun, F., and B. Blumberg. 2006. Environmental obesogens: Organotins and endocrine disruption via nuclear receptor signaling. *Endocrinology* 147:s50–55.

———. 2009. Minireview: The case for obesogens. *Molecular Endocrinology* 23:1127–34.

Grun, F., H. Watanabe, Z. Zamanian, L. Maeda, K. Arima, R. Cubacha, D. M. Gardiner, J. Kanno, T. Iguchi, and B. Blumberg. 2006. Endocrine-disrupting organotin compounds are potent inducers of adipogenesis in vertebrates. *Molecular Endocrinology* 20:2141–55.

Grundy, S., J. Cleeman, and C. Bairey Merz. 2004. Implications of recent clinical trials for the National Cholesterol Education Program Adult Treatment Panel III guidelines. *Circulation* 110:227–39.

Guthman, J. 2003. Fast food/organic food: Reflexive tastes and the making of "yuppie chow." *Journal of Social and Cultural Geography* 4:43–56.

———. 2004. *Agrarian dreams? The paradox of organic farming in California.* Berkeley: University of California Press.

———. 2008a. "If they only knew": Colorblindness and universalism in California alternative food institutions. *Professional Geographer* 60:387–97.

———. 2008b. Thinking inside the neoliberal box: The micro-politics of agro-food philanthropy. *Geoforum* 39:1241–53.

Guthman, J., A. W. Morris, and P. Allen. 2006. Squaring farm security and food security in two types of alternative food institutions. *Rural Sociology* 71:662–84.

Hacking, I. 1990. *The taming of chance.* Cambridge: Cambridge University Press.

Hajer, M. A. 1995. *The politics of environmental discourse: Ecological modernization and the policy process.* New York: Oxford University Press.

Hall, S. 1992. The West and the rest: Discourse and power. In *Formations of modernity,* ed. S. Hall and B. Gieben, 275–320. Cambridge: Polity Press.

Hamilton, C., and G. Filardo. 2006. The dangers of categorizing body mass index. *European Heart Journal* 27:2903–4.

Hamin, M. T. 1999. Constitutional types, institutional forms: Reconfiguring diagnostic and therapeutic approaches to obesity in early twentieth-century biomedical investigation. In *Weighty issues: Fatness and thinness as social problems*, ed. J. Sobal and D. Maurer, 53–73. New York: Aldine De Gruyer.

Haraway, D. 1991. *Simians, cyborgs, and women: The reinvention of nature.* New York: Routledge.

Harper, J. 2004. Breathless in Houston: A political ecology of health approach to understanding environmental health concerns. *Medical Anthropology: Cross-Cultural Studies in Health and Illness* 23:295–326.

Harrison, J. 2008a. Abandoned bodies and spaces of sacrifice: Pesticide drift activism and the contestation of neoliberal environmental politics in California. *Geoforum* 30:1197–1214.

——. 2008b. Lessons learned from pesticide drift: A call to bring production agriculture, farm labor, and social justice back into agrifood research and activism. *Agriculture and Human Values* 25:163–67.

Harvey, D. 1982. *Limits to capital.* Chicago: University of Chicago Press.

——. 1989. *The condition of postmodernity.* Cambridge, MA: Blackwell.

——. 1998. The body as an accumulation strategy. *Environment and Planning D: Society and Space* 16:401–21.

——. 2003. *The new imperialism.* Oxford: Oxford University Press.

——. 2005. *A brief history of neoliberalism.* New York: Oxford University Press.

Harvey, D., and D. Haraway. 1995. Nature, politics, and possibilities: A debate and discussion with David Harvey and Donna Haraway. *Environment and Planning D: Society and Space* 13:507–27.

Hassanein, N. 2003. Practicing food democracy: A pragmatic politics of transformation. *Journal of Rural Studies* 19:77–86.

Hatch, E. E., J. W. Nelson, R. W. Stahlhut, and T. F. Webster. 2010. Association of endocrine disruptors and obesity: Perspectives from epidemiological studies. *International Journal of Andrology* 33:324–32.

Hayes-Conroy, J. 2009. Visceral reactions: Alternative food and social difference in American and Canadian schools. PhD dissertation, Pennsylvania State University.

Heffernan, W. 1998. Agriculture and monopoly capital. *Monthly Review* 50:46–59.

Heindel, J. J. 2003. Endocrine disruptors and the obesity epidemic. *Toxicological Sciences* 76:247–49.

Herrick, C. 2007. Risky bodies: Public health, social marketing and the governance of obesity. *Geoforum* 38:90–102.

Hess, D. J. 1997. *Science studies: An advanced introduction.* New York: New York University Press.

Hill, J. O., and J. C. Peters. 1998. Environmental contributions to the obesity epidemic. *Science* 280:1371–74.

Hines, E. P., S. S. White, J. P. Stanko, E. A. Gibbs-Flournoy, C. Lau, and S. E. Fenton. 2009. Phenotypic dichotomy following developmental exposure to perfluorooctanoic acid (PFOA) in female CD-1 mice: Low doses induce elevated serum leptin and insulin, and overweight in mid-life. *Molecular and Cellular Endocrinology* 304:97–105.

INCITE! Women of Color Against Violence, ed. 2006. *The revolution will not be funded: Beyond the non-profit industrial complex.* Cambridge, MA: South End Press.

Jackson, J. E., M. P. Doescher, A. F. Jerant, and L. G. Hart. 2005. A national study of obesity prevalence and trends by type of rural county. *Journal of Rural Health* 21:140–48.

Jasanoff, S. 2004. *States of knowledge: The co-production of science and social order.* London: Routledge.

Jasanoff, S., and B. Wynne. 1998. Science and decision-making. In *Human choice and climate change*, ed. S. Rayner and E. Malone, 1:1–87. Columbus, OH: Batelle Press.

Jekanowski, M. D. 1999. Causes and consequences of fast food sales growth. *Food Review*, January–April:11–16.

Jessop, B. 2002. Liberalism, neoliberalism, and urban governance: A state theoretical perspective. *Antipode* 34:452–72.

Johnston, J. 2008. The citizen-consumer hybrid: Ideological tensions and the case of Whole Foods Market. *Theory and Society* 37:229–70.

Julier, A. 2008. The political economy of obesity: The fat pay all. In *Food and culture: A reader*, ed. C. Counihan and P. Van Esterik, 482–99. New York: Routledge.

Kautsky, K. 1988. *The agrarian question.* London: Zwan Press.

Kavanagh, K., K. L. Jones, J. Sawyer, K. Kelley, J. J. Carr, J. D. Wagner, and L. L. Rudel. 2007. Trans fat diet induces abdominal obesity and changes in insulin sensitivity in monkeys. *Obesity* 15:1675–84.

Kearns, R., and G. Moon. 2002. From medical to health geography: Novelty, place and theory after a decade of change. *Progress in Human Geography* 26:605–25.

Kegley, S., S. Orme, and L. Neumeister. 2000. Hooked on poison: Pesticide use in California, 1991–98. San Francisco: Californians for Pesticide Reform. www.panna.org/sites/default/files/HookedonPoison2000.pdf.

Kelly, E. 2006. *Obesity.* Westport, CT: Greenwood.

Kershaw, E. E., and J. S. Flier. 2004. Adipose tissue as an endocrine organ. *Journal of Clinical Endocrinology and Metabolism* 89:2548–56.

Kim, J., K. E. Peterson, K. S. Scanlon, G. M. Fitzmaurice, A. Must, E. Oken, S. L. Rifas-Shiman, J. W. Rich-Edwards, and M. W. Gillman. 2006. Trends in overweight from 1980 through 2001 among preschool-aged children enrolled in a health maintenance organization. *Obesity* 14:1107–12.

King corn. 2007. Directed by Aaron Woolf, produced by Ian Cheney and Curt Ellis. Mosaic Films. www.kingcorn.net.

Kirchner, S., T. Kieu, C. Chow, S. Casey, and B. Blumberg. 2010. Prenatal exposure to the environmental obesogen tributyltin predisposes multipotent stem cells to become adipocytes. *Molecular Endocrinology* 24:526–39.

Kirkland, A. 2010. The environmental account of obesity: A case for feminist skepticism. *Signs: A Journal of Women in Culture and Society* 35:463–85.

Klein, R. 2010. What is health and how do you get it? In *Against health: Resisting the invisible morality*, ed. J. Metzl and A. Kirkland, 15–25. New York: New York University Press.

Kloppenberg, J. J., J. Henrickson, and G. W. Stevenson. 1996. Coming into the food-shed. *Agriculture and Human Values* 13:33–42.

Kloppenburg, J. 2005. *First the seed: The political economy of plant biotechnology.* Madison: University of Wisconsin Press.

Kobayashi, A., and L. Peake. 2000. Racism out of place: Thoughts on whiteness and an anti-racist geography in the new millennium. *Annals of the Association of American Geographers* 90:392–403.

Komlos, J., and M. Brabec. 2010. The trend of BMI values among US adults. Social Science Research Network eLibrary, National Bureau of Economic Research. http://ssrn.com/paper=1573500.Krimsky, S. 2000. *Hormonal chaos: The scientific and social origins of the environmental endocrine hypothesis.* Baltimore: Johns Hopkins University Press.

Kuczmarski, R. J., and K. M. Flegal. 2000. Criteria for definition of overweight in transition: Background and recommendations for the United States. *American Journal of Clinical Nutrition* 72:1074–91.

Kuczmarski, R. J., K. M. Flegal, S. M. Campbell, and C. L. Johnson. 1994. Increasing prevalence of overweight among US adults: The National Health and Nutrition Examination Surveys, 1960 to 1991. *JAMA* 272:205–11.

Kuhn, T. 1962. *The structure of scientific revolutions.* Chicago: University of Chicago Press.

Landau, E. 2009. Thin is better to curb global warming, study says. Retrieved from http://edition.cnn.com/2009/HEALTH/04/20/thin.global.warming/index.html on April 20, 2009.

Langston, N. 2010. *Toxic bodies: Hormone disrupters and the legacy of DES.* New Haven, CT: Yale University Press.

LeBesco, K. 2004. *Revolting bodies? The struggle to redefine fat identity.* Amherst: University of Massachusetts.

Lee, H. 2006. Obesity among California adults: Racial and ethnic differences. Public Policy Institute of California. www.ppic.org/content/pubs/report/R_906HLR .pdf.

Levenstein, H. A. 1988. *Revolution at the table: The transformation of the American diet.* New York: Oxford University Press.

Limerick, P. 1987. *The legacy of conquest: The unbroken past of the American West.* New York: Norton.

Lipsitz, G. 1998. *The possessive investment in whiteness.* Philadelphia: Temple University Press.

Lopez, R. 2004. Urban sprawl and risk for being overweight or obese. *American Journal of Public Health* 94:1574–79.

Lupton, D. 1997. Foucault and the medicalisation critique. In *Foucault, health and medicine*, ed. A. Petersen and R. Bunton, 94–110. New York: Routledge.

Lyson, T. A. 2004. *Civic agriculture: Reconnecting farm, food, and community.* Lebanon, NH: Tufts University Press.

Maddock, J. 2004. The relationship between obesity and the prevalence of fast food restaurants: State-level analysis. *American Journal of Health Promotion* 19:137–43.

Mansfield, B. 2011. Is fish health food or poison? Farmed fish and the material production of un/healthy nature. *Antipode* 43:413–34.

Mapes, K. 2009. *Sweet tyranny: Migrant labor, industrial agriculture, and imperial politics.* Urbana: University of Illinois Press.

Martin, E. 1991. The egg and the sperm: How science constructed a romance based on stereotypical male-female roles. *Signs: Journal of Women in Culture and Society* 16:485–501.

———. 1994. *Flexible bodies: Tracking immunity in American culture from the days of polio to the age of AIDS.* Boston: Beacon Press.

Massey, D. S., and N. A. Denton. 1998. *American apartheid: Segregation and the making of the underclass.* Cambridge, MA: Harvard University Press.

Masuno, H., T. Kidani, K. Sekiya, K. Sakayama, T. Shiosaka, H. Yamamoto, and K. Honda. 2002. Bisphenol A in combination with insulin can accelerate the conversion of 3T3-L1 fibroblasts to adipocytes. *Journal of Lipid Research* 43:676–84.

Matfin, G. 2008. Challenges in developing drugs for the metabolic syndrome. *Current Diabetes Reports* 8:31–36.

Maurer, D. 1999. Too skinny or vibrant and healthy? Weight management in the vegetarian movement. In *Weighty issues: Fatness and thinness as social problems,* ed. J. Sobal and D. Maurer, 209–30. New York: Aldine De Gruyer.

Mayer, J. D. 1996. The political ecology of disease as one new focus for medical geography. *Progress in Human Geography* 20:441–56.

McCarthy, J., and S. Prudham. 2004. Neoliberal nature and the nature of neoliberalism. *Geoforum* 35:275–83.

McConnell, G. 1953. *The decline of agrarian democracy.* Berkeley: University of California Press.

McCullum-Gomez, C., C. Benbrook, and R. Theuer. 2009. That first step—Organic food and a healthier future. The Organic Center. www.organic-center.org/reportfiles/That_First_Step_Full.pdf.

McKinney, K. D. 2005. *Being white: Stories of race and racism.* New York: Routledge.

McMichael, P. 2004. *Development and social change.* Thousand Oaks, CA: Sage.

McNalley, D. 2011. *Global slump: The economics and politics of crisis and resistance.* Oakland, CA: PM Press.

McWilliams, J. 2009. *Just food: Where locavores get it wrong and how we can truly eat responsibly.* Boston: Little, Brown.

Metzl, J. 2010. Introduction: Why against health? In *Against health: Resisting the invisible morality,* ed. J. Metzl and A. Kirkland, 1–11. New York: New York University Press.

Miller, P., and N. Rose. 1997. Mobilizing the consumer: Assembling the subject of consumption. *Theory, Culture, and Society* 14:1–36.

Mokdad, A. H., E. S. Ford, B. A. Bowman, W. H. Dietz, F. Vinicor, V. S. Bales, and J. S. Marks. 2003. Prevalence of obesity, diabetes, and obesity-related health risk factors, 2001. *JAMA* 289:76–79.

Mokdad, A. H., J. S. Marks, D. F. Stroup, and J. L. Gerberding. 2004. Actual causes of death in the United States, 2000. *JAMA* 291:1238–45.

Montague, C. T., and S. O'Rahilly. 2000. The perils of portliness: Causes and consequences of visceral adiposity. *Diabetes* 49:883–88.

Moore, D. S., A. Pandian, and J. Kosek. 2003. Introduction: The cultural politics of race and nature: Terrains of power and practice. In *Race, nature, and the politics of difference*, ed. D. S. Moore, J. Kosek, and A. Pandian, 1–70. Durham, NC: Duke University Press.

Morrison, T. 1992. *Playing in the dark: Whiteness and the literary imagination.* Cambridge, MA: Harvard University Press.

Morse, J. M. 1995. The significance of saturation. *Qualitative Health Research* 5:147–49.

Nash, L. 2007. *Inescapable ecologies: A history of environment, disease, and knowledge.* Berkeley: University of California Press.

National Task Force on the Prevention and Treatment of Obesity. 2002. Medical care for obese patients: Advice for health care professionals. *American Family Physician* 65:81–88.

Nestle, M. 2002. *Food politics: How the food industry influences nutrition and health.* Berkeley: University of California Press.

———. 2003. *Safe food: Bacteria, biotechnology and bioterrorism.* Berkeley: University of California Press.

———. 2006. *What to eat.* New York: North Point Press.

Neumann, R. 1998. *Imposing wilderness: Struggles over livelihood and nature preservation in Africa.* Berkeley: University of California Press.

Nevins, J. 2001. *Operation gatekeeper: The rise of the "illegal alien" and the remaking of the U.S.–Mexico boundary.* London: Routledge.

Newbold, R., E. Padilla-Banks, W. Jefferson, and J. Heindel. 2008. Effects of endocrine disruptors on obesity. *International Journal of Andrology* 31:201–8.

O'Connor, J. 1989. Capitalism, nature, socialism: A theoretical introduction. *Capitalism, Nature, Socialism* 1:11–38.

Ogden, C. L., M. D. Carroll, L. R. Curtin, M. M. Lamb, and K. M. Flegal. 2010. Prevalence of high body mass index in US children and adolescents, 2007–2008. *JAMA* 303:242–49.

Ogden, C. L., M. D. Carroll, L. R. Curtin, M. A. McDowell, C. J. Tabak, and K. M. Flegal. 2006. Prevalence of overweight and obesity in the United States, 1999–2004. *JAMA* 295:1549–55.

Ogden, C. L., K. M. Flegal, M. D. Carroll, and C. L. Johnson. 2002. Prevalence and trends in overweight among US children and adolescents, 1999–2000. *JAMA* 288:1728–32.

Oliver, J. E. 2006. *Fat politics: The real story behind America's obesity epidemic.* New York: Oxford University.

Papas, M. A., A. J. Alberg, R. Ewing, K. J. Helzlsouer, T. L. Gary, and A. C. Klassen. 2007. The built environment and obesity. *Epidemiologic Reviews* 29:129–43.

Peck, J., and A. Tickell. 2002. Neoliberalizing space. *Antipode* 34:380–404.

Petersen, A. 1997. Risk, governance, and the new public health. In *Foucault, health and medicine*, ed. A. Petersen and R. Bunton, 189–206. New York: Routledge.

Petersen, A., and D. Lupton. 1996. *The new public health: Health and self in the age of risk*. Thousand Oaks, CA: Sage.

Petersen, K. F., D. Befroy, S. Dufour, J. Dziura, C. Ariyan, D. L. Rothman, L. DiPietro, G. W. Cline, and G. I. Shulman. 2003. Mitochondrial dysfunction in the elderly: Possible role in insulin resistance. *Science* 300:1140–42.

Philpott, T. 2007. It's the agronomy, stupid: Why gutting subsidies shouldn't be the focus of Farm Bill reform efforts. *Grist*, November 8. www.grist.org/article/its-the-agronomy-stupid.

Pijl, H., and A. E. Meinders. 1996. Bodyweight change as an adverse effect of drug treatment: Mechanisms and management. *Drug Safety: An International Journal of Medical Toxicology and Drug Experience* 14:329–42.

Plantinga, A. J., and S. Bernell. 2005. A spatial economic analysis of urban land use and obesity. *Journal of Regional Science* 45:473–92.

Pollan, M. 2006. *The omnivore's dilemma: A natural history of four meals*. New York: Penguin.

———. 2007. You are what you grow. *New York Times*, April 22.

———. 2008a. Farmer in chief. *New York Times Magazine*, October 9.

———. 2008b. *In defense of food: An eater's manifesto*. New York: Penguin.

———. 2009a. Big food vs. big insurance. *New York Times*, September 10.

———. 2009b. *Food rules: An eater's manual*. New York Penguin.

———. 2009c. Out of the kitchen, onto the couch. *New York Times*, July 29.

Pool, R. 2001. *Fat: Fighting the obesity epidemic*. Oxford: Oxford University Press.

Poortinga, W. 2006. Perceptions of the environment, physical activity, and obesity. *Social Science and Medicine* 63:2835–46.

Popkin, B. 2008. *The world is fat: The fads, trends, policies, and products that are fattening the human race*. New York: Avery.

Poppendieck, J. 1998. *Sweet charity? Emergency food and the end of entitlement*. New York: Penguin.

———. 2010. *Free for all: Fixing school food in America*. Berkeley: University of California.

Power, M. L., and J. Schulkin. 2009. *The evolution of obesity*. Baltimore: Johns Hopkins University Press.

Pudup, M. B. 2008. It takes a garden: Cultivating citizen-subjects in organized garden projects. *Geoforum* 39:1228–40.

Puhl, R., and K. D. Brownell. 2001. Bias, discrimination, and obesity. *Obesity* 9:788–805.

Pulido, L. 2000. Rethinking environmental racism: White privilege and urban development in southern California. *Annals of the Association of American Geographers* 90:12–40.

Quadagno, J. S. 1996. *The color of welfare: How racism undermined the war on poverty.* Oxford: Oxford University Press.

Quastel, N. 2009. Political ecologies of gentrification. *Urban Geography* 30:694–725.

Quinn, J. W., K. M. Neckerman, A. G. Rundle, and C. Weiss. 2007. Does park access and park quality predict adult obesity in New York City? Paper presented at the Annual Meeting of the Association of American Geographers, San Francisco.

Raja, S., Y. Li, J. Roemmich, M. Changxing, L. Epstein, P. Yadav, and A. B. Ticoalu. 2010. Food environment, built environment, and women's BMI: Evidence from Erie County, New York. *Journal of Planning Education and Research* 29:444–60.

Raloff, J. 2002. Hormones: Here's the beef: Environmental concerns reemerge over steroids given to livestock—Animal excretions release synthetic hormones into environment. *Science News* 161:10.

Reardon, J. 2005. *Race to the finish: Identity and governance in an age of genomics.* Princeton, NJ: Princeton University Press.

Ritzer, G. 1993. *The McDonaldization of society.* Thousand Oaks, CA: Pine Forge Press.

Robbins, P. 2004. *Political ecology.* Oxford: Blackwell.

———. 2007. *Lawn people: How grasses, weeds, and chemicals make us who we are.* Philadelphia: Temple University.

Robert, S. A., and E. N. Reither. 2004. A multilevel analysis of race, community disadvantage, and body mass index among adults in the US. *Social Science and Medicine* 59:2421–34.

Roberts, D. 1998. *Killing the black body: Race, reproduction, and the meaning of liberty.* New York: Pantheon.

Rome, E. S., and S. Ammerman. 2003. Medical complications of eating disorders: An update. *Journal of Adolescent Health* 33:418–26.

Romm, J. 2001. The coincidental order of environmental injustice. In *Justice and natural resources: Concepts, strategies, and applications,* ed. K. M. Mutz, G. C. Bryner, and D. S. Kennedy, 117–37. Covelo, CA: Island Press.

Rose, G. 1985. Sick individuals and sick populations. *International Journal of Epidemiology* 14:32–38.

Rose, N. 1999. *Powers of freedom: Reframing political thought.* Cambridge: Cambridge University Press.

———. 2007. Molecular biopolitics, somatic ethics, and the spirit of biocapital. *Social Theory and Health* 5:3–29.

Rosenberger, R. S., Y. Sneh, and T. T. Phipps. 2005. A spatial analysis of linkages between health care expenditures, physical inactivity, obesity and recreation supply. *Journal of Leisure Research* 37:216–35.

Rosmond, R. 2005. Role of stress in the pathogenesis of the metabolic syndrome. *Psychoneuroendocrinology* 30:1–10.

Ross, B. 2005. Fat or fiction? Weighing the obesity epidemic. In *The obesity epidemic: Science, morality, and ideology,* ed. M. Gard and J. Wright, 86–100. London: Routledge.

Ross, E. B. 1998. *The Malthus factor: Poverty, politics, and population in capitalist development*. London: Zed Books.

Rubin, B. S., and A. M Soto. 2009. Bisphenol A: Perinatal exposure and body weight. *Molecular and Cellular Endocrinology* 304:55–62.

Ruzzin, J., R. Petersen, E. Meugnier, L. Madsen, E.-J. Lock, H. Lillefosse, T. Ma, S. Pesenti, S. B. Sonne, T. T. Marstrand, M. K. Malde, Z.-Y. Du, C. Chavey, L. Fajas, A.-K. Lundebye, C. L. Brand, H. Vidal, K. Kristiansen, and L. Froyland. 2009. Persistent organic pollutant exposure leads to insulin resistance syndrome. *Environmental Health Perspectives* 118:465–71.

Saguy, A. C., and K. W. Riley. 2005. Weighing both sides: Morality, mortality, and framing contests over obesity. *Journal of Health Politics, Policy and Law* 30:869–923.

Sayer, A. 1992. *Method in social science*. London: Routledge.

Schein, R. H. 2006. Race and landcape in the United States. In *Landscape and race in the United States*, ed. R. H. Schein, 1–21. New York: Routledge.

Schlosser, E. 2001. *Fast food nation: The dark side of the American meal*. Boston: Houghton Mifflin.

Schrag, P. 1998. *Paradise lost: California's experience, America's future*. Berkeley: University of California Press.

Scrinis, G. 2008. On the ideology of nutritionism. *Gastronomica* 8:39–48.

Seidman, I. E. 2006. *Interviewing as qualitative research: A guide for researchers in education and the social sciences*. New York: Teachers College Press.

Short, A., J. Guthman, and S. Raskin. 2007. Food deserts, oases, or mirages? Small markets and community food security in the San Francisco Bay Area. *Journal of Planning Education and Research* 26:352–64.

Shrader-Frechette, K. 2005. *Environmental justice: Creating equality, reclaiming democracy*. New York: Oxford University Press.

Singer, N. 2010. Eat an apple (doctor's orders). *New York Times*, August 12.

Sklair, L. 1995. *Sociology of the global system*. 2nd ed. Baltimore: Johns Hopkins University Press.

Skrabanek, P. 1994. *Death of humane medicine and the rise of coercive healthism*. [Edmonds, Suffolk, UK]: Social Affairs Unit.

Smith, N. 1996. *The new urban frontier: Gentrification and the revanchist city*. London: Routledge.

Sobal, J. 1995. The medicalization and demedicalization of obesity. In *Eating agendas: Food and nutrition as social problems*, ed. J. Sobal and D. Maurer, 79–90. New York: Aldine De Gruyer.

———. 1999. The size acceptance movement and the social construction of body weight. In *Weighty issues: Fatness and thinness as social problems*, ed. J. Sobal and D. Maurer, 231–49. New York: Aldine De Gruyer.

Stahlhut, R. W., E. van Wijngaarden, T. D. Dye, S. Cook, and S. H. Swan. 2007. Concentrations of urinary phthalate metabolites are associated with increased waist circumference and insulin resistance in adult U.S. males. *Environmental Health Perspectives* 115:876–82.

Stanhope, K. L., and P. J. Havel. 2010. Fructose consumption: Recent results and their potential implications. *Annals of the New York Academy of Sciences* 1190:15–24.

Stein, R. 2004. CDC study overestimated deaths from obesity. *Washington Post*, November 24.

Steingraber, S. 1997. *Living downstream: An ecologist looks at cancer and the environment*. New York: Addison-Wesley.

———. 2003. *Having faith: An ecologist's journey to motherhood*. New York: Berkley Publishing Group.

Stern, A. M. 1999. Buildings, boundaries, and blood: Medicalization and nation-building on the U.S.-Mexico border, 1910–1930. *Hispanic American Historical Review* 79:41–82.

Stettler, N., V. A. Stallings, A. B. Troxel, J. Zhao, R. Schinnar, S. E. Nelson, E. E. Ziegler, and B. L. Strom. 2005. Weight gain in the first week of life and overweight in adulthood: A cohort study of European American subjects fed infant formula. *Circulation* 111:1897–1903.

Stoler, A. L. 1995. *Race and the education of desire*. Durham, NC: Duke University Press.

Stull, D. D., and M. J. Broadway. 2004. *Slaughterhouse blues: The meat and poultry industry in North America*. Belmont, CA: Thomson/Wadsworth.

Sullivan, S. 2006. *Revealing whiteness: The unconscious habits of racial privilege*. Indianapolis: Indiana University Press.

Swan, S. H., F. Liu, J. W. Overstreet, C. Brazil, and N. E. Skakkebaek. 2007. Semen quality of fertile US males in relation to their mothers' beef consumption during pregnancy. *Human Reproduction* 22:1497–1502.

Swinburn, B., G. Egger, and F. Raza. 1999. Dissecting obesogenic environments: The development and application of a framework for identifying and prioritizing environmental interventions for obesity. *Preventative Medicine* 29:563–70.

Szasz, A. 2007. *Shopping our way to safety: How we changed from protecting the environment to protecting ourselves*. Minneapolis: University of Minnesota Press.

Sze, J. 2007. *Noxious New York: The racial politics of urban health and environmental politics*. Cambridge, MA: MIT Press.

Tabb, M. M., and B. Blumberg. 2006. New modes of action for endocrine-disrupting chemicals. *Molecular Endocrinology* 20:475–82.

Tattenham, K. 2006. Food politics and the food justice movement. Senior thesis, University of California, Santa Cruz.

Taubes, G. 2007. Do we really know what makes us healthy? *New York Times Magazine*, September 16.

Taylor, P., and F. H. Buttel. 1992. How do we know we have global environmental problems? Science and globalization of environmental discourse. *Geoforum* 23:405–16.

Unger, R. H., and P. E. Scherer. 2010. Gluttony, sloth and the metabolic syndrome: A roadmap to lipotoxicity. *Trends in Endocrinology and Metabolism* 21:345–52.

United Soybean Board. 2007. Animal ag brochure. Retrieved from www.unitedsoybean.org/Public/SoyResources.aspx on November 2, 2007.

US Agency for International Development. 2004. Fifty years of food for peace: The history of America's food aid. Retrieved from www.usaid.gov/our_work/humanitarian_assistance/ffp/50th/history.html on October 30, 2007.

US Department of Agriculture. 2002. *Consumption in America: Agriculture factbook, 2001–2002.* Washington, DC: US Department of Agriculture. Retrieved from www.usda.gov/factbook.

US Department of Agriculture, National Agricultural Statistics Service. 2001. *Trends in US agriculture: Corn hybridization.* Washington, DC: US Department of Agriculture, National Agricultural Statistics Service. Retrieved from www.usda.gov/nass/pubs/trends/cornhybridization.htm.

——. 2007. Crops and plants, search by commodity. Retrieved from www.nass.usda.gov/QuickStats/indexbysubject.jsp?Text1 = &site = NASS_MAIN&select = Select+a+State&Pass_name = &Pass_group = Crops+%26+Plants&Pass_subgroup = Field+Crops&list = Beans+All+Dry+Edible on October 16, 2007.

——. 2009. *Trends in U.S. agriculture.* Retrieved from www.nass.usda.gov/Publications/Trends_in_U.S._Agriculture/productivity.asp on March 13, 2009.

US Department of Agriculture, Economic Research Service. 2009. *Food CPI, prices and expenditures: Food expenditures by families and individuals as a share of disposable personal income.* Retrieved from www.ers.usda.gov/Briefing/CPIFoodAnd Expenditures/Data/table7.htm on March 13, 2009.

——. 2010. *Agricultural trade multipliers: Effects of trade on the U.S. economy.* Retrieved from www.ers.usda.gov/Data/TradeMultiplier/econeffects/2008overview.aspx on October 29. 2010.

US Department of Health and Human Services. 2001. *The Surgeon General's call to action to prevent and decrease overweight and obesity.* Rockville, MD: US Department of Health and Human Services, Public Health Service, Office of the Surgeon General.

Villanueva, E. 2001. The validity of self-reported weight in US adults: A population based cross-sectional study. *BMC Public Health* 1:1–11.

Wang, Y., and M. A. Beydoun. 2007. The obesity epidemic in the United States—Gender, age, socioeconomic, racial/ethnic, and geographic characteristics: A systematic review and meta-regression analysis. *Epidemiologic Reviews* 29: 6–28.

Wargo, J. 1998. *Our children's toxic legacy.* New Haven, CT: Yale University Press.

Watts, M. J. 1993. Life under contract: Contract farming, agrarian restructuring, and flexible accumulation. In *Living under contract,* ed. M. J. Watts and P. Little, 21–78. Madison: University of Wisconsin Press.

Wells, M. 1996. *Strawberry fields: Politics, class, and work in California agriculture.* Ithaca, NY: Cornell University Press.

White, R. 1991. *"It's your misfortune and none of my own": A new history of the American West.* Norman: University of Oklahoma Press.

White House Task Force on Childhood Obesity. 2010. Solving the problem of childhood obesity within a generation. Retrieved from www.letsmove.gov/pdf/

TaskForce_on_Childhood_Obesity_May2010_FullReport.pdf on October 8, 2010.

Whitley-Putz, L. 2004. Calorie "counter" publics: Rhetoric in fat activist practice. PhD dissertation, Rensselaer Polytechnic Institute.

Williams, R. 1980. *Problems in materialism and culture*. London: Verso.

Winson, A. 2004. Bringing political economy into the debate on the obesity epidemic. *Agriculture and Human Values* 21:299–312.

Working Life (n.d.) Wages and benefits: Real wages (1964–2004). Retrieved from www.workinglife.org/wiki/Wages+and+Benefits%3A+Real+Wages+%281964–2004%29, on October 13, 2010.

World Health Organization. 2011. Retrieved from www.who.int/topics/obesity/en/ on March 23, 2011.

World Health Organization Expert Consultation. 2004. Appropriate body-mass index for Asian populations and its implications for policy and intervention strategies. *Lancet* 363:157–63.

Worster, D. 1979. *Dust bowl: The southern plains in the 1930s*. New York: Oxford University Press.

Zhang, Q., and Y. Wang. 2004. Socioeconomic inequality of obesity in the United States: Do gender, age, and ethnicity matter? *Social Science and Medicine* 58:1171–80.

INDEX

adiposity, 26–29, 35–36, 98, 100, 104, 188;
toxins and, 100, 104, 107, 112, 192
African Americans, 61, 71, 89, 94, 111, 135,
167; BMIs of, 28, 81, 92, 97; food justice
movement and, 154
Agency for International Development, US,
121
Agricultural Adjustment Acts (1933; 1938),
120
Agricultural Labor Relations Act (1975), 137
Agriculture, US Department of (USDA), 91,
94, 112, 129–30, 133, 148, 186; Economic
Research Service, 116; National Agricultural Statistics Service, 116, 124; National
Organic Program, 149
Allen, Patricia, 151, 198n1
Allison, D. B., 33
alternative food movement, 3–5, 19, 22, 23,
140–62, 184–86, 188, 196; food justice
movement and, 153–59; food security and,
177; healthism and, 131, 141, 146, 156,
160–61; limits of, 163, 164, 186, 193–94
Althusser, Louis, 197n2
appropriationism, 123, 125
Aramark Corporation, 137
Arizona, 96, 138
Armstrong, David, 38–40
Asian Americans, 92, 97, 99, 198n2
"at risk," notion of, 36–38, 44, 58, 157, 179
attention deficit hyperactivity disorder
(ADHD), 104

Baillie-Hamilton, Paula, 94, 95, 100, 111,
152–53
Bangalore (India), 170

Bangladesh, 170
bariatric surgery, 64
Barker, Karen, 25, 61
Barker hypothesis, 103
Behavioral Risk Factor Surveillance system
(BFRSS), 37, 70, 76
Beijing Olympics, 172
Belasco, Warren, 130, 142, 145
bell curves, 15, 20, 31, 40–42, 98, 102
Berkeley (California) public school system,
4, 177
Bernell, S., 73, 76
Bhattacharya, Jayanta, 49
big-box stores, 73–74, 77, 81, 84, 137, 177
Biggest Loser, The (television series), 54, 157,
179, 187
biopower, 55
bisphenol A (BPA), 107, 109, 114
blacks. See African Americans
Blair, Dorothy, 7
blood glucose levels, 3, 35, 38–39, 96
Blumberg, Bruce, 100, 104–6, 108, 110, 111,
113, 114
body mass index (BMI), 26–35, 51, 91–92,
103, 116, 188–90; construction of epidemic with, 29–32; energy balance model
and, 93, 94; exposure to chemicals and
food substances and, 110–12; genetics and,
95, 97; morality associated with, 33–35;
obesogenic environment and, 68–72, 74,
75, 77–79, 81, 84; risk factors associated
with, 37–38; statistical analysis of, 40–42,
98; treatment costs and, 48; variation in,
45
Bordo, Susan, 53; Unbearable Weight, 146–47

soy, 106, 109–11, 123, 126, 128; subsidies for, 116, 120, 173
spatial analysis, 70
Specter, S. E., 116–17, 122
Splenda, 179
sprawl. *See* suburban sprawl
Steingraber, Sandra, 11–12, 112
stroke, 29, 33
subsidies: commodity (*see* commodity subsidies); indirect, 124, 128–34
substitutionsim, 123, 125, 127–28, 132–34, 138
suburban sprawl, 73, 75–78, 84, 86
Sullivan, Shannon, 199n3
Supplemental Nutritional Assistance Program (SNAP), 175–76
supply-side interventions, 75, 87–89
Surgeon General's Call to Action to Prevent and Decrease Overweight and Obesity, 48
surveillance medicine, 40
Survivor (television series), 53
Sweden, 80
Szasz, Andy, 88, 89, 152; *Shopping Our Way to Safety*, 152

Tanzania, 12
Taubes, Gary, 35–37
technologies, agricultural, 124–25
Texas, 136, 138
Thatcher, Margaret, 168
thyroid disease, 3, 39, 108, 121
Time magazine, 114
Toxic Substances Control Act (1976), 131
toxins, environmental, 3, 11–12, 21, 22, 65, 92, 100–101, 112–15, 152 (*see also* obesogens; *specific toxins*); endocrine-disrupting chemicals (EDCs), 101–14
Tracy (California), 77, 79, 81, 82, 89, 93
Trader Joe's, 79, 127, 153
tributyltin (TBT), 105–7, 109–10, 127
Tufts School of Medicine, 105
Tyson Corporation, 126, 179

Unilever Corporation, 126
unions, 17, 136–37, 169–70, 173
United Farm Workers, 136
United Kingdom, 54, 168
University of California, 135; Berkeley, 3, 91; Irvine, 105; San Francisco, 99; Santa Cruz, 2, 3, 197n1

Vermont, 136
Vietnam, 170
Vietnam War, 167

Wagner Act (1935), 137
Wall Street Journal, 49
Wal-Mart, 137, 149, 150, 153, 170, 173
Wann, Marilyn, 47, 50–51
Washington, 136
Waters, Alice, 4, 143, 158
Weight Watchers, 179
welfare state, 55
West Virginia, 71, 76
White House Task Force on Childhood Obesity, 49
whites, 92, 118, 135–36, 158, 191, 199; BMIs of, 97; spatial patterns of obesity and, 71, 89; working-class, 94, 153, 192
Whole Foods, 49, 79, 81, 82, 153, 176, 179, 185
Wisconsin, 136
Women, Infants, and Children Supplemental Nutrition Program (WIC), 129, 175
working class, 153, 168, 192; BMI of, 94; suburban, 84
Working Life, 169
World Health Organization (WHO), 26, 30–31
World War I, 119
Wright, Jan, 22, 24, 45, 93–94, 96, 114

X-rays, 28
Xenical, 179

"yo-yo" dieting, 64

CALIFORNIA STUDIES IN FOOD AND CULTURE

Darra Goldstein, Editor

TEXT
10.5/14 Jenson

DISPLAY
Jenson Pro (Open Type) + Benton Gothic Regular and Light

COMPOSITOR
Toppan Best-set Premedia Limited

INDEXER
Ruth Elwell

CARTOGRAPHER
Red Shoe Design

PRINTER AND BINDER
Maple-Vail Book Manufacturing Group